X-RAY ROBOT™

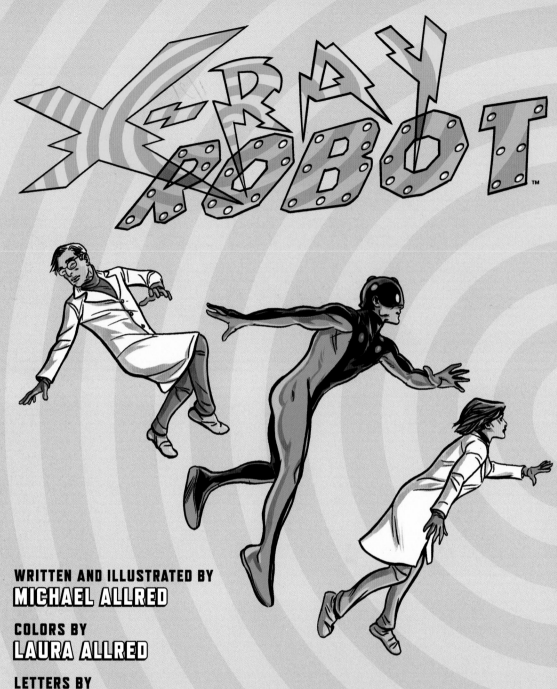

X-RAY ROBOT

WRITTEN AND ILLUSTRATED BY
MICHAEL ALLRED

COLORS BY
LAURA ALLRED

LETTERS BY
NATE PIEKOS

3D CONVERSIONS BY
CHRISTIAN LeBLANC

X-RAY ROBOT CREATED BY
MICHAEL ALLRED

COVER AND CHAPTER BREAKS BY
MICHAEL ALLRED WITH **LAURA ALLRED**

3D COVERS ON PAGES 107–116! BRING YOUR 3D GLASSES!*
*3D GLASSES NOT INCLUDED

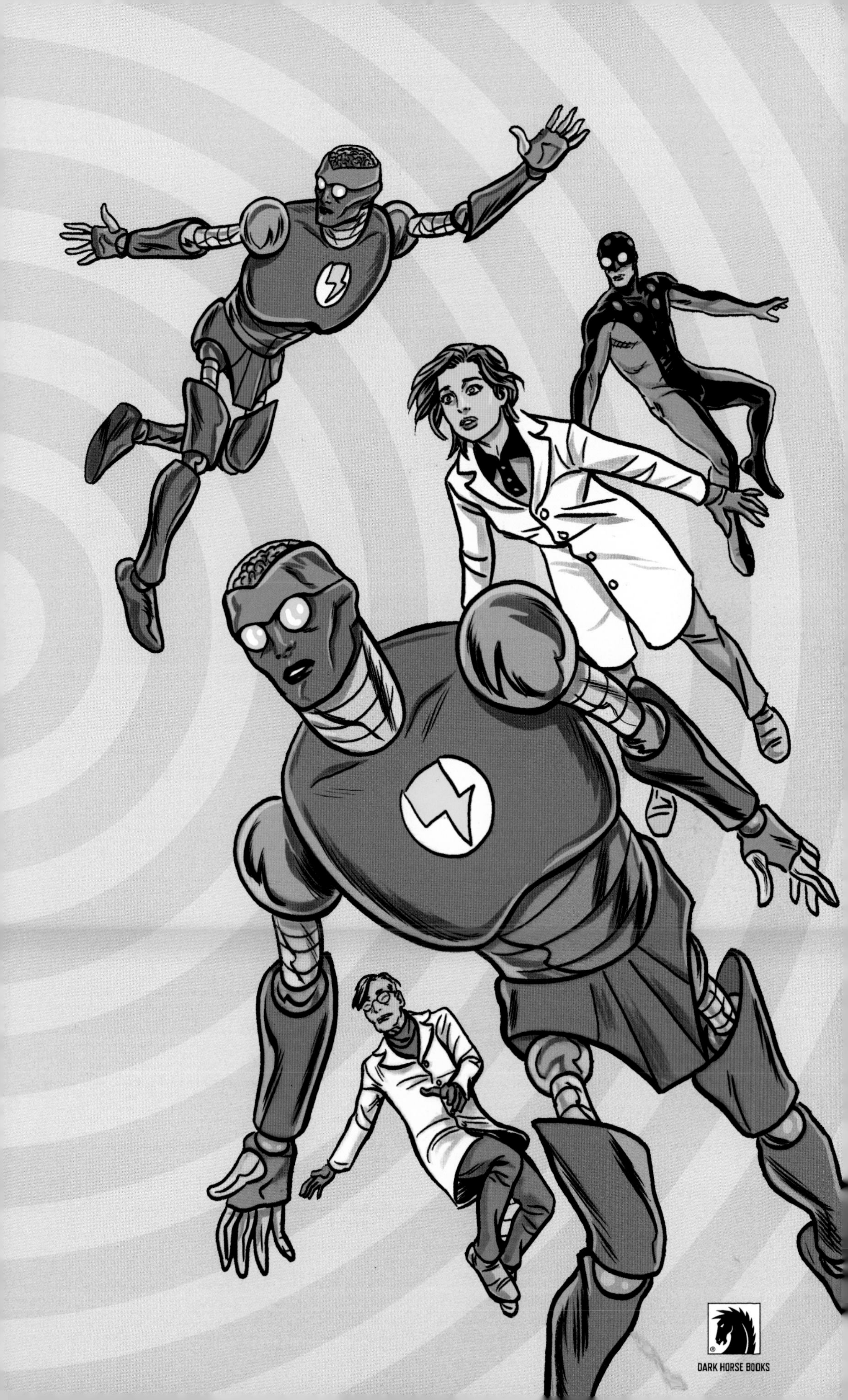

DARK HORSE BOOKS

PRESIDENT & PUBLISHER
MIKE RICHARDSON

EDITOR
DANIEL CHABON

ASSISTANT EDITOR
CHUCK HOWITT

DESIGNER
BRENNAN THOME

DIGITAL ART TECHNICIAN
ADAM PRUETT

X-RAY ROBOT

Collects issues #1–#4 of the Dark Horse Comics series *X-Ray Robot*.

Published by Dark Horse Books / A division of Dark Horse Comics LLC / 10956 SE Main Street / Milwaukie, OR 97222

DarkHorse.com

To find a comics shop in your area, visit comicshoplocator.com

First edition: November 2020
Ebook ISBN 978-1-50671-062-4 / Trade paperback ISBN 978-1-50671-078-5

1 3 5 7 9 10 8 6 4 2
Printed in China

Neil Hankerson Executive Vice President • Tom Weddle Chief Financial Officer • Randy Stradley Vice President of Publishing • Nick McWhorter Chief Business Development Officer • Dale LaFountain Chief Information Officer • Matt Parkinson Vice President of Marketing • Vanessa Todd-Holmes Vice President of Production and Scheduling • Mark Bernardi Vice President of Book Trade and Digital Sales • Ken Lizzi General Counsel • Dave Marshall Editor in Chief • Davey Estrada Editorial Director • Chris Warner Senior Books Editor • Cary Grazzini Director of Specialty Projects • Lia Ribacchi Art Director • Matt Dryer Director of Digital Art and Prepress • Michael Gombos Senior Director of Licensed Publications • Kari Yadro Director of Custom Programs • Kari Torson Director of International Licensing • Sean Brice Director of Trade Sales

Library of Congress Cataloging-in-Publication Data
Names: Allred, Mike (Mike Dalton), writer, illustrator. | Allred, Laura, colourist. | Piekos, Nate, letterer.
Title: X-ray robot / written and illustrated by Michael Allred ; colors by Laura Allred ; letters by Nate Piekos.
Description: First edition. | Milwaukie, OR : Dark Horse Books, 2020.
Identifiers: LCCN 2020019763 (print) | LCCN 2020019764 (ebook) | ISBN 9781506710785 (trade paperback) | ISBN 9781506710624 (ebook)
Subjects: LCSH: Comic books, strips, etc.
Classification: LCC PN6728.X28 A55 2020 (print) | LCC PN6728.X28 (ebook) | DDC 741.5/973--dc23
LC record available at https://lccn.loc.gov/2020019763
LC ebook record available at https://lccn.loc.gov/2020019764

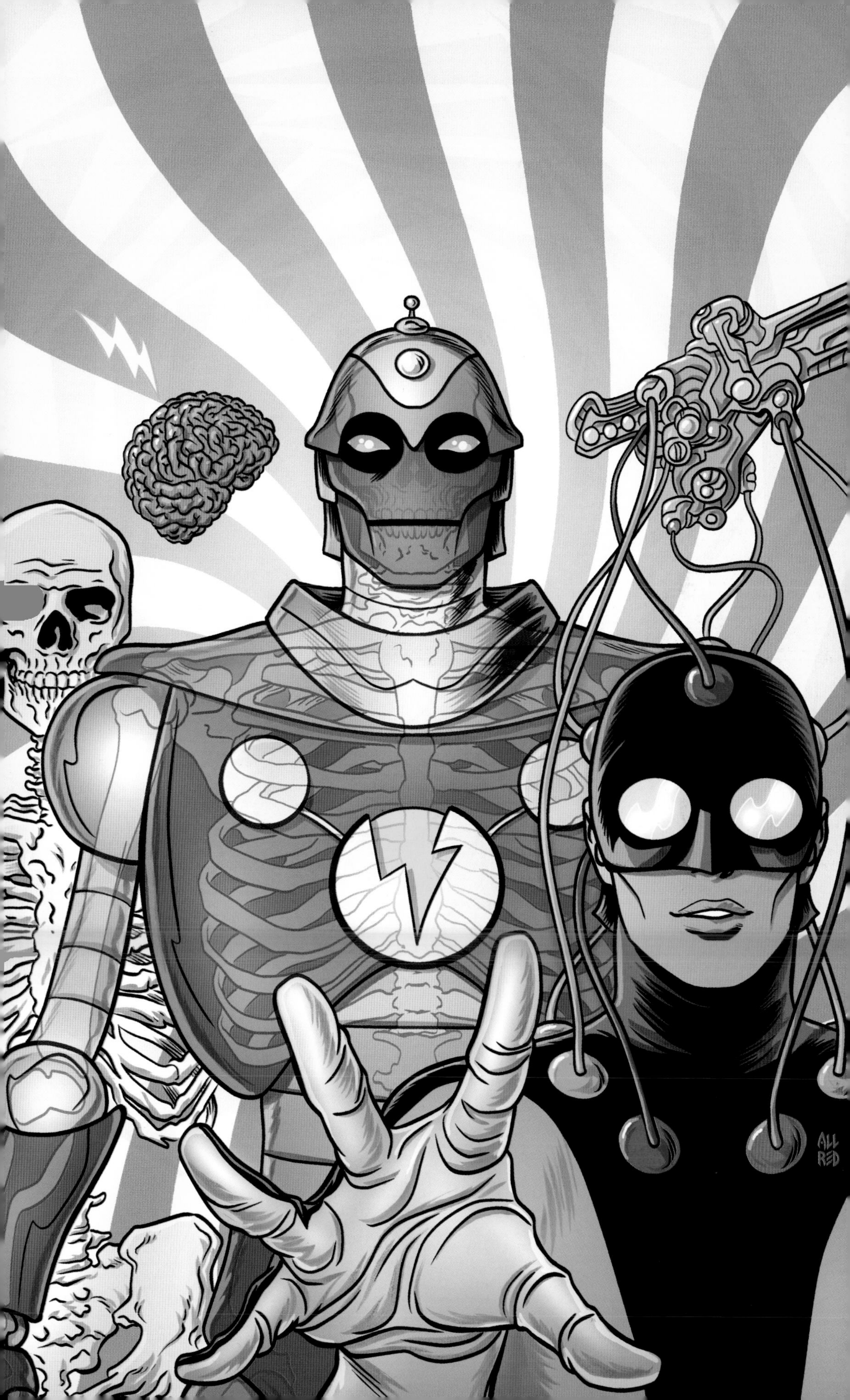
ALL
RED

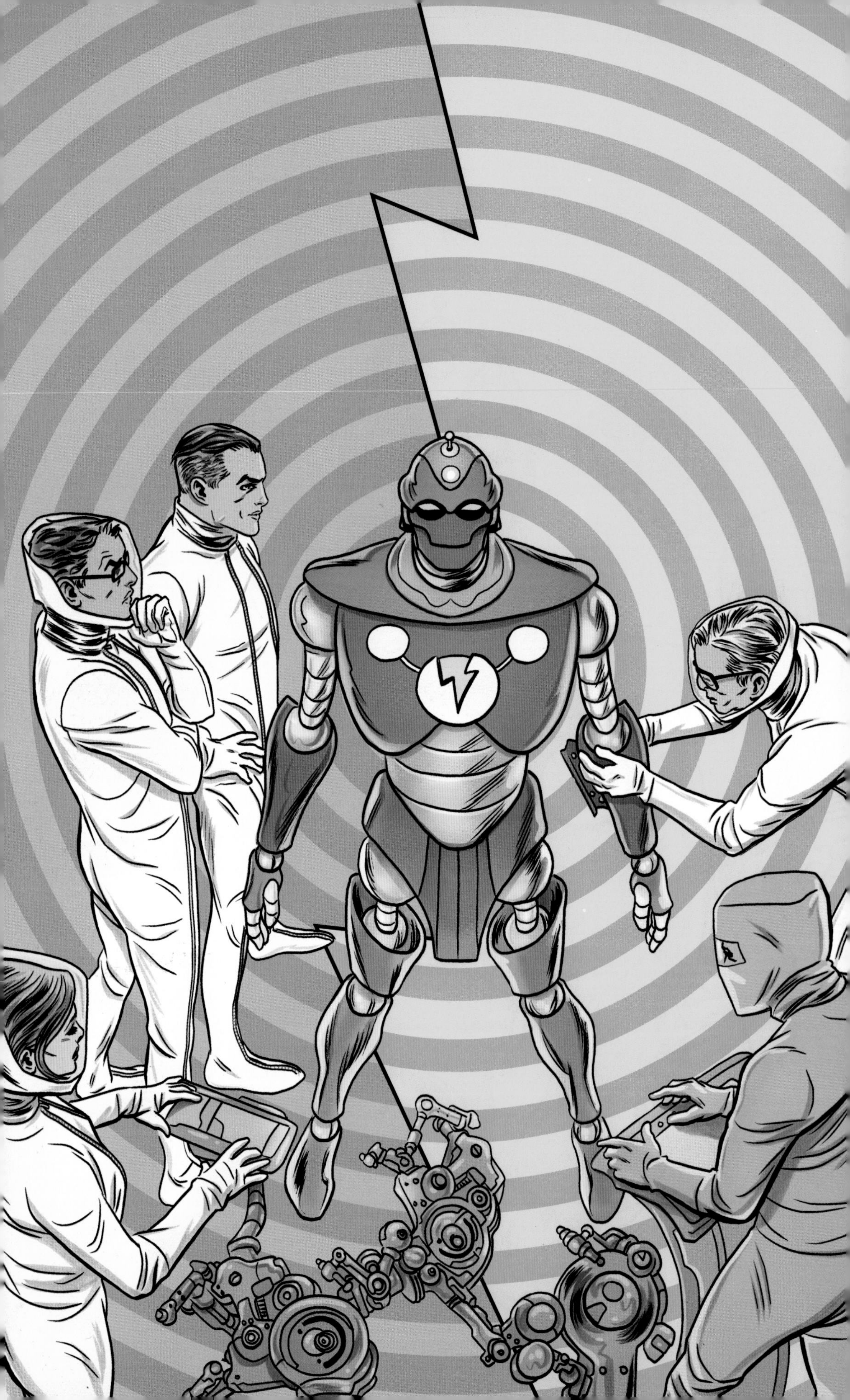

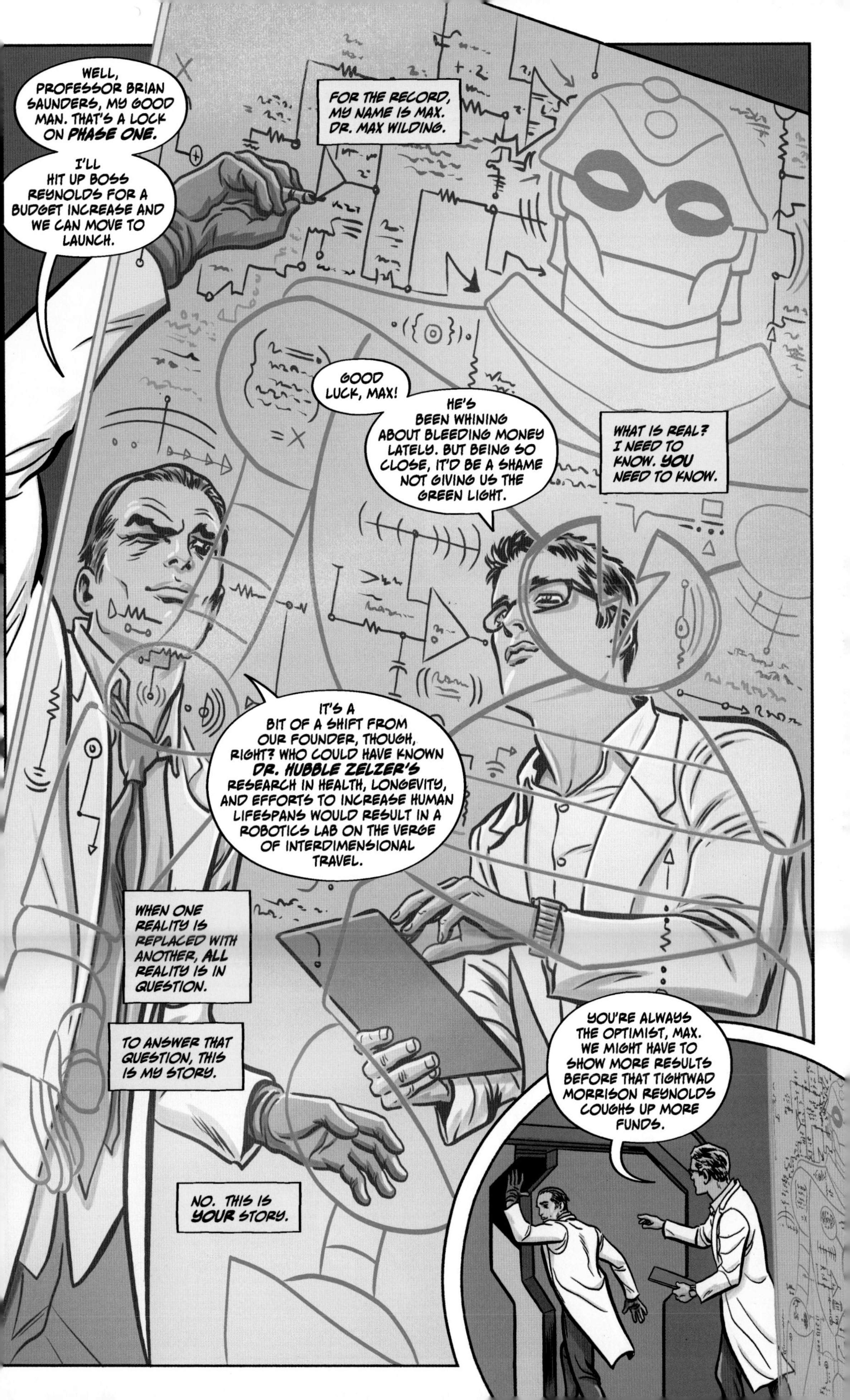

WELL, PROFESSOR BRIAN SAUNDERS, MY GOOD MAN. THAT'S A LOCK ON **PHASE ONE.**
I'LL HIT UP BOSS REYNOLDS FOR A BUDGET INCREASE AND WE CAN MOVE TO LAUNCH.
FOR THE RECORD, MY NAME IS MAX. DR. MAX WILDING.
GOOD LUCK, MAX!
HE'S BEEN WHINING ABOUT BLEEDING MONEY LATELY. BUT BEING SO CLOSE, IT'D BE A SHAME NOT GIVING US THE GREEN LIGHT.
WHAT IS REAL? I NEED TO KNOW. **YOU** NEED TO KNOW.
IT'S A BIT OF A SHIFT FROM OUR FOUNDER, THOUGH, RIGHT? WHO COULD HAVE KNOWN **DR. HUBBLE ZELZER'S** RESEARCH IN HEALTH, LONGEVITY, AND EFFORTS TO INCREASE HUMAN LIFESPANS WOULD RESULT IN A ROBOTICS LAB ON THE VERGE OF INTERDIMENSIONAL TRAVEL.
WHEN ONE REALITY IS REPLACED WITH ANOTHER, **ALL** REALITY IS IN QUESTION.
TO ANSWER THAT QUESTION, THIS IS MY STORY.
NO. THIS IS **YOUR** STORY.
YOU'RE ALWAYS THE OPTIMIST, MAX. WE MIGHT HAVE TO SHOW MORE RESULTS BEFORE THAT TIGHTWAD MORRISON REYNOLDS COUGHS UP MORE FUNDS.

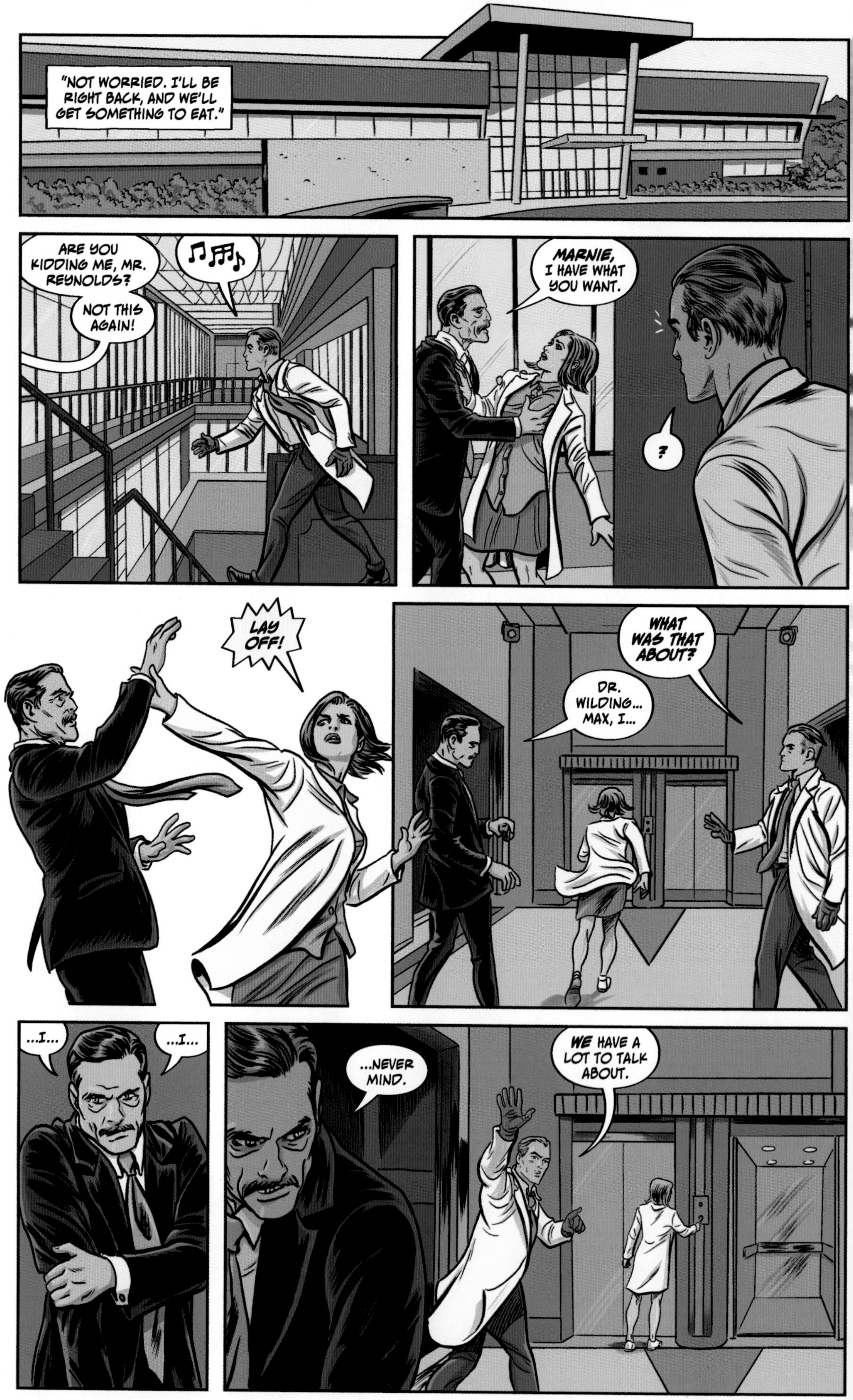
"NOT WORRIED. I'LL BE RIGHT BACK, AND WE'LL GET SOMETHING TO EAT."
ARE YOU KIDDING ME, MR. REYNOLDS?
NOT THIS AGAIN!
♫♬♪
MARNIE, I HAVE WHAT YOU WANT.
?
LAY OFF!
WHAT WAS THAT ABOUT?
DR. WILDING... MAX, I...
...I...
...I...
...NEVER MIND.
WE HAVE A LOT TO TALK ABOUT.

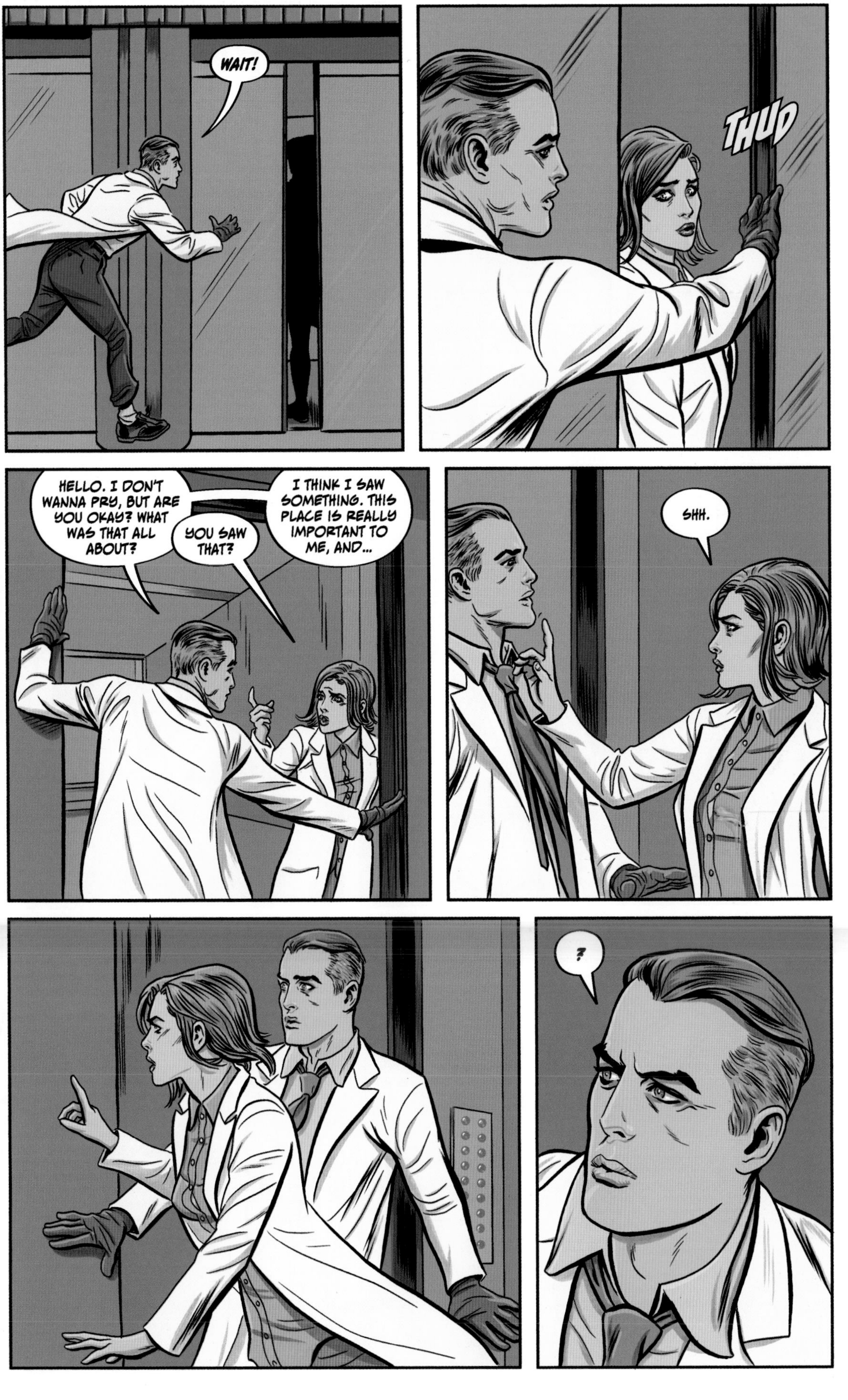
WAIT!
THUD
HELLO. I DON'T WANNA PRY, BUT ARE YOU OKAY? WHAT WAS THAT ALL ABOUT?
YOU SAW THAT?
I THINK I SAW SOMETHING. THIS PLACE IS REALLY IMPORTANT TO ME, AND...
SHH.
?

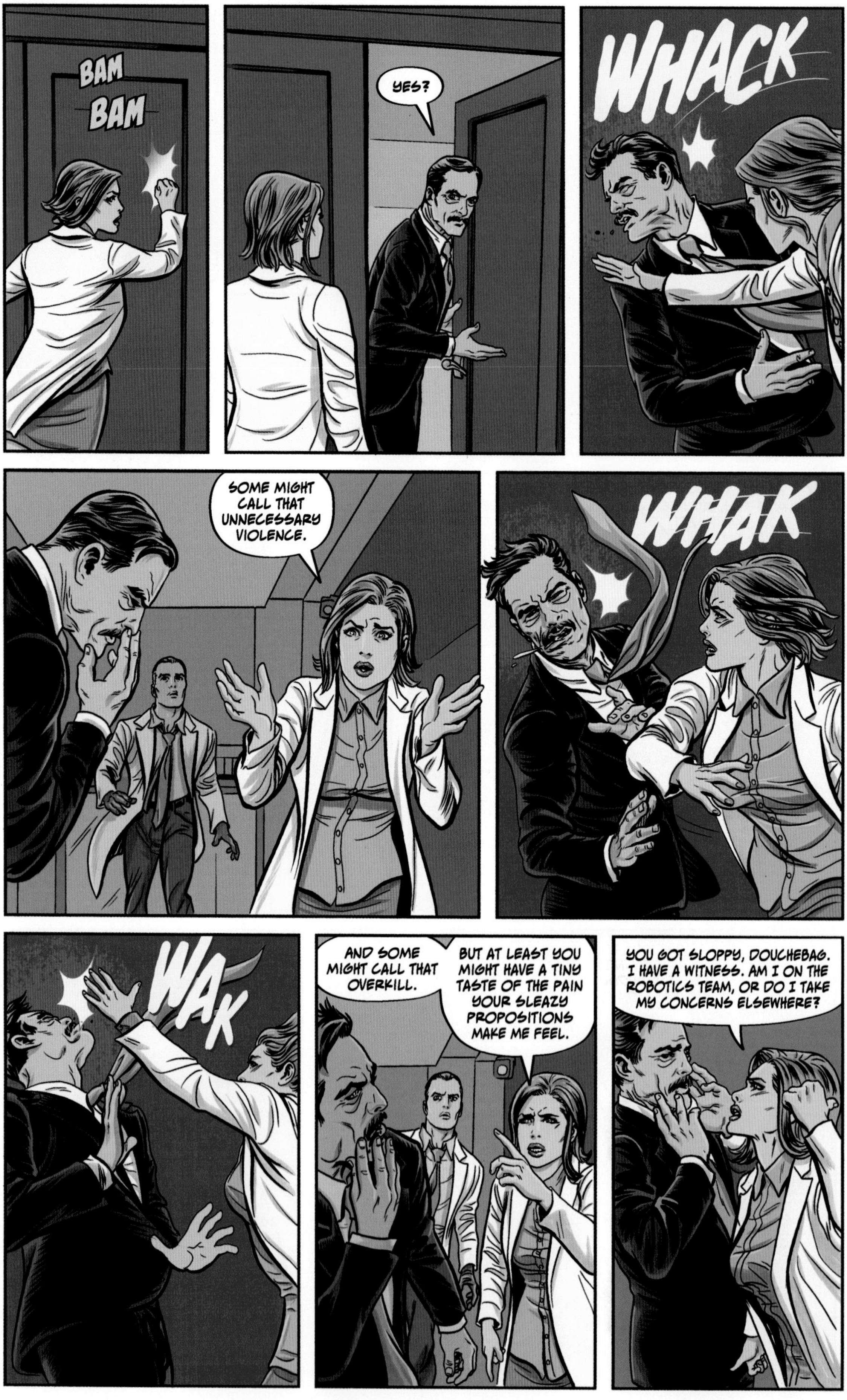
BAM
BAM
YES?
WHACK
SOME MIGHT CALL THAT UNNECESSARY VIOLENCE.
WHAK
WAK
AND SOME MIGHT CALL THAT OVERKILL.
BUT AT LEAST YOU MIGHT HAVE A TINY TASTE OF THE PAIN YOUR SLEAZY PROPOSITIONS MAKE ME FEEL.
YOU GOT SLOPPY, DOUCHEBAG. I HAVE A WITNESS. AM I ON THE ROBOTICS TEAM, OR DO I TAKE MY CONCERNS ELSEWHERE?

FINE. YOU'RE ON THE TEAM.

THANK YOU FOR THE OPPORTUNITY.

I TOOK CARE OF IT. THANKS!

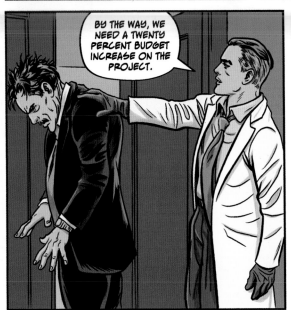
BY THE WAY, WE NEED A TWENTY PERCENT BUDGET INCREASE ON THE PROJECT.

CATCH YA LATER.

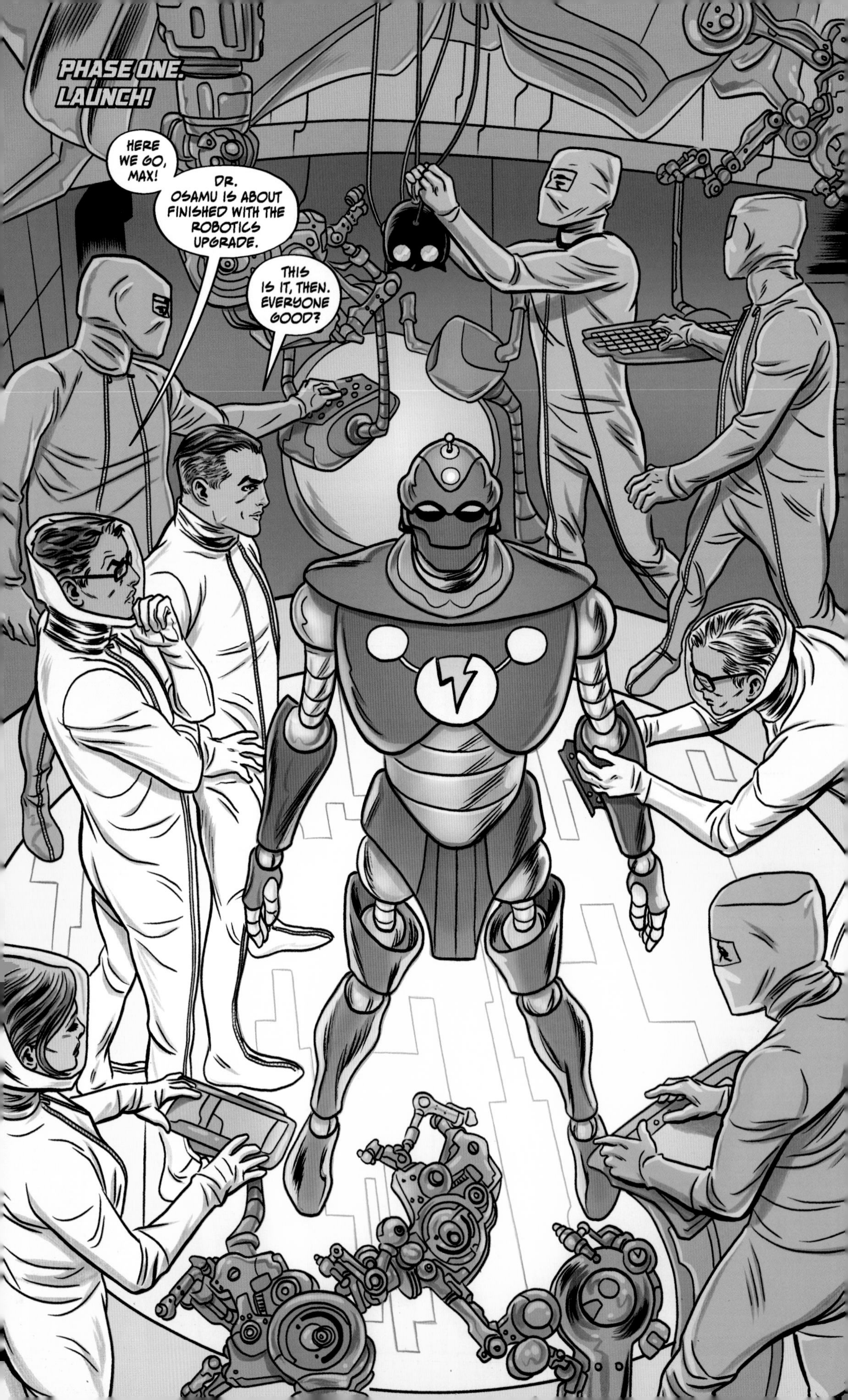
PHASE ONE. LAUNCH!
HERE WE GO, MAX!
DR. OSAMU IS ABOUT FINISHED WITH THE ROBOTICS UPGRADE.
THIS IS IT, THEN. EVERYONE GOOD?

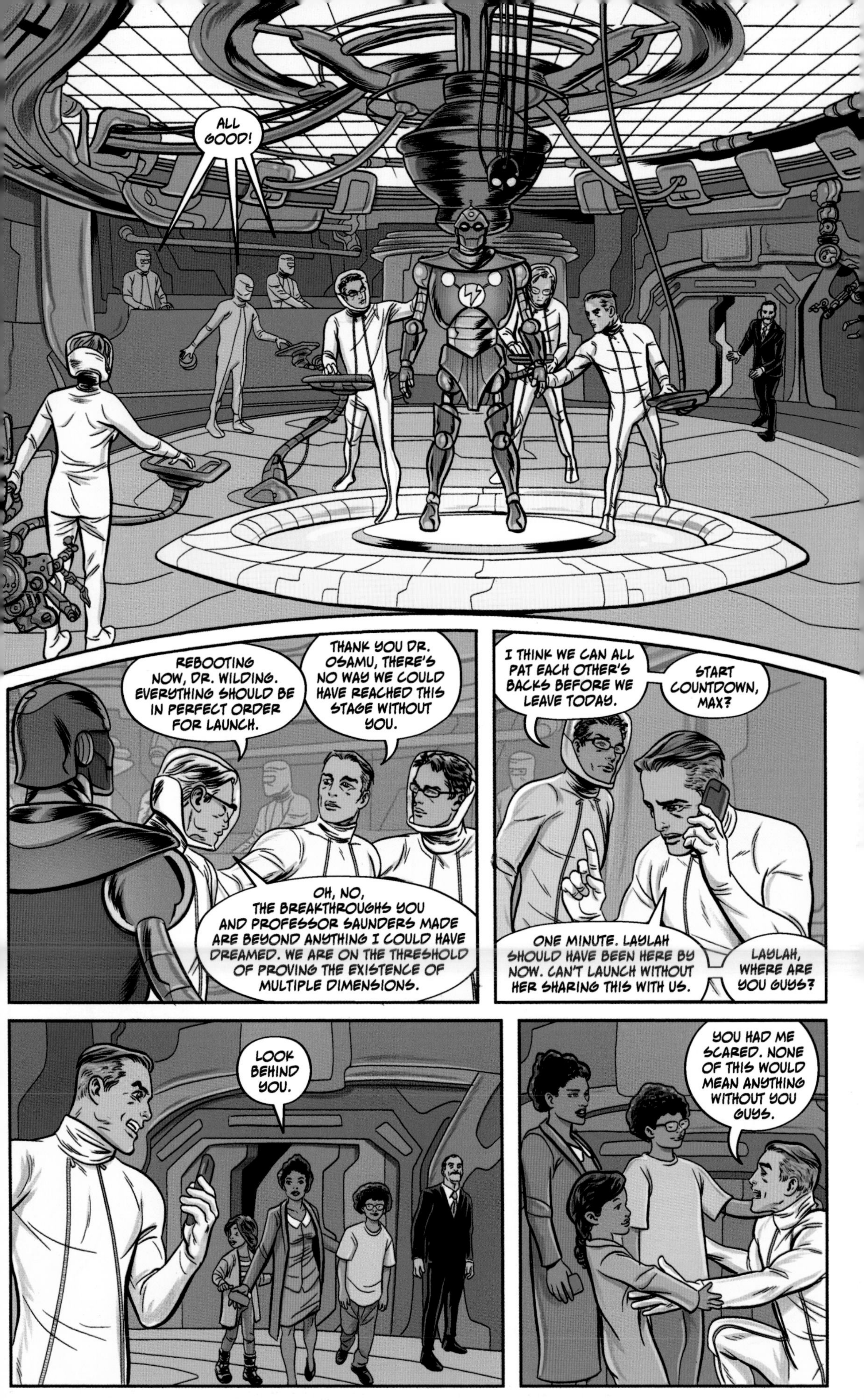
ALL GOOD!
REBOOTING NOW, DR. WILDING. EVERYTHING SHOULD BE IN PERFECT ORDER FOR LAUNCH.
THANK YOU DR. OSAMU, THERE'S NO WAY WE COULD HAVE REACHED THIS STAGE WITHOUT YOU.
OH, NO, THE BREAKTHROUGHS YOU AND PROFESSOR SAUNDERS MADE ARE BEYOND ANYTHING I COULD HAVE DREAMED. WE ARE ON THE THRESHOLD OF PROVING THE EXISTENCE OF MULTIPLE DIMENSIONS.
I THINK WE CAN ALL PAT EACH OTHER'S BACKS BEFORE WE LEAVE TODAY.
START COUNTDOWN, MAX?
ONE MINUTE. LAYLAH SHOULD HAVE BEEN HERE BY NOW. CAN'T LAUNCH WITHOUT HER SHARING THIS WITH US.
LAYLAH, WHERE ARE YOU GUYS?
LOOK BEHIND YOU.
YOU HAD ME SCARED. NONE OF THIS WOULD MEAN ANYTHING WITHOUT YOU GUYS.

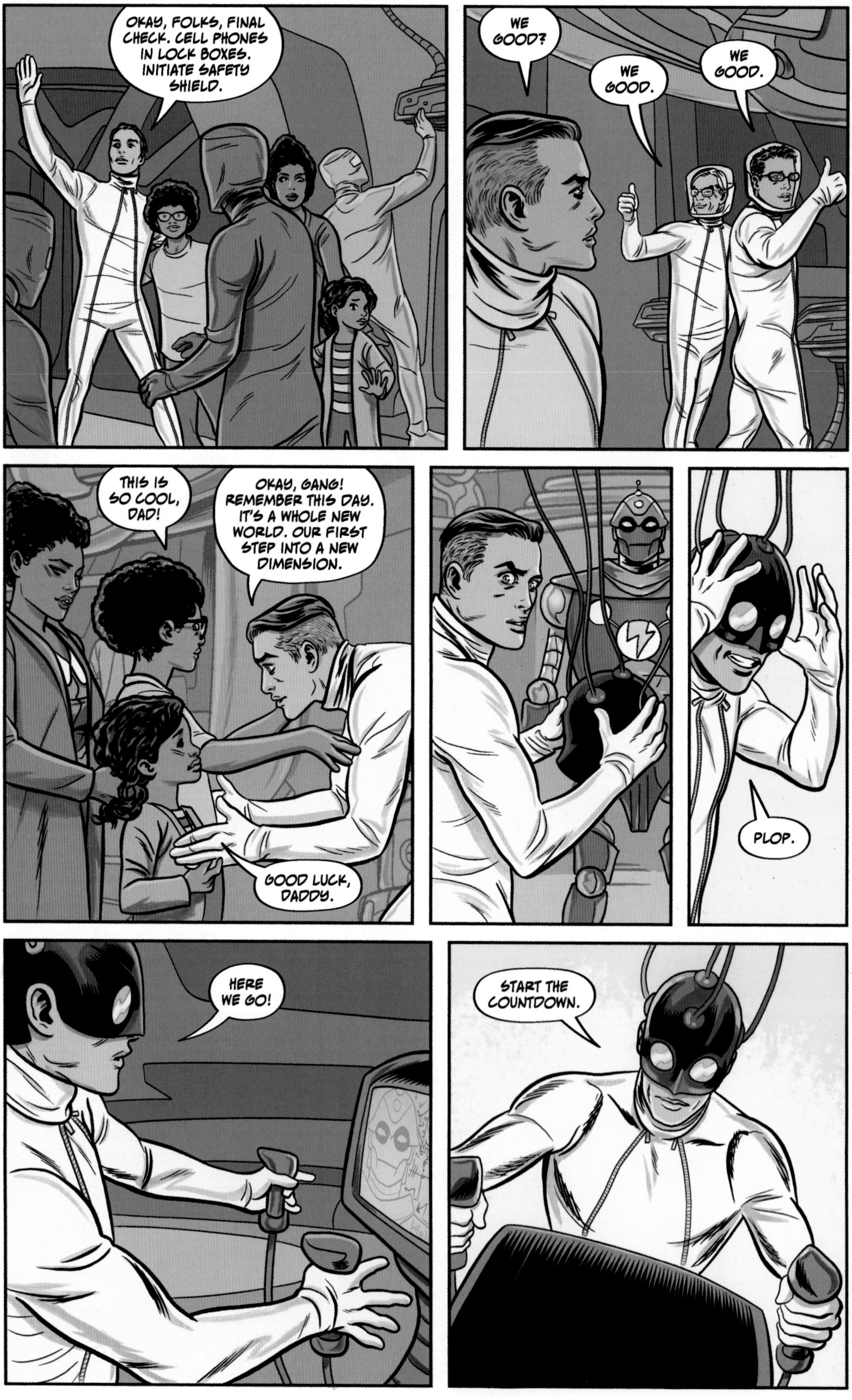
OKAY, FOLKS, FINAL CHECK. CELL PHONES IN LOCK BOXES. INITIATE SAFETY SHIELD.
WE GOOD?
WE GOOD.
WE GOOD.
THIS IS SO COOL, DAD!
OKAY, GANG! REMEMBER THIS DAY. IT'S A WHOLE NEW WORLD. OUR FIRST STEP INTO A NEW DIMENSION.
GOOD LUCK, DADDY.
PLOP.
HERE WE GO!
START THE COUNTDOWN.

10-9-8-7-6-5-4-3-2-1
VRRRRRRRRR
CHK
CHK
CHK
WHOOSH
WHERE'S THE ROBOT? WAS THIS SUPPOSED TO HAPPEN?
PLEASE STEP BACK, MR. REYNOLDS! YOU'RE NOT WEARING ANY PROTECTION, AND THERE ARE TOO MANY UNKNOWNS AT THIS POINT.
THROUGH HIS HELMET, DR. WILDING CAN SEE WHERE THE ROBOT IS TRAVELING. IT SHOULD RETURN VERY QUICKLY AT THIS STAGE.

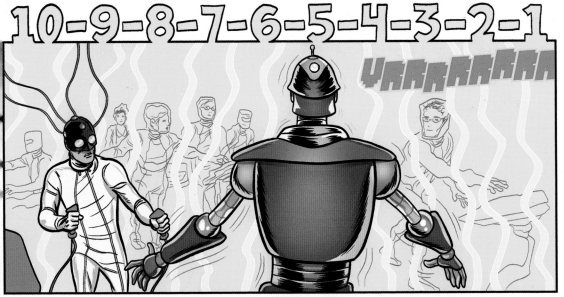

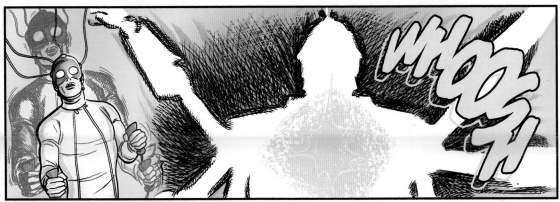

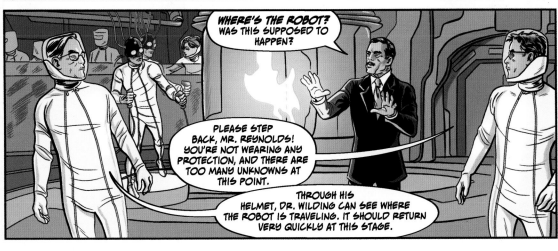

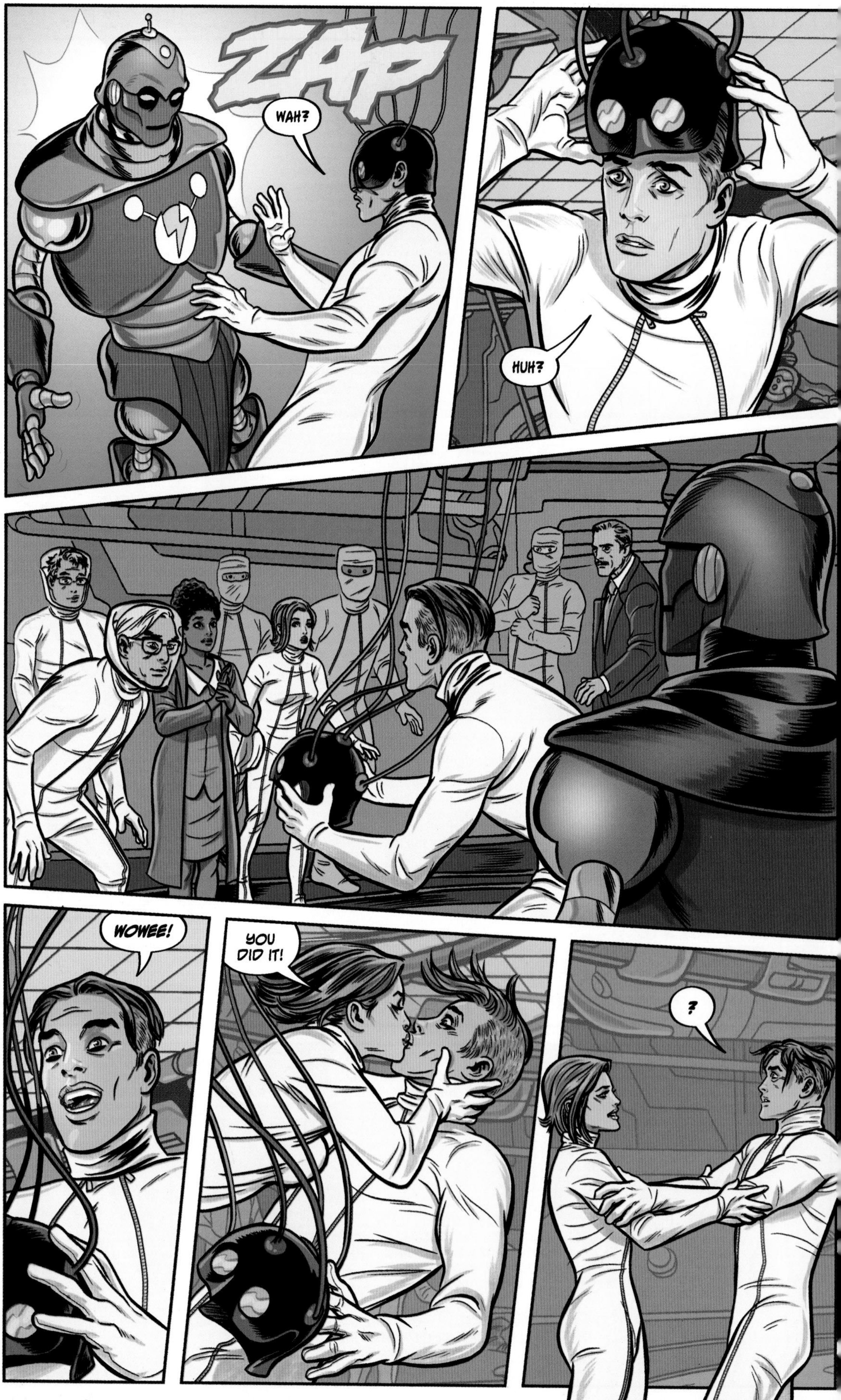
ZAP
WAH?
HUH?
WOWEE!
YOU DID IT!
?

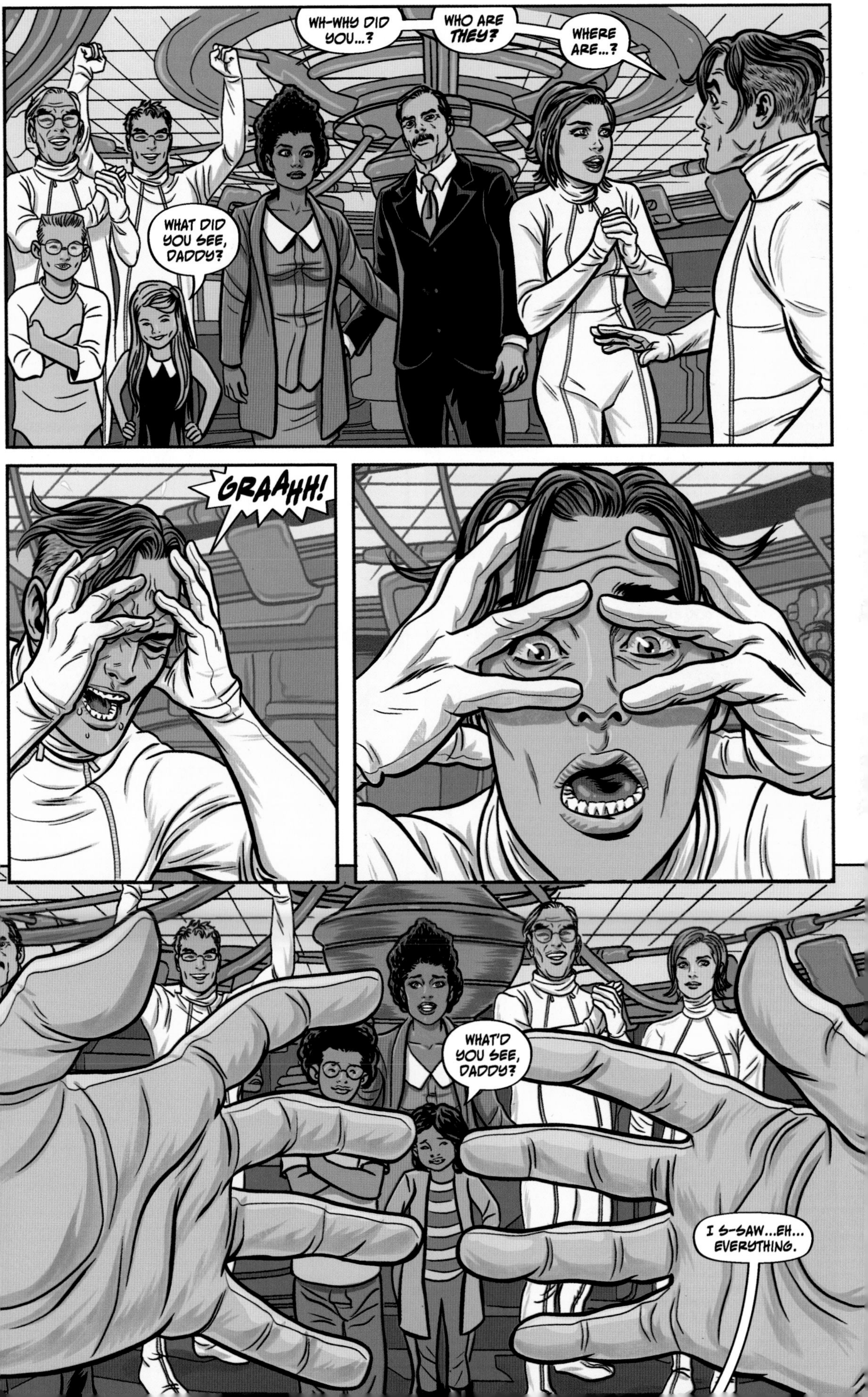
WH-WHY DID YOU...?
WHO ARE THEY?
WHERE ARE...?
WHAT DID YOU SEE, DADDY?
GRAAHH!
WHAT'D YOU SEE, DADDY?
I S-SAW...EH... EVERYTHING.

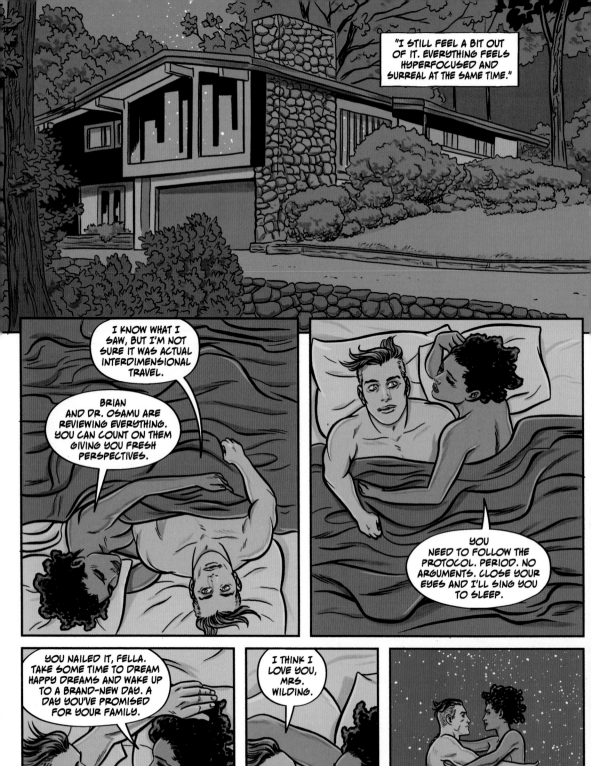

"I STILL FEEL A BIT OUT OF IT. EVERYTHING FEELS HYPERFOCUSED AND SURREAL AT THE SAME TIME."

I KNOW WHAT I SAW, BUT I'M NOT SURE IT WAS ACTUAL INTERDIMENSIONAL TRAVEL.

BRIAN AND DR. OSAMU ARE REVIEWING EVERYTHING. YOU CAN COUNT ON THEM GIVING YOU FRESH PERSPECTIVES.

YOU NEED TO FOLLOW THE PROTOCOL. PERIOD. NO ARGUMENTS. CLOSE YOUR EYES AND I'LL SING YOU TO SLEEP.

YOU NAILED IT, FELLA. TAKE SOME TIME TO DREAM HAPPY DREAMS AND WAKE UP TO A BRAND-NEW DAY. A DAY YOU'VE PROMISED FOR YOUR FAMILY.

IN A COUPLE DAYS YOU'LL ALL COMPARE NOTES AS OBJECTIVELY AS POSSIBLE AND KNOW EXACTLY WHAT YOUR NEXT BIG LEAP IS.

I THINK I LOVE YOU, MRS. WILDING.

I KNOW YOU DO, DR. WILDING.

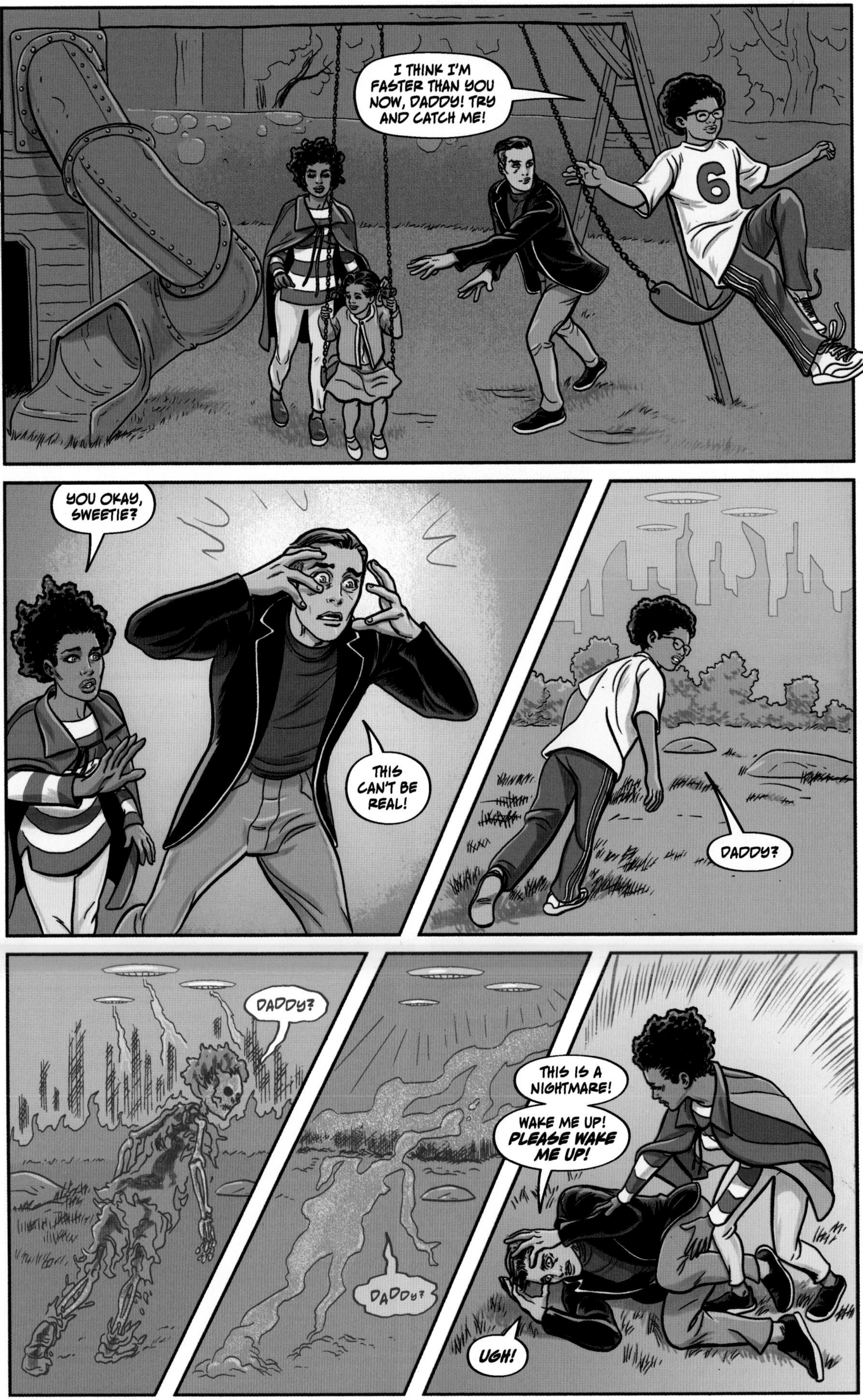
I THINK I'M FASTER THAN YOU NOW, DADDY! TRY AND CATCH ME!
6
YOU OKAY, SWEETIE?
THIS CAN'T BE REAL!
DADDY?
DADDY?
DADDY?
THIS IS A NIGHTMARE!
WAKE ME UP! PLEASE WAKE ME UP!
UGH!

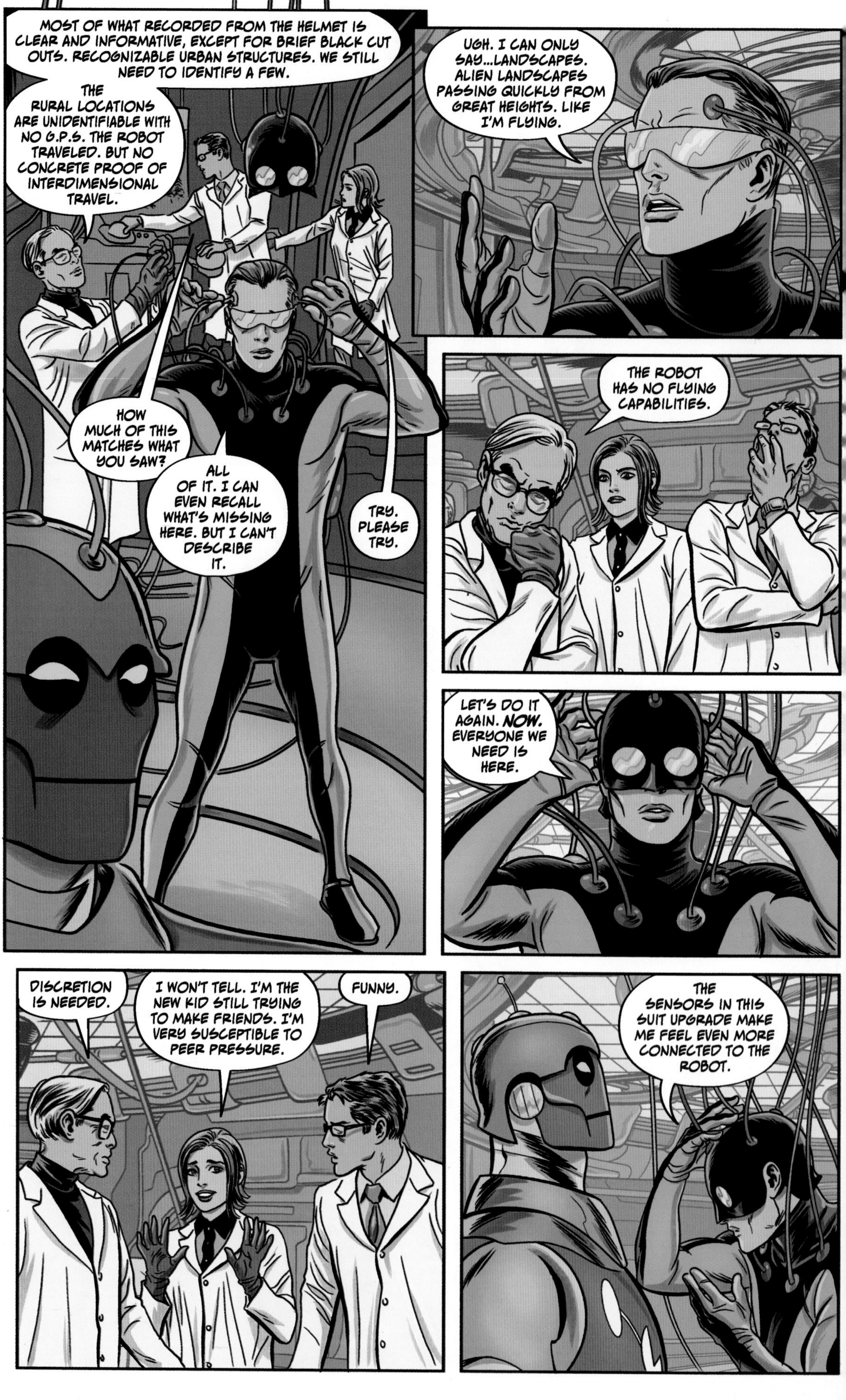
MOST OF WHAT RECORDED FROM THE HELMET IS CLEAR AND INFORMATIVE, EXCEPT FOR BRIEF BLACK CUT OUTS. RECOGNIZABLE URBAN STRUCTURES. WE STILL NEED TO IDENTIFY A FEW.
THE RURAL LOCATIONS ARE UNIDENTIFIABLE WITH NO G.P.S. THE ROBOT TRAVELED. BUT NO CONCRETE PROOF OF INTERDIMENSIONAL TRAVEL.
HOW MUCH OF THIS MATCHES WHAT YOU SAW?
ALL OF IT. I CAN EVEN RECALL WHAT'S MISSING HERE. BUT I CAN'T DESCRIBE IT.
TRY. PLEASE TRY.
UGH. I CAN ONLY SAY...LANDSCAPES. ALIEN LANDSCAPES PASSING QUICKLY FROM GREAT HEIGHTS. LIKE I'M FLYING.
THE ROBOT HAS NO FLYING CAPABILITIES.
LET'S DO IT AGAIN. NOW. EVERYONE WE NEED IS HERE.
DISCRETION IS NEEDED.
I WON'T TELL. I'M THE NEW KID STILL TRYING TO MAKE FRIENDS. I'M VERY SUSCEPTIBLE TO PEER PRESSURE.
FUNNY.
THE SENSORS IN THIS SUIT UPGRADE MAKE ME FEEL EVEN MORE CONNECTED TO THE ROBOT.

10-9-8-7-6-5-4-3-2-1
WHOA.
WHOA!
WHOA!
VVVVVRRRRRRRRRRRRRR
WHAT'S THIS?
ZAP
NO!
HOLY SH--!

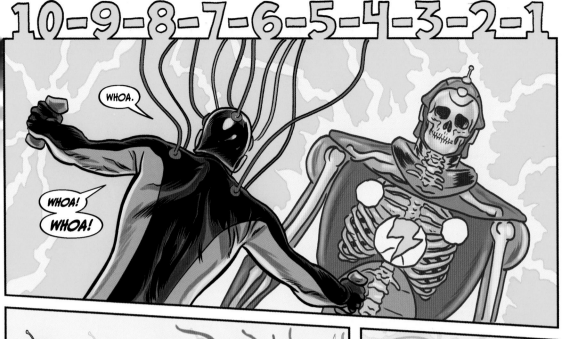

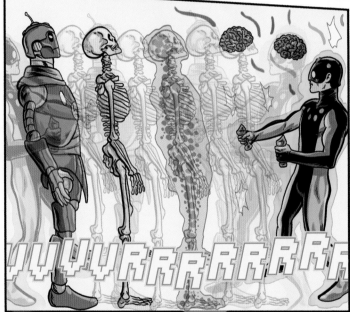

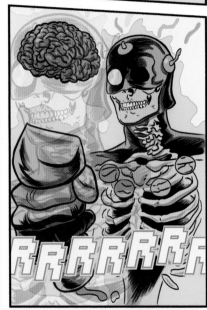

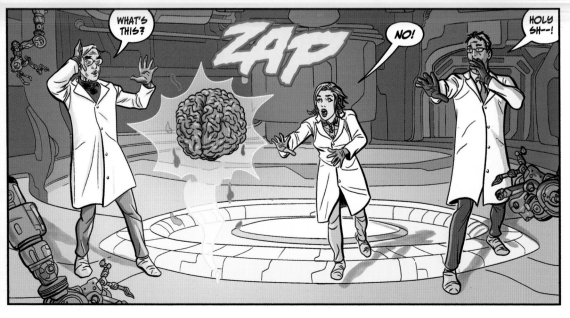

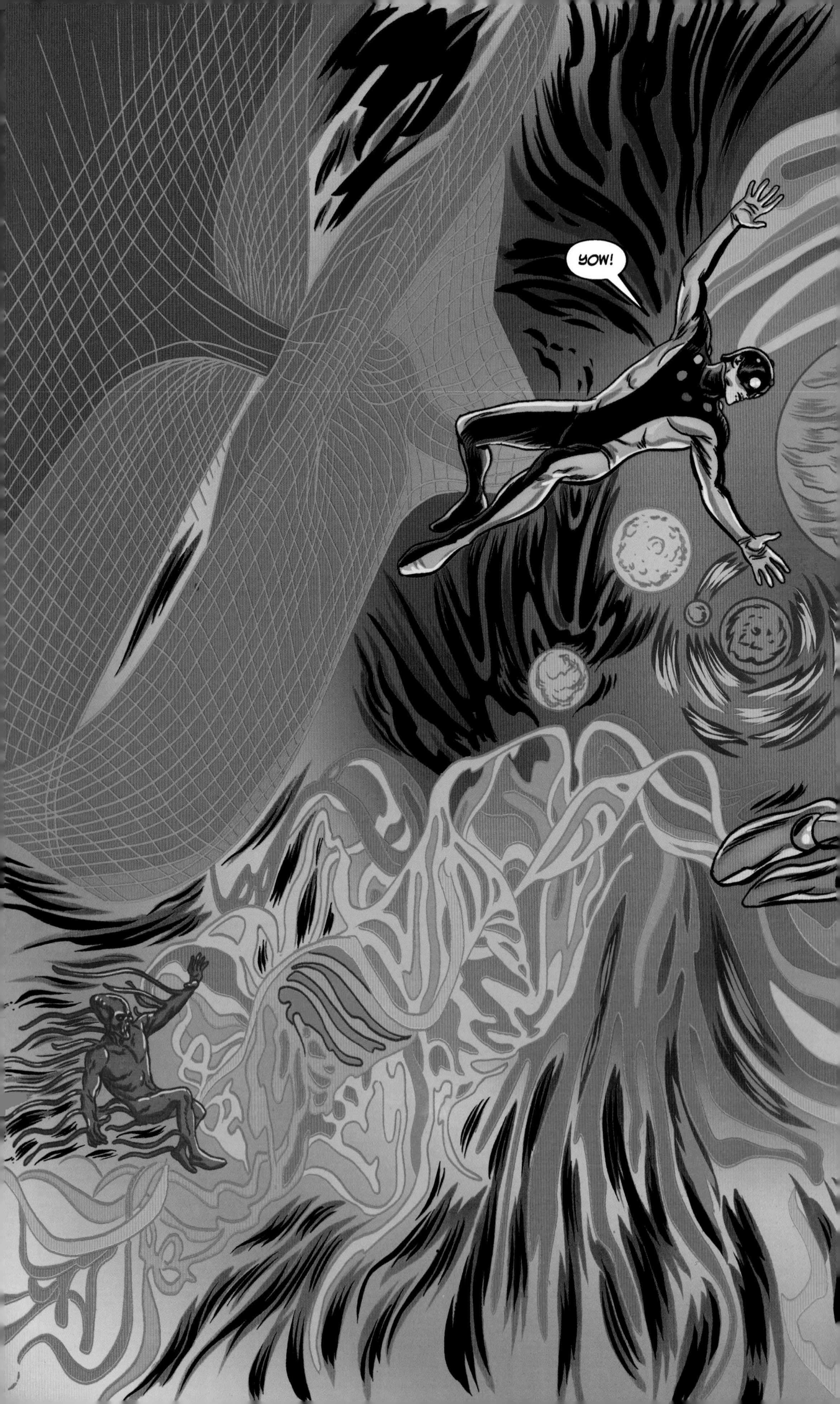
YOW!

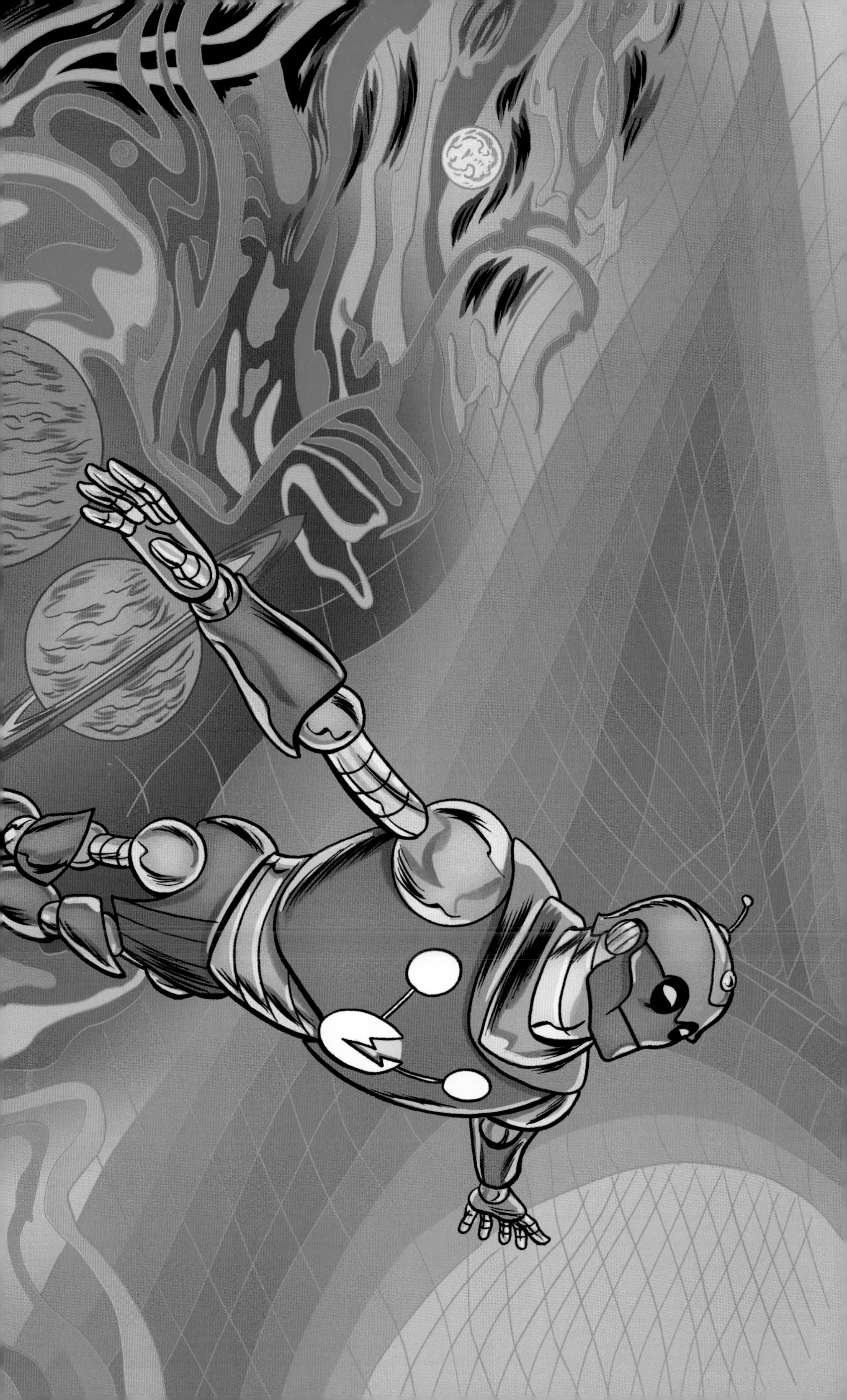

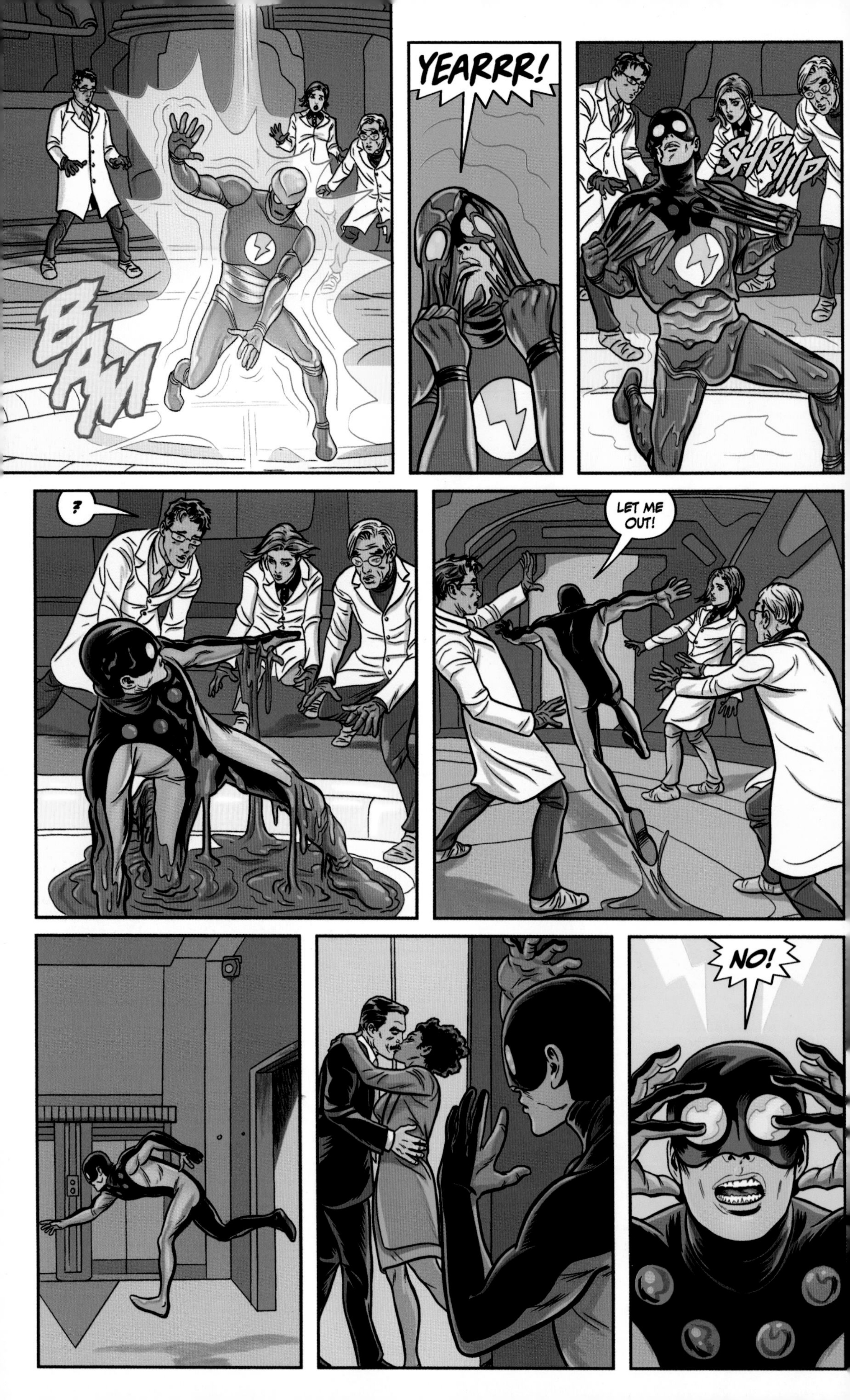
BAM
YEARRR!
SHRIIIP
?
LET ME OUT!
NO!

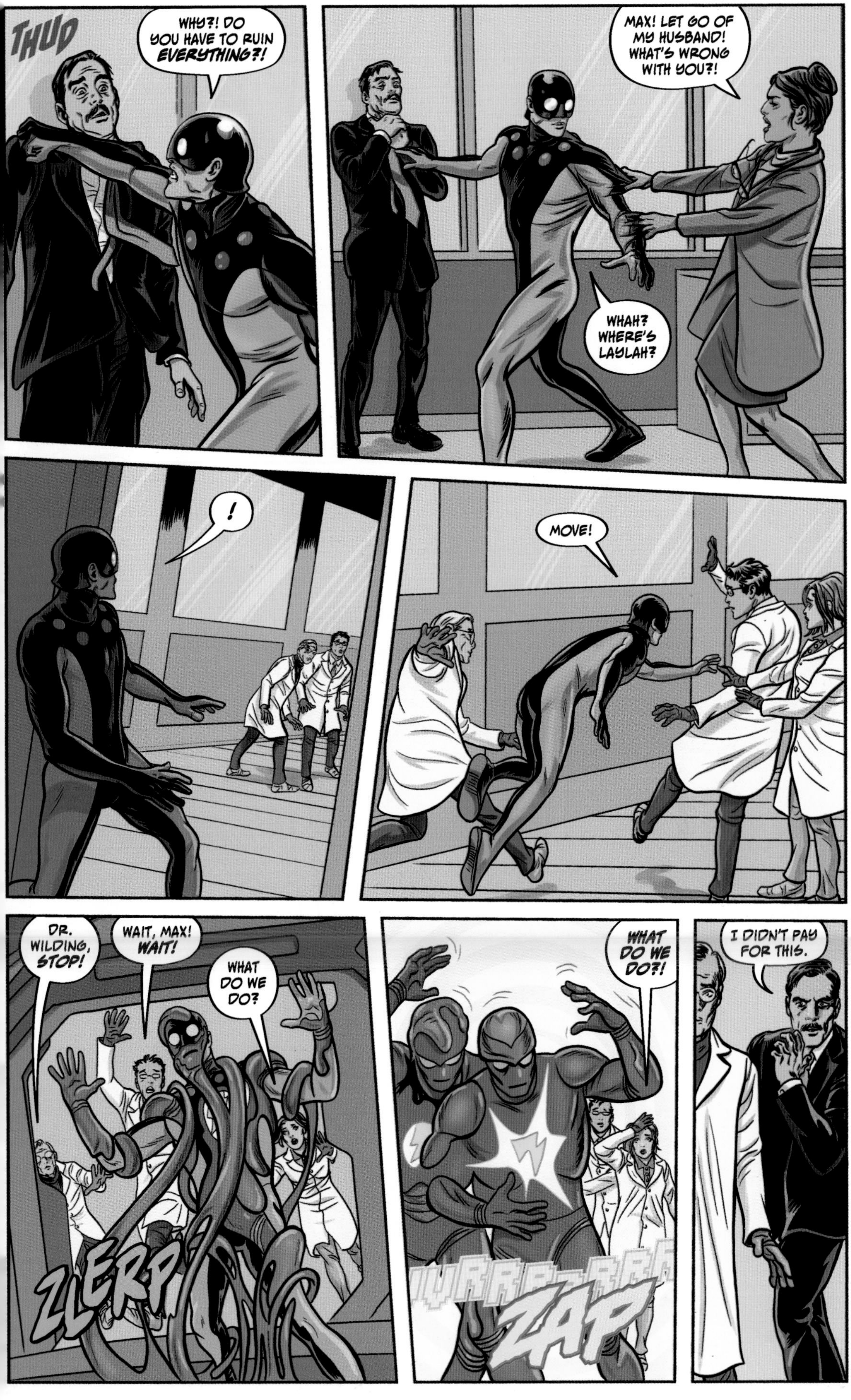
THUD
WHY?! DO YOU HAVE TO RUIN EVERYTHING?!
MAX! LET GO OF MY HUSBAND! WHAT'S WRONG WITH YOU?!
WHAH? WHERE'S LAYLAH?
!
MOVE!
DR. WILDING, STOP!
WAIT, MAX! WAIT!
WHAT DO WE DO?
ZLERP
WHAT DO WE DO?!
ZAP
I DIDN'T PAY FOR THIS.

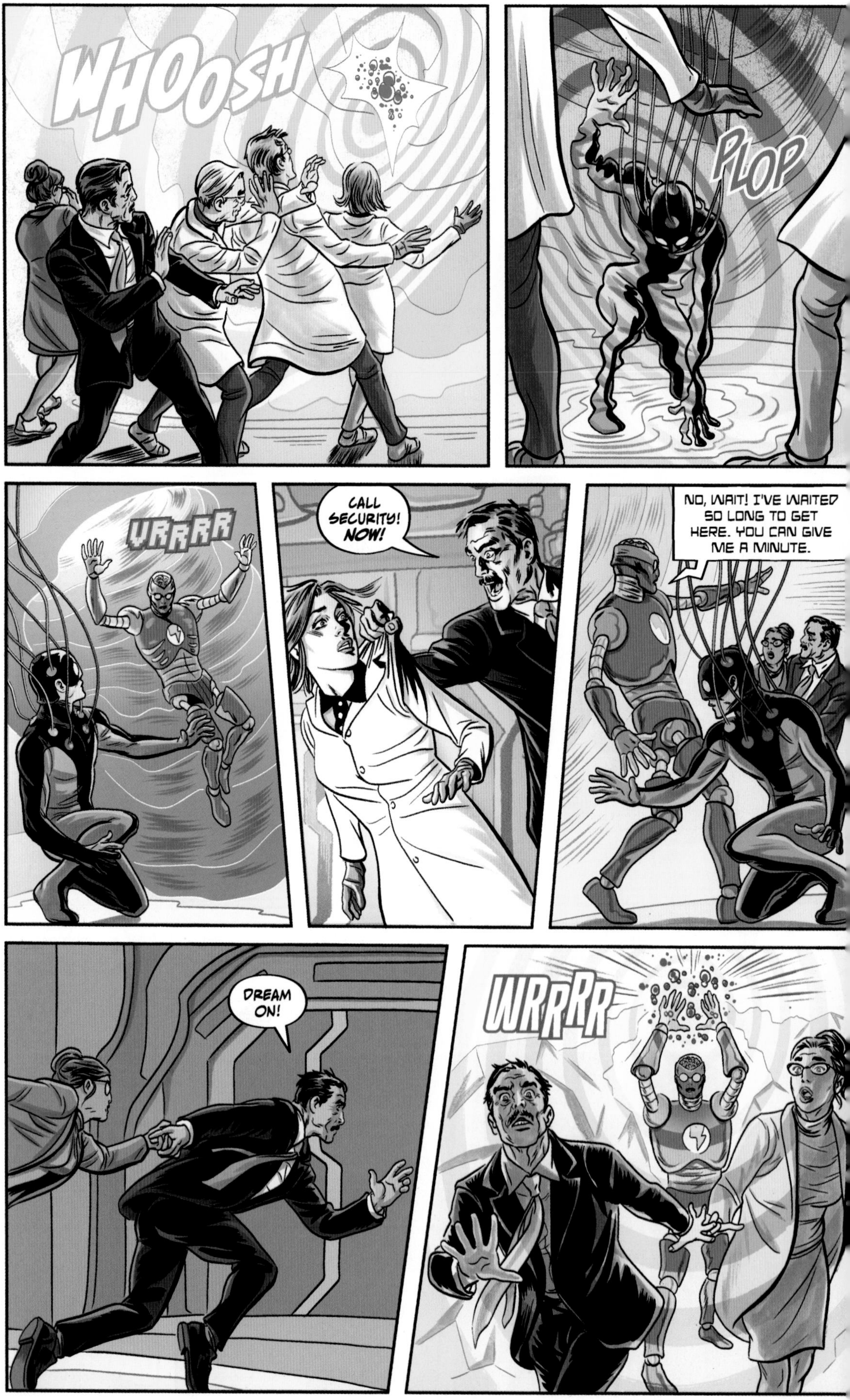
WHOOSH
PLOP
VRRRR
CALL SECURITY! NOW!
NO, WAIT! I'VE WAITED SO LONG TO GET HERE. YOU CAN GIVE ME A MINUTE.
DREAM ON!
WRRRR

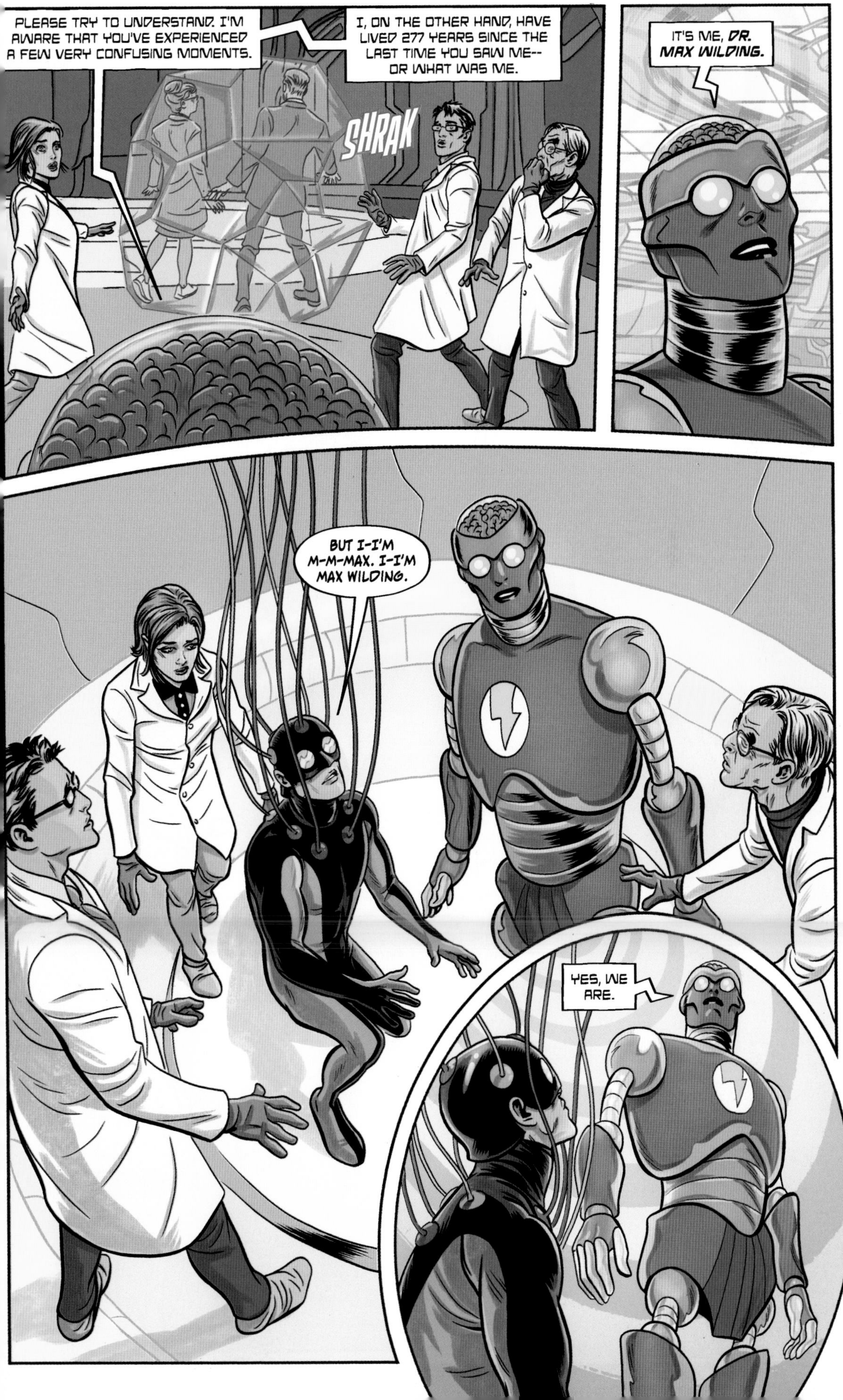
PLEASE TRY TO UNDERSTAND. I'M AWARE THAT YOU'VE EXPERIENCED A FEW VERY CONFUSING MOMENTS.
I, ON THE OTHER HAND, HAVE LIVED 277 YEARS SINCE THE LAST TIME YOU SAW ME-- OR WHAT WAS ME.
SHRAK
IT'S ME, DR. MAX WILDING.
BUT I-I'M M-M-MAX. I-I'M MAX WILDING.
YES, WE ARE.

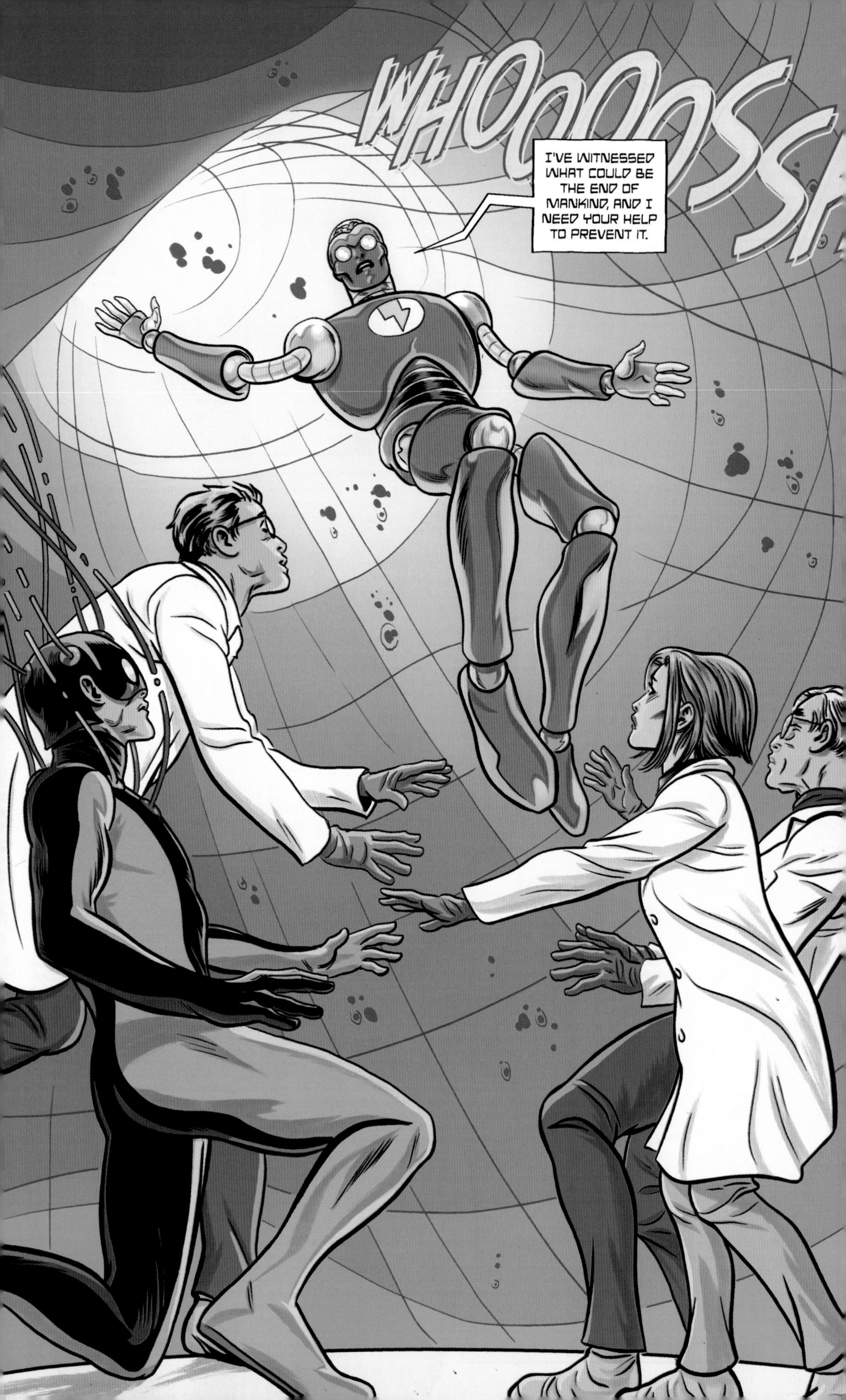
WHOOOOOSH!
I'VE WITNESSED WHAT COULD BE THE END OF MANKIND, AND I NEED YOUR HELP TO PREVENT IT.

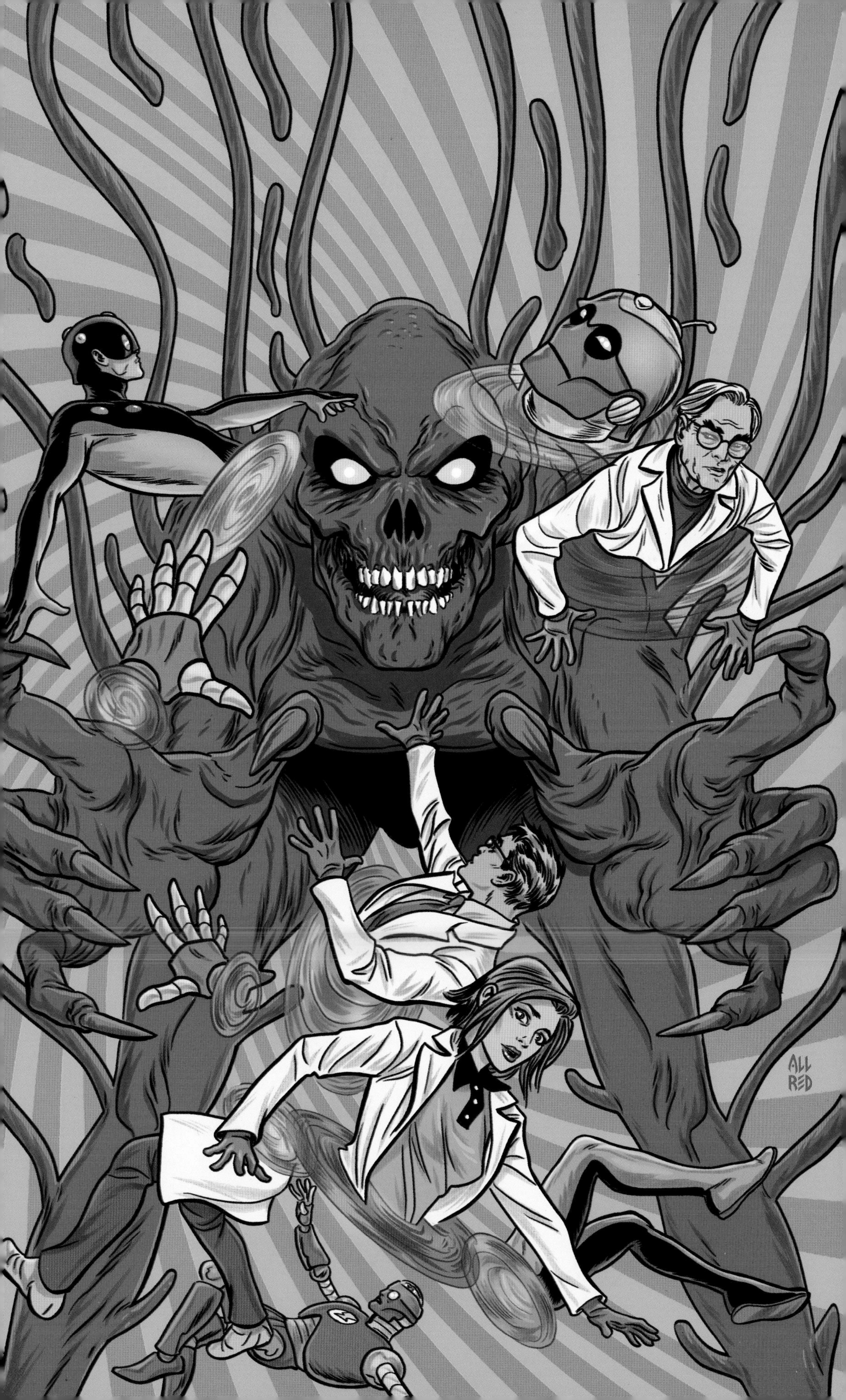
ALL
RED

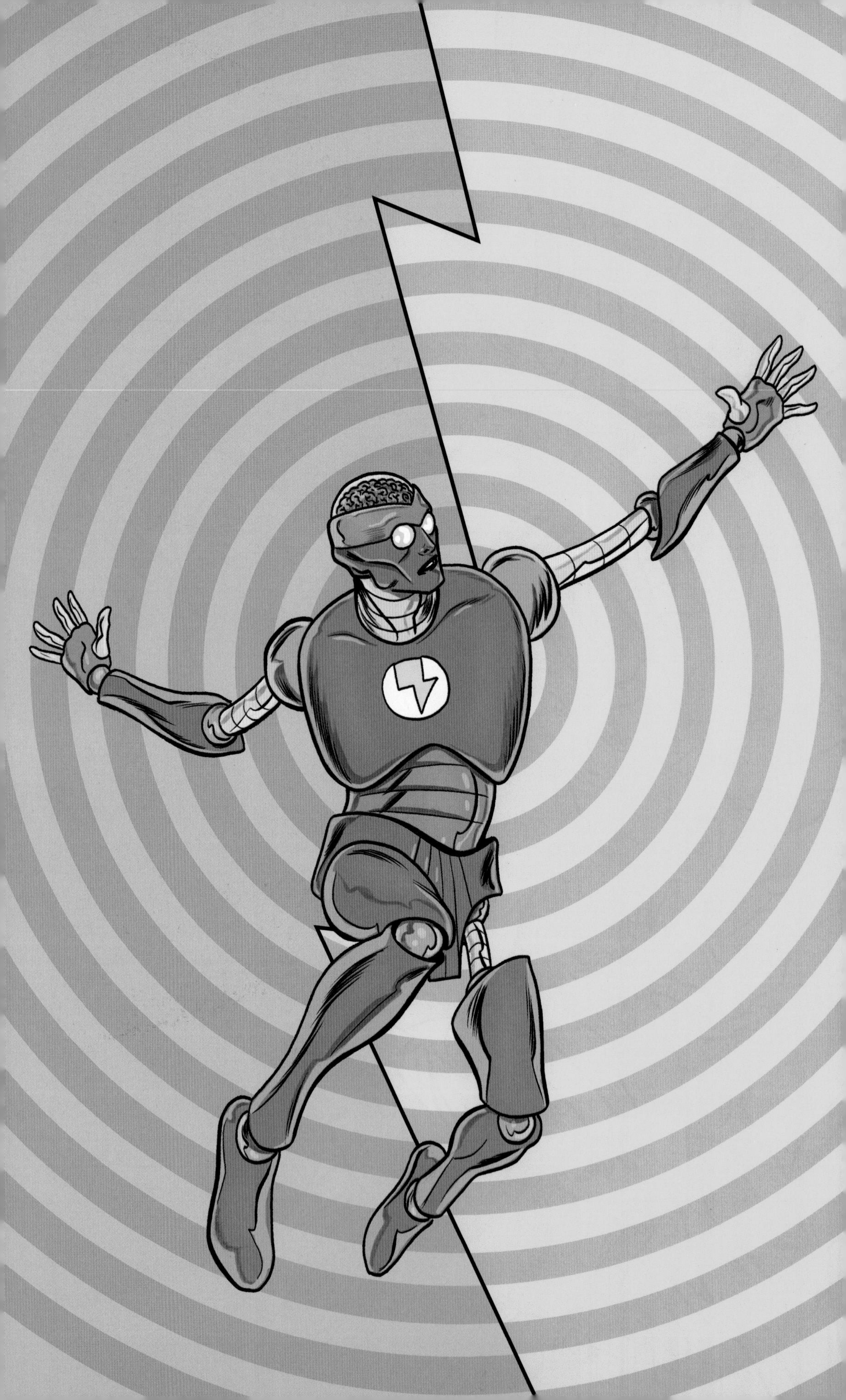

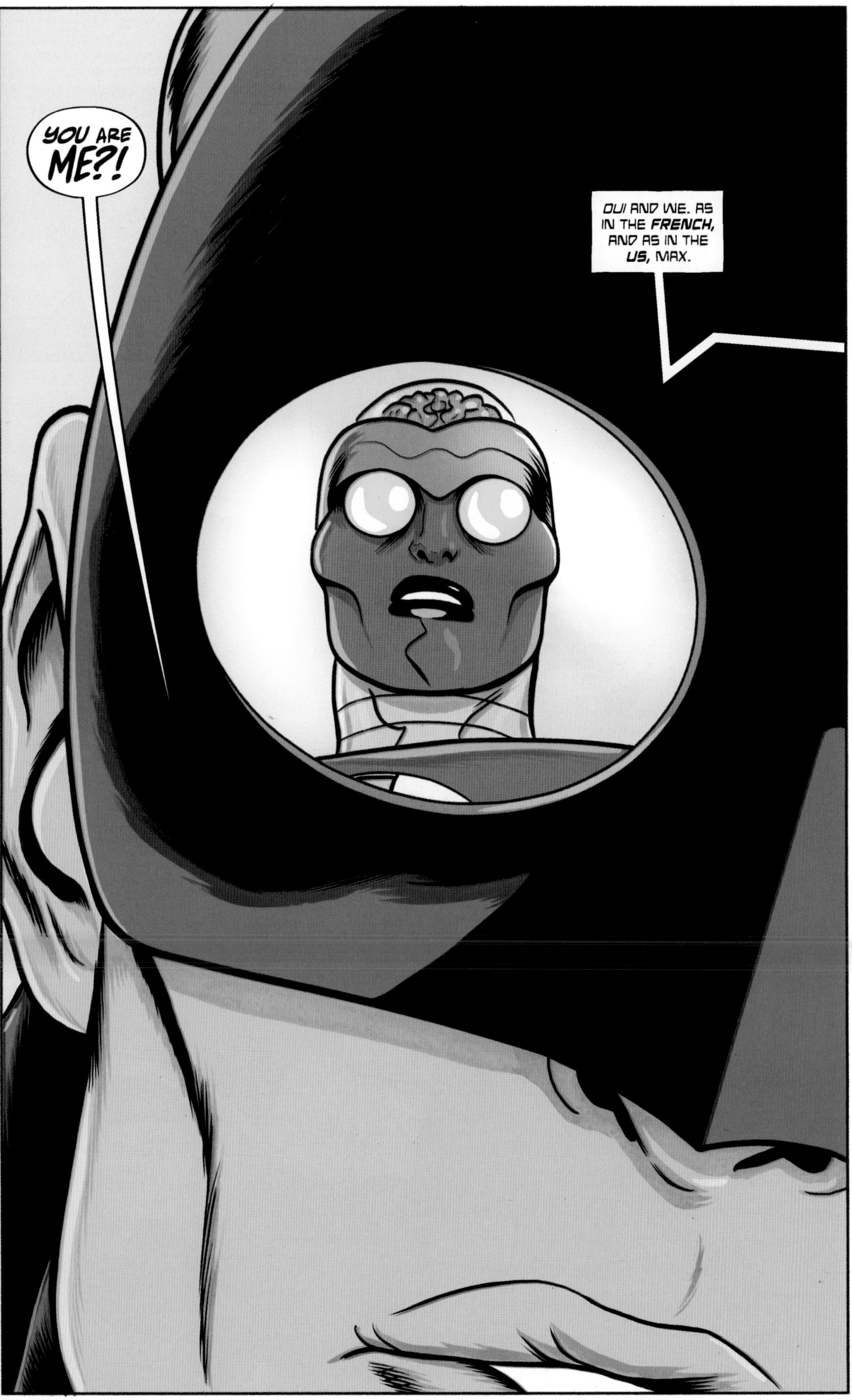
YOU ARE ME?!
OUI AND WE. AS IN THE FRENCH, AND AS IN THE US, MAX.

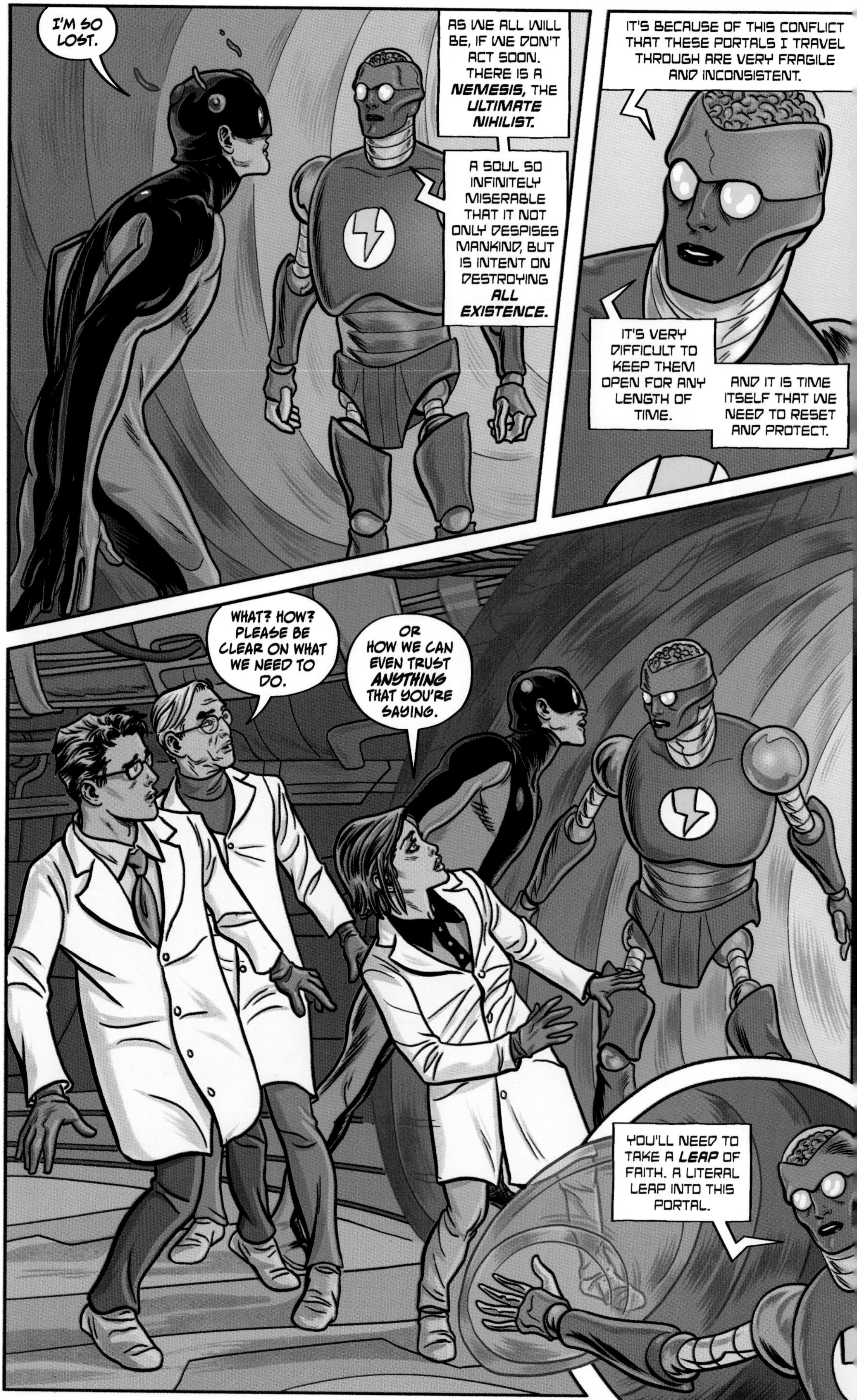
I'M SO LOST.
AS WE ALL WILL BE, IF WE DON'T ACT SOON. THERE IS A NEMESIS, THE ULTIMATE NIHILIST.
A SOUL SO INFINITELY MISERABLE THAT IT NOT ONLY DESPISES MANKIND, BUT IS INTENT ON DESTROYING ALL EXISTENCE.
IT'S BECAUSE OF THIS CONFLICT THAT THESE PORTALS I TRAVEL THROUGH ARE VERY FRAGILE AND INCONSISTENT.
IT'S VERY DIFFICULT TO KEEP THEM OPEN FOR ANY LENGTH OF TIME.
AND IT IS TIME ITSELF THAT WE NEED TO RESET AND PROTECT.
WHAT? HOW? PLEASE BE CLEAR ON WHAT WE NEED TO DO.
OR HOW WE CAN EVEN TRUST ANYTHING THAT YOU'RE SAYING.
YOU'LL NEED TO TAKE A LEAP OF FAITH. A LITERAL LEAP INTO THIS PORTAL.

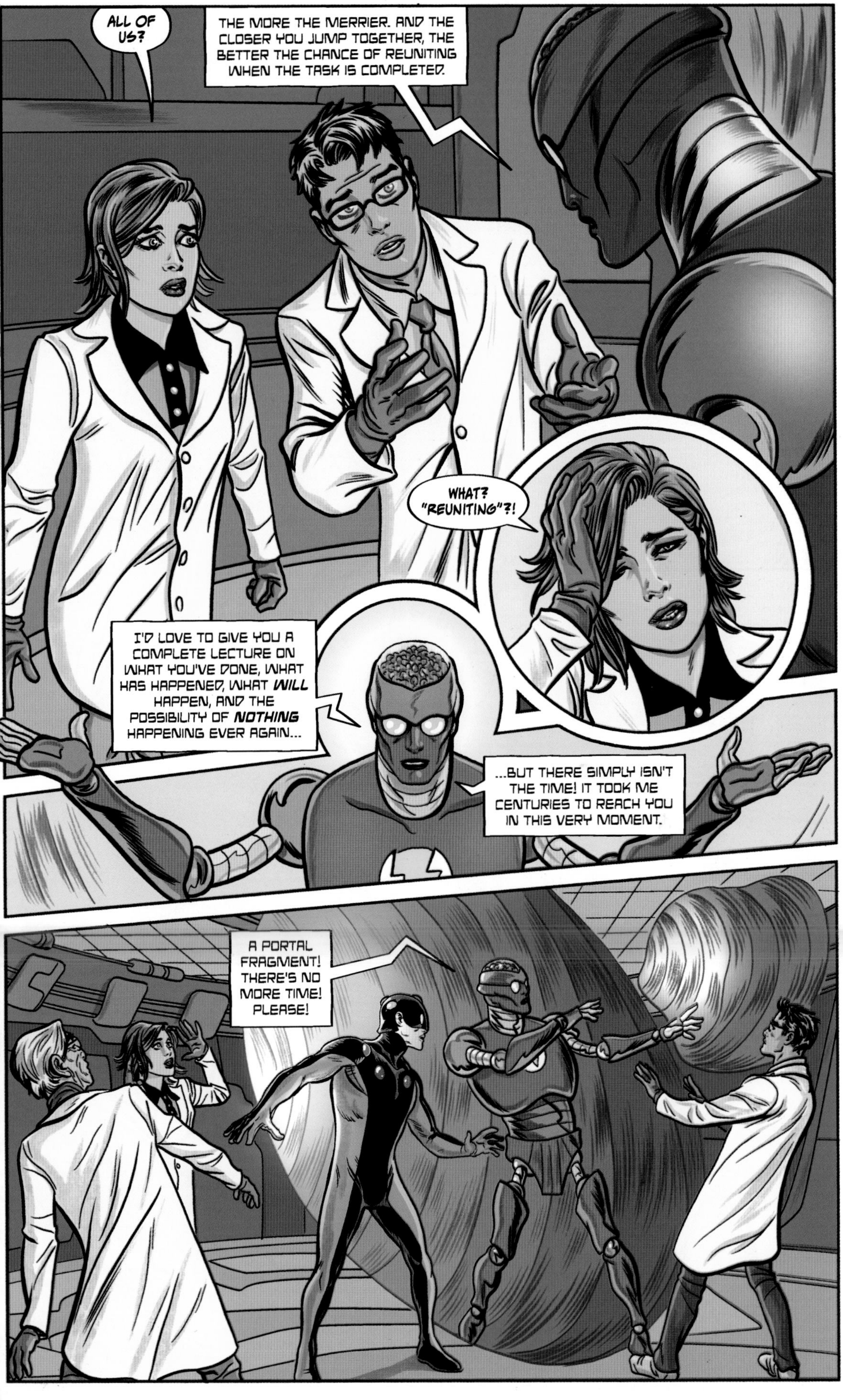

ALL OF US?
THE MORE THE MERRIER. AND THE CLOSER YOU JUMP TOGETHER, THE BETTER THE CHANCE OF REUNITING WHEN THE TASK IS COMPLETED.
WHAT? "REUNITING"?!
I'D LOVE TO GIVE YOU A COMPLETE LECTURE ON WHAT YOU'VE DONE, WHAT HAS HAPPENED, WHAT *WILL* HAPPEN, AND THE POSSIBILITY OF *NOTHING* HAPPENING EVER AGAIN...
...BUT THERE SIMPLY ISN'T THE TIME! IT TOOK ME CENTURIES TO REACH YOU IN THIS VERY MOMENT.
A PORTAL FRAGMENT! THERE'S NO MORE TIME! PLEASE!

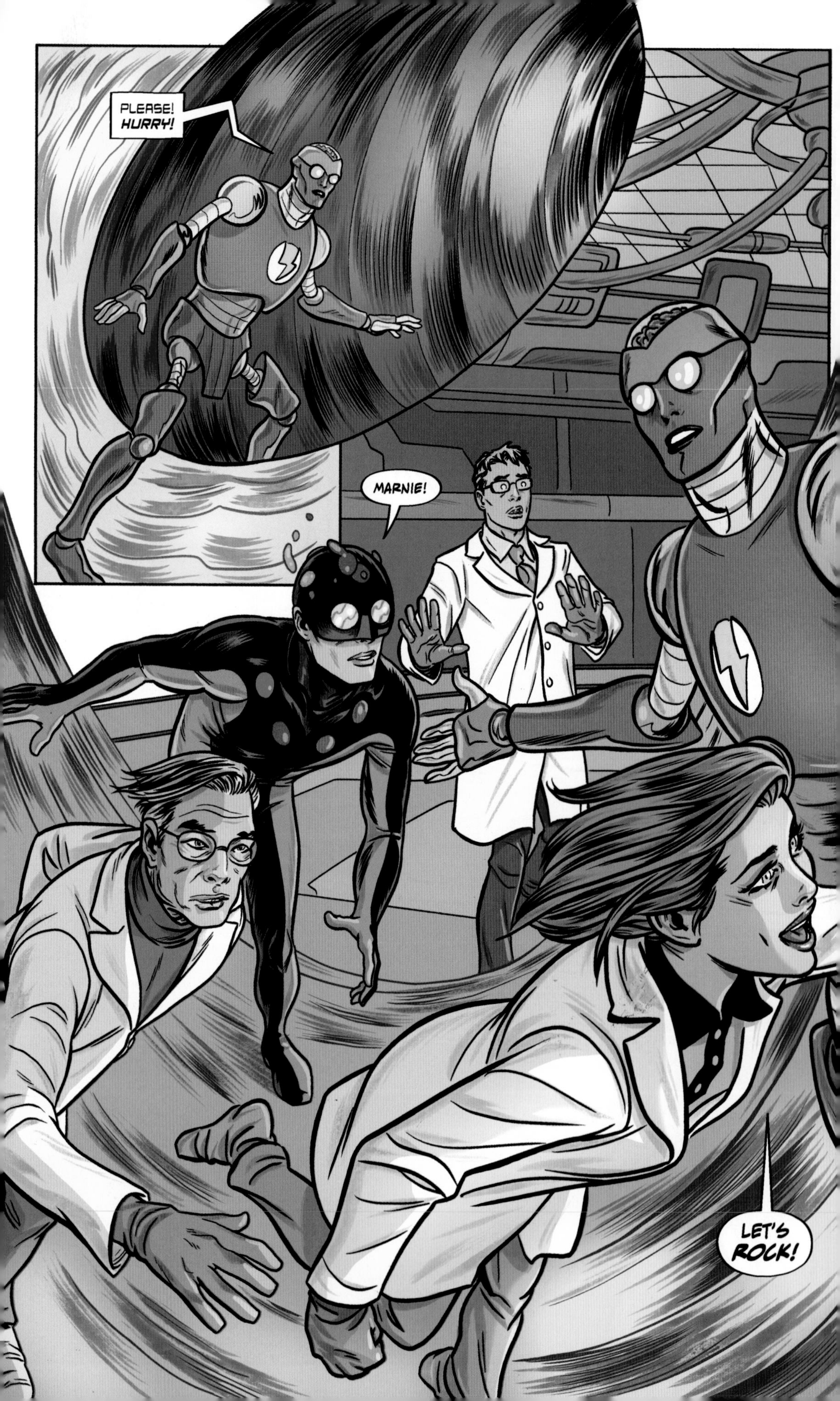
PLEASE! HURRY!
MARNIE!
LET'S ROCK!

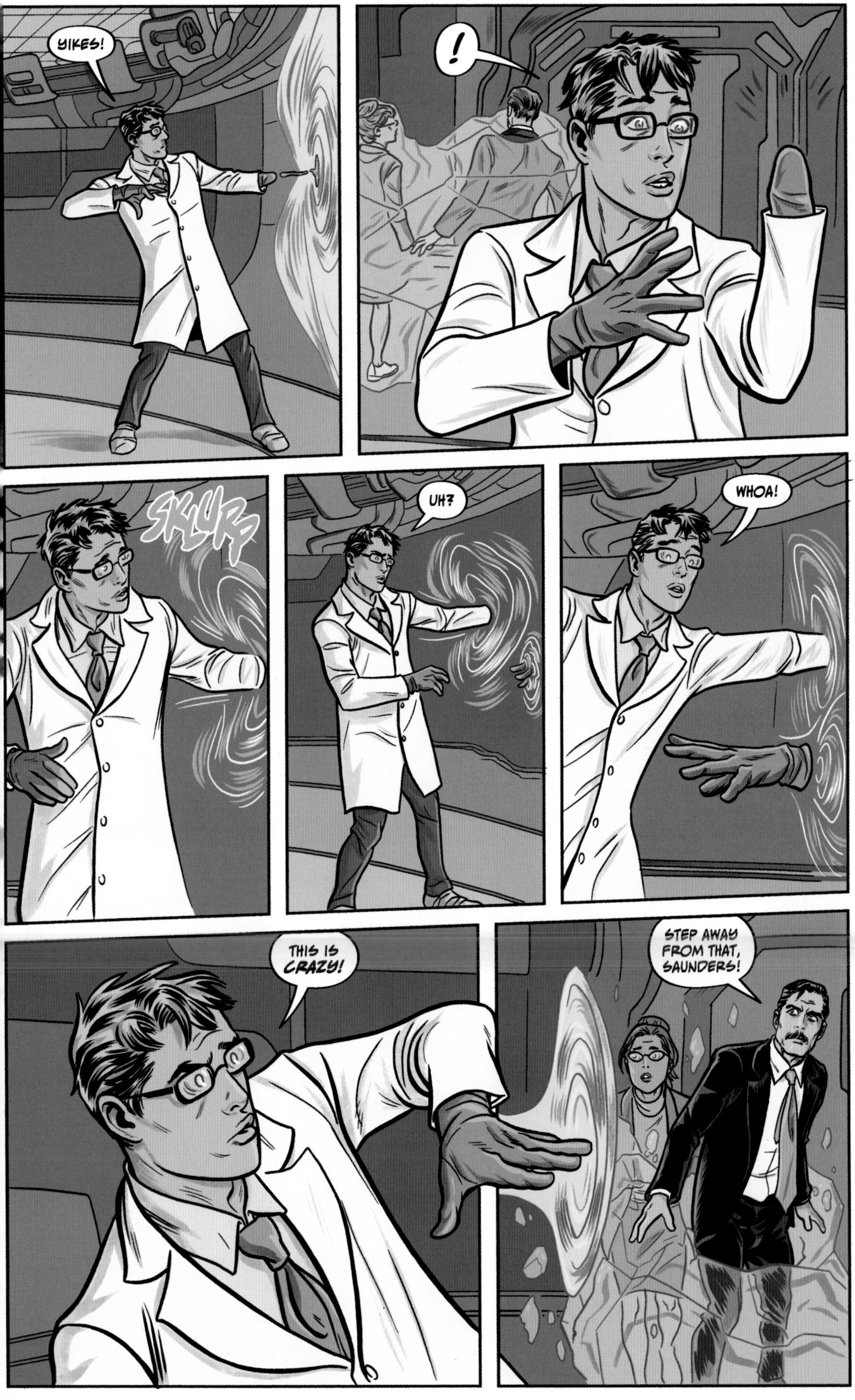
YIKES!
!
SKLURB
UH?
WHOA!
THIS IS CRAZY!
STEP AWAY FROM THAT, SAUNDERS!

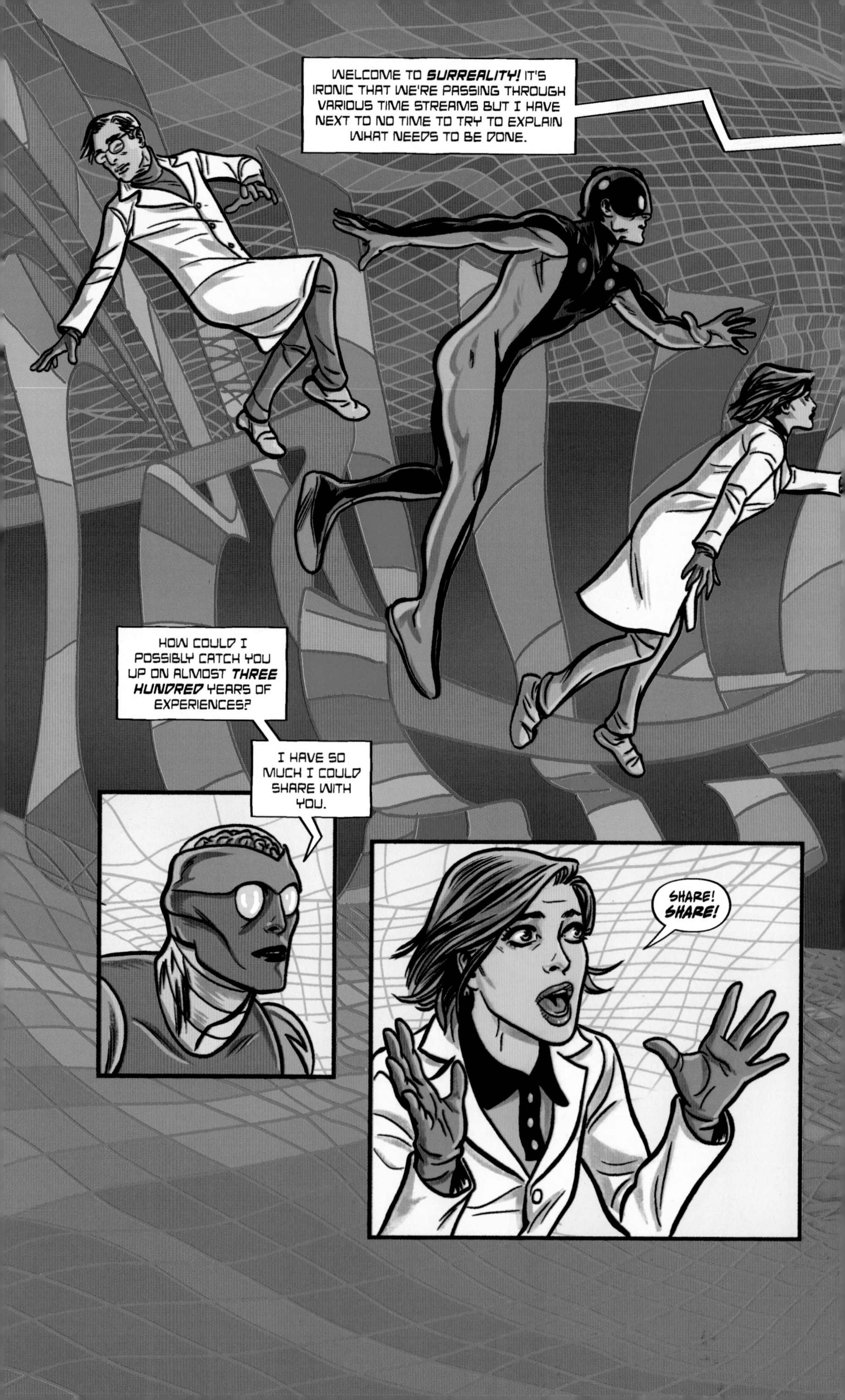
WELCOME TO SURREALITY! IT'S IRONIC THAT WE'RE PASSING THROUGH VARIOUS TIME STREAMS BUT I HAVE NEXT TO NO TIME TO TRY TO EXPLAIN WHAT NEEDS TO BE DONE.
HOW COULD I POSSIBLY CATCH YOU UP ON ALMOST THREE HUNDRED YEARS OF EXPERIENCES?
I HAVE SO MUCH I COULD SHARE WITH YOU.
SHARE! SHARE!

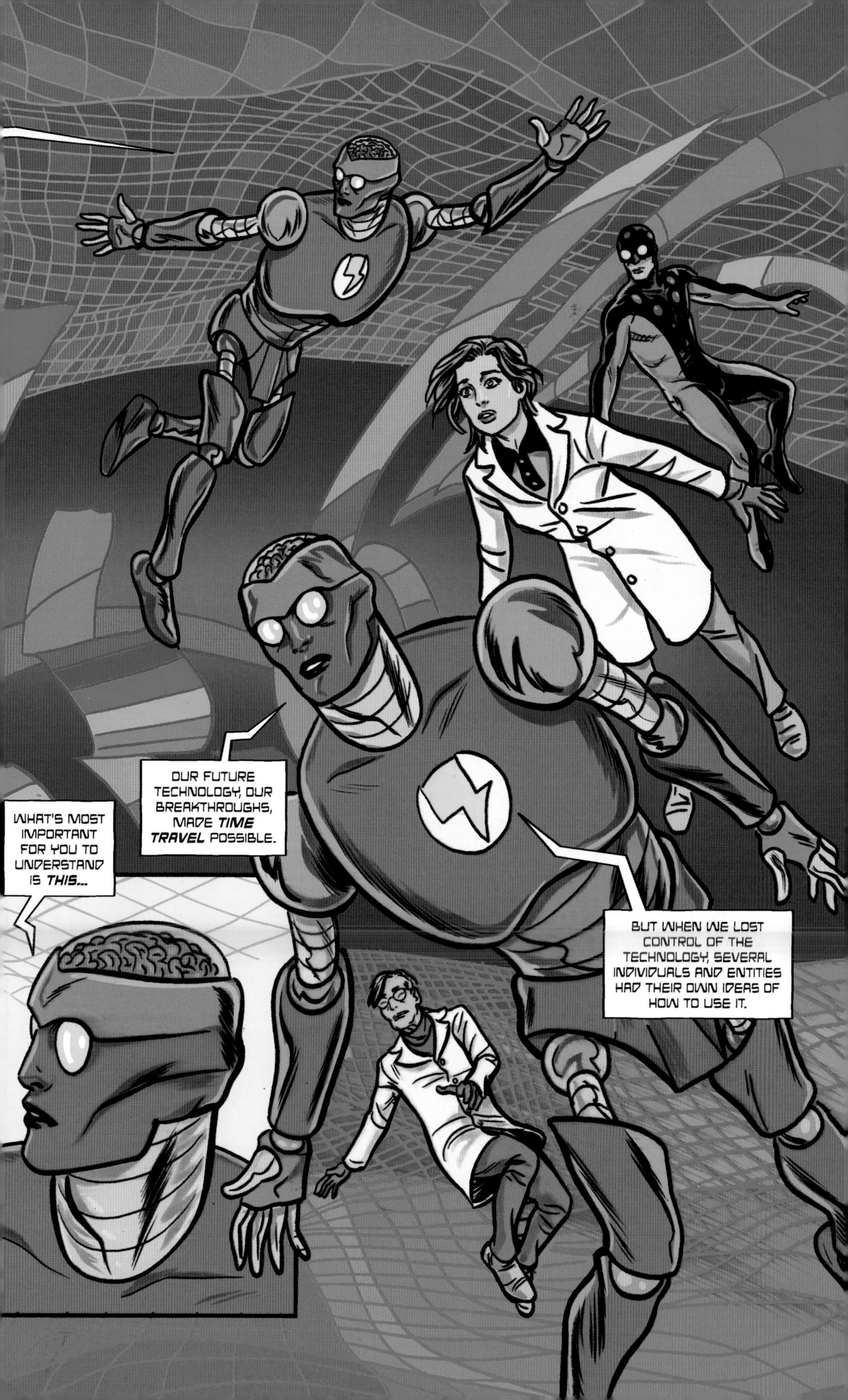
OUR FUTURE TECHNOLOGY, OUR BREAKTHROUGHS, MADE *TIME TRAVEL* POSSIBLE.
BUT WHEN WE LOST CONTROL OF THE TECHNOLOGY, SEVERAL INDIVIDUALS AND ENTITIES HAD THEIR OWN IDEAS OF HOW TO USE IT.
WHAT'S MOST IMPORTANT FOR YOU TO UNDERSTAND IS *THIS...*

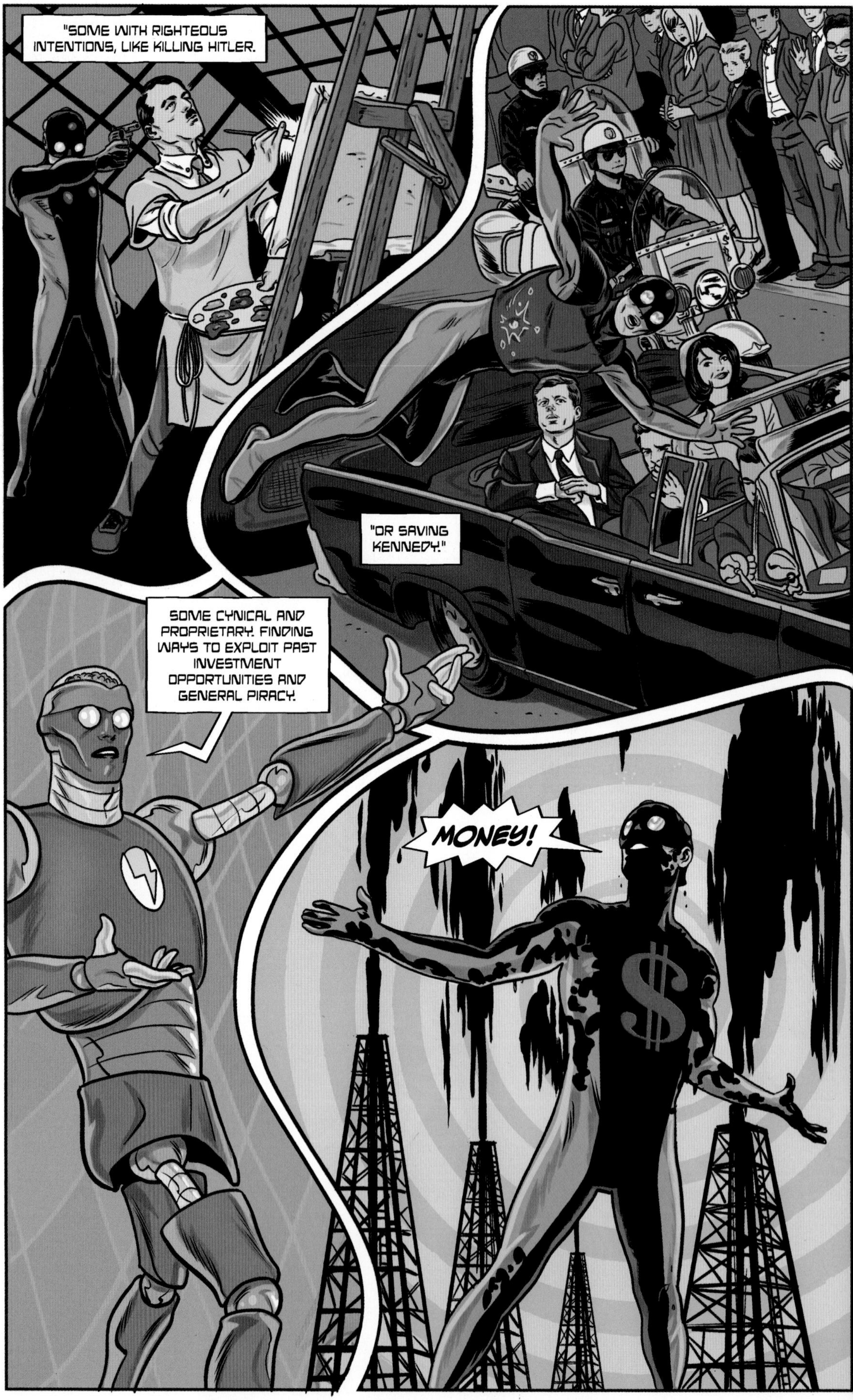
"SOME WITH RIGHTEOUS INTENTIONS, LIKE KILLING HITLER.
"OR SAVING KENNEDY."
SOME CYNICAL AND PROPRIETARY. FINDING WAYS TO EXPLOIT PAST INVESTMENT OPPORTUNITIES AND GENERAL PIRACY.
MONEY!

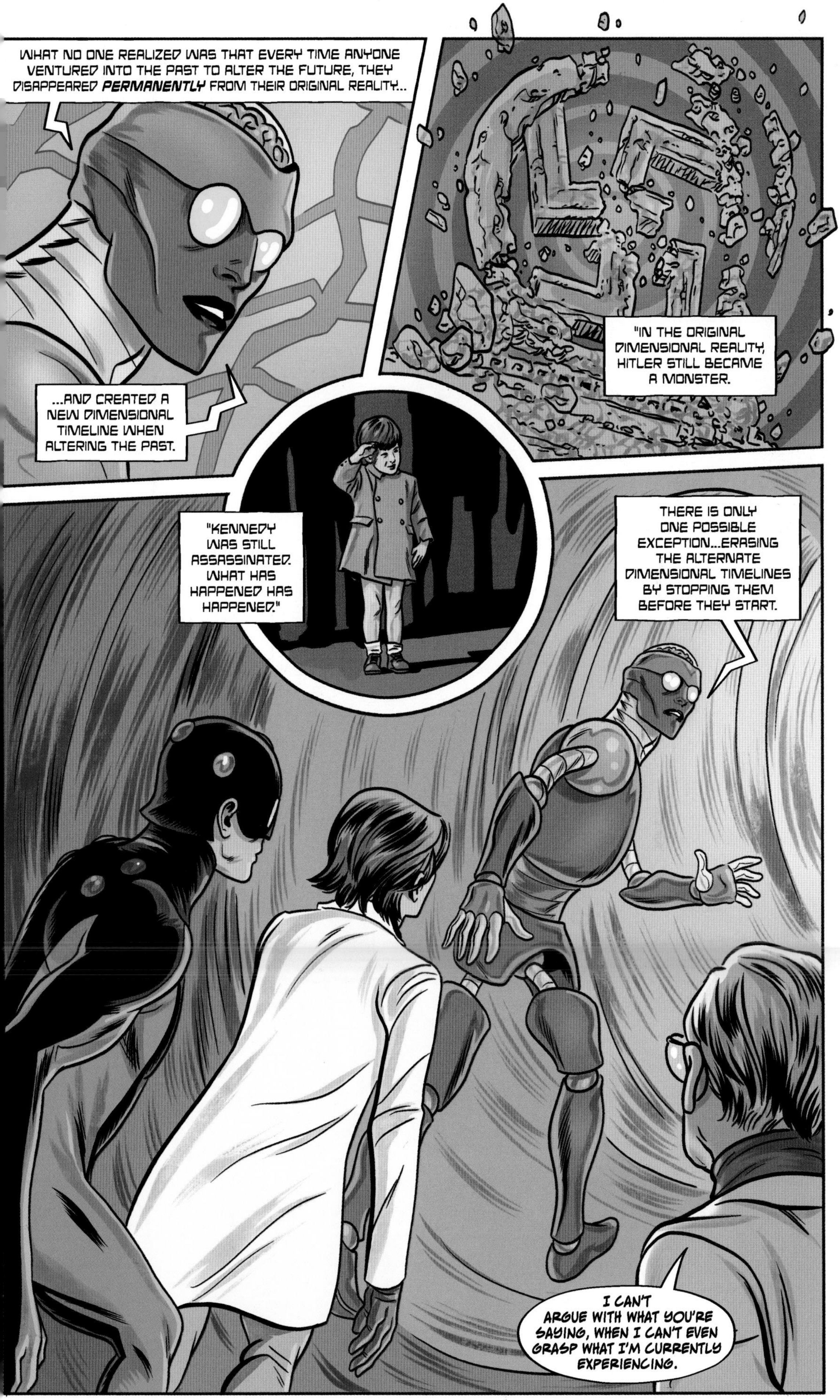
WHAT NO ONE REALIZED WAS THAT EVERY TIME ANYONE VENTURED INTO THE PAST TO ALTER THE FUTURE, THEY DISAPPEARED PERMANENTLY FROM THEIR ORIGINAL REALITY...
...AND CREATED A NEW DIMENSIONAL TIMELINE WHEN ALTERING THE PAST.
"IN THE ORIGINAL DIMENSIONAL REALITY, HITLER STILL BECAME A MONSTER.
"KENNEDY WAS STILL ASSASSINATED. WHAT HAS HAPPENED HAS HAPPENED."
THERE IS ONLY ONE POSSIBLE EXCEPTION...ERASING THE ALTERNATE DIMENSIONAL TIMELINES BY STOPPING THEM BEFORE THEY START.
I CAN'T ARGUE WITH WHAT YOU'RE SAYING, WHEN I CAN'T EVEN GRASP WHAT I'M CURRENTLY EXPERIENCING.

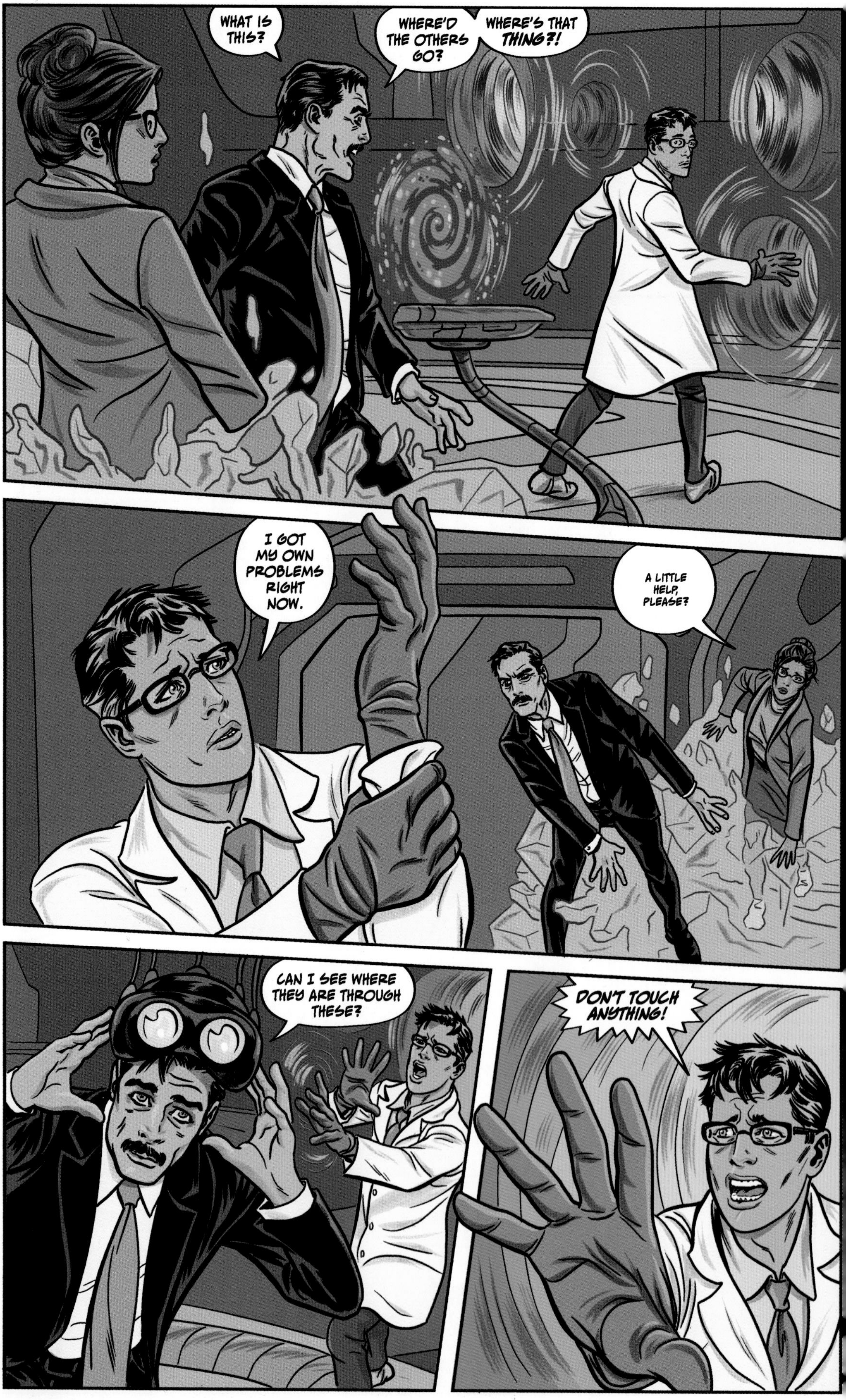
WHAT IS THIS?
WHERE'D THE OTHERS GO?
WHERE'S THAT THING?!
I GOT MY OWN PROBLEMS RIGHT NOW.
A LITTLE HELP, PLEASE?
CAN I SEE WHERE THEY ARE THROUGH THESE?
DON'T TOUCH ANYTHING!

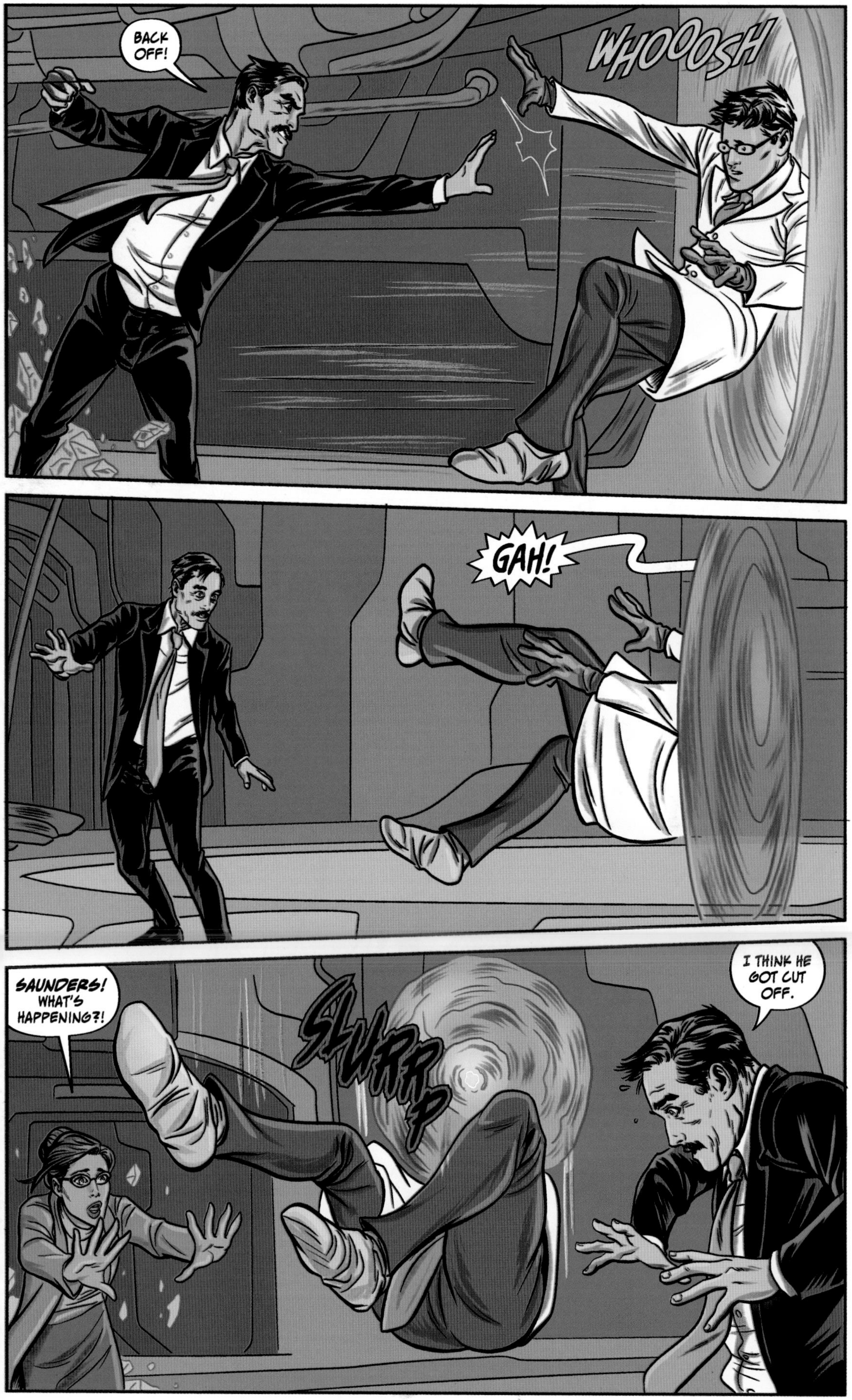
BACK OFF!
WHOOOSH
GAH!
SAUNDERS! WHAT'S HAPPENING?!
SLURRP
I THINK HE GOT CUT OFF.

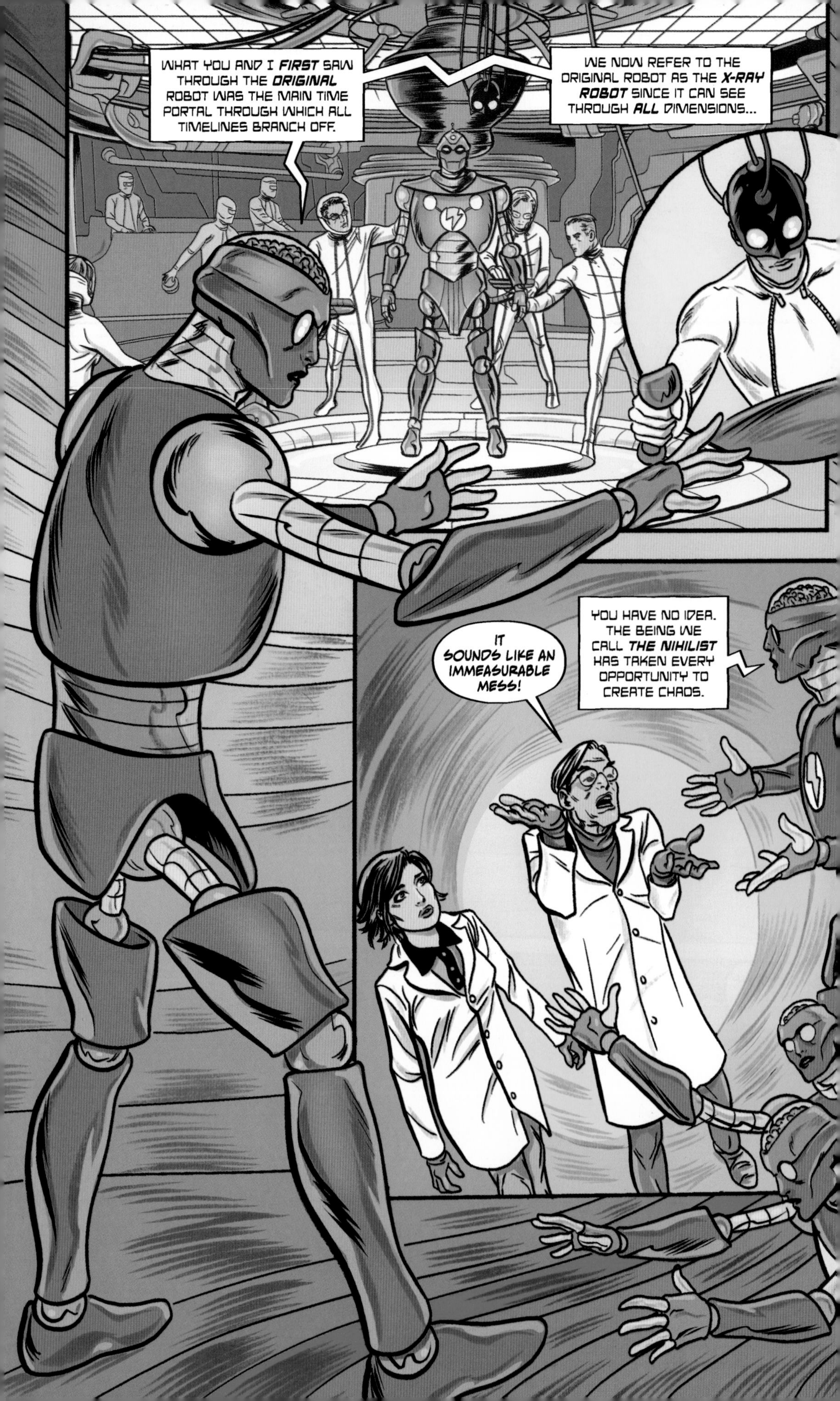
WHAT YOU AND I FIRST SAW THROUGH THE ORIGINAL ROBOT WAS THE MAIN TIME PORTAL THROUGH WHICH ALL TIMELINES BRANCH OFF.
WE NOW REFER TO THE ORIGINAL ROBOT AS THE X-RAY ROBOT SINCE IT CAN SEE THROUGH ALL DIMENSIONS...
IT SOUNDS LIKE AN IMMEASURABLE MESS!
YOU HAVE NO IDEA. THE BEING WE CALL THE NIHILIST HAS TAKEN EVERY OPPORTUNITY TO CREATE CHAOS.

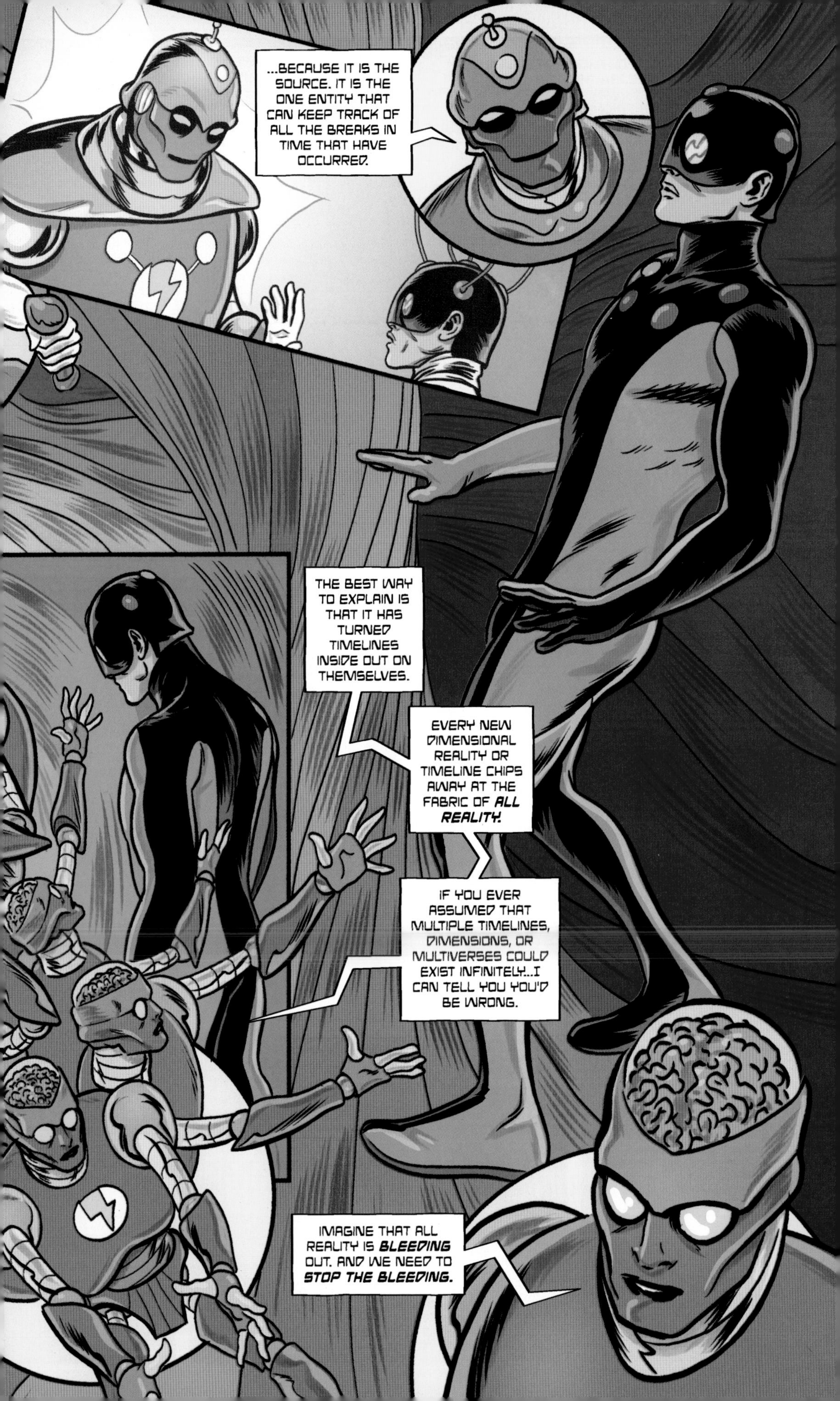
...BECAUSE IT IS THE SOURCE. IT IS THE ONE ENTITY THAT CAN KEEP TRACK OF ALL THE BREAKS IN TIME THAT HAVE OCCURRED.
THE BEST WAY TO EXPLAIN IS THAT IT HAS TURNED TIMELINES INSIDE OUT ON THEMSELVES.
EVERY NEW DIMENSIONAL REALITY OR TIMELINE CHIPS AWAY AT THE FABRIC OF ALL REALITY.
IF YOU EVER ASSUMED THAT MULTIPLE TIMELINES, DIMENSIONS, OR MULTIVERSES COULD EXIST INFINITELY...I CAN TELL YOU YOU'D BE WRONG.
IMAGINE THAT ALL REALITY IS BLEEDING OUT. AND WE NEED TO STOP THE BLEEDING.

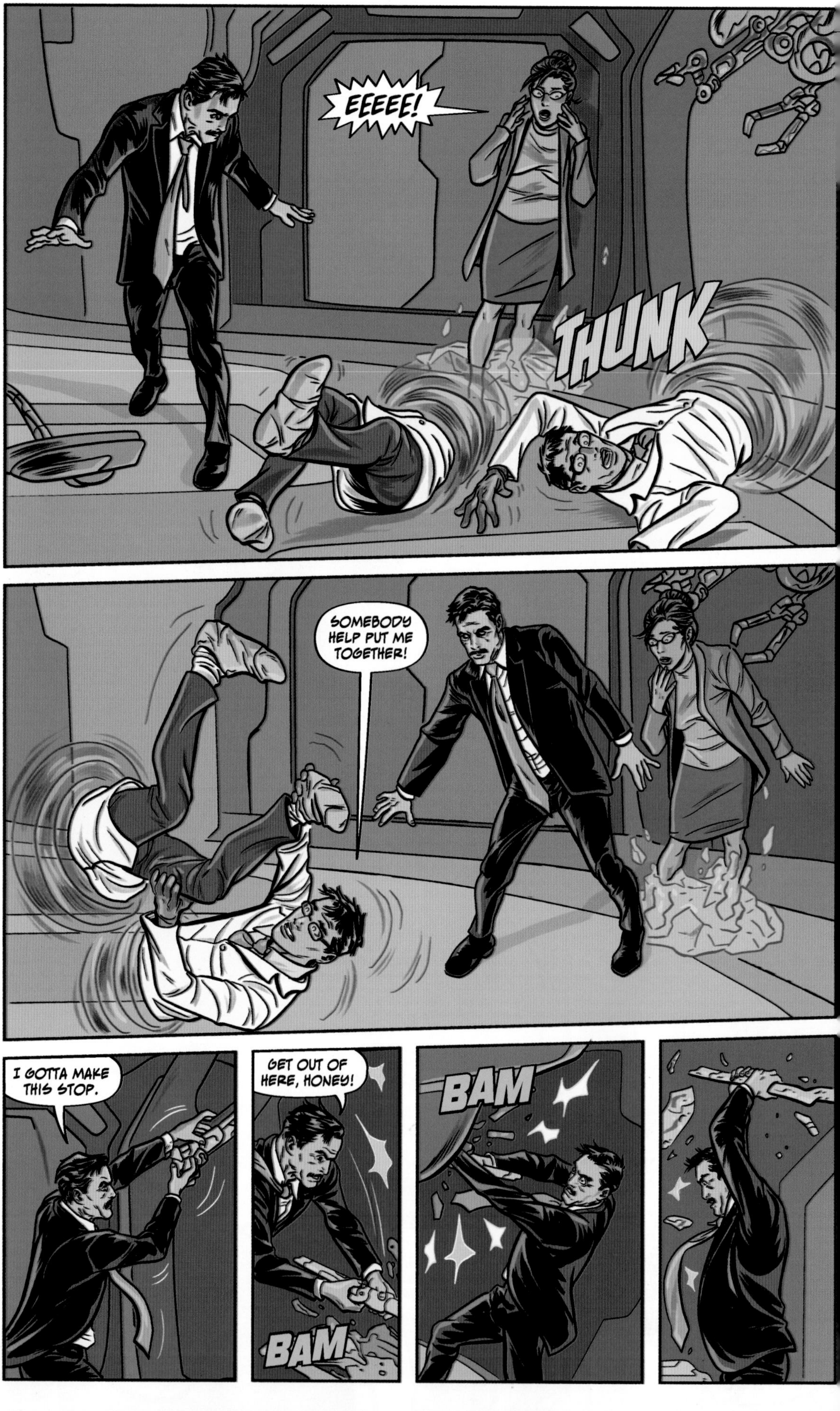
EEEEE!
THUNK
SOMEBODY HELP PUT ME TOGETHER!
I GOTTA MAKE THIS STOP.
GET OUT OF HERE, HONEY!
BAM
BAM

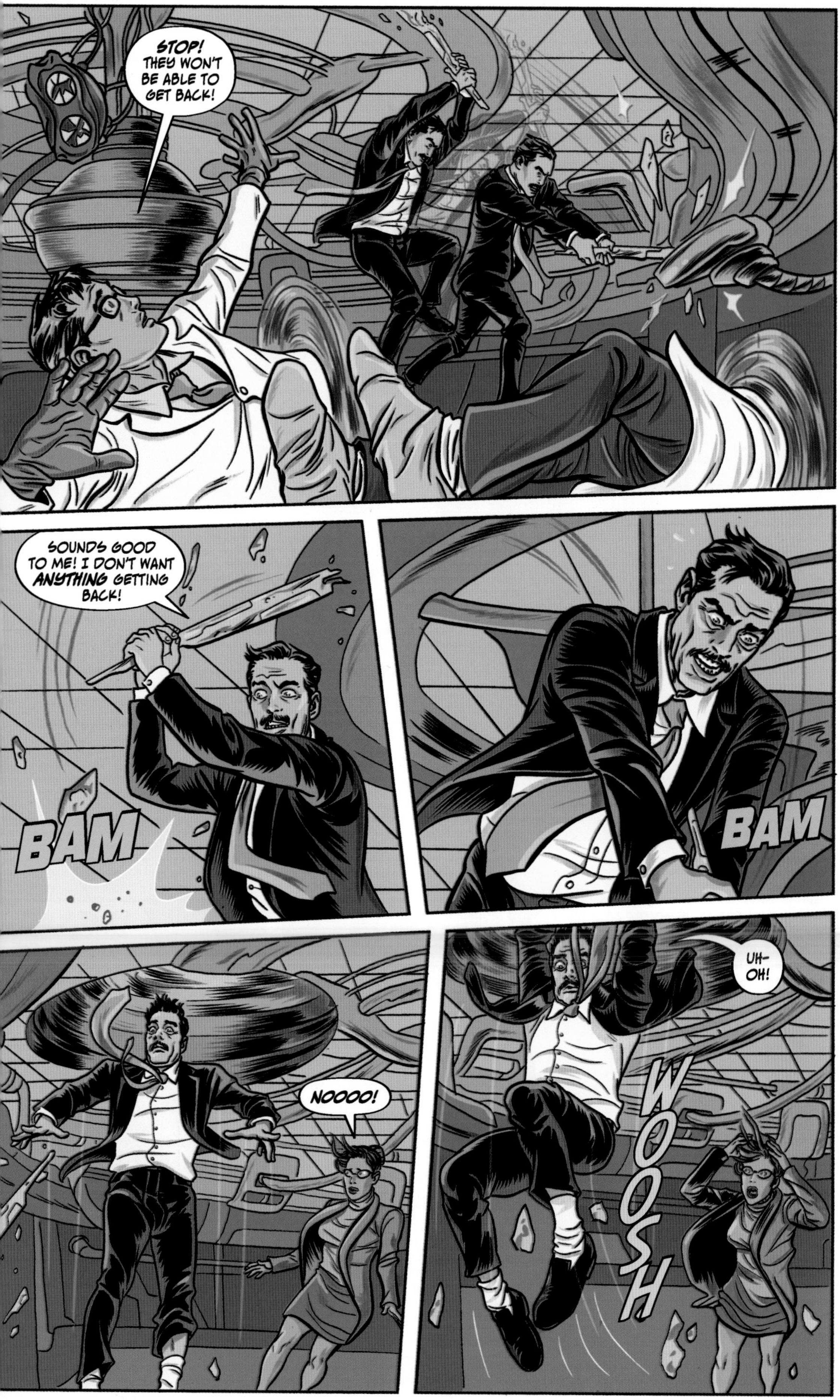
STOP! THEY WON'T BE ABLE TO GET BACK!
SOUNDS GOOD TO ME! I DON'T WANT ANYTHING GETTING BACK!
BAM
BAM
NOOOO!
UH-OH!
WOOSH

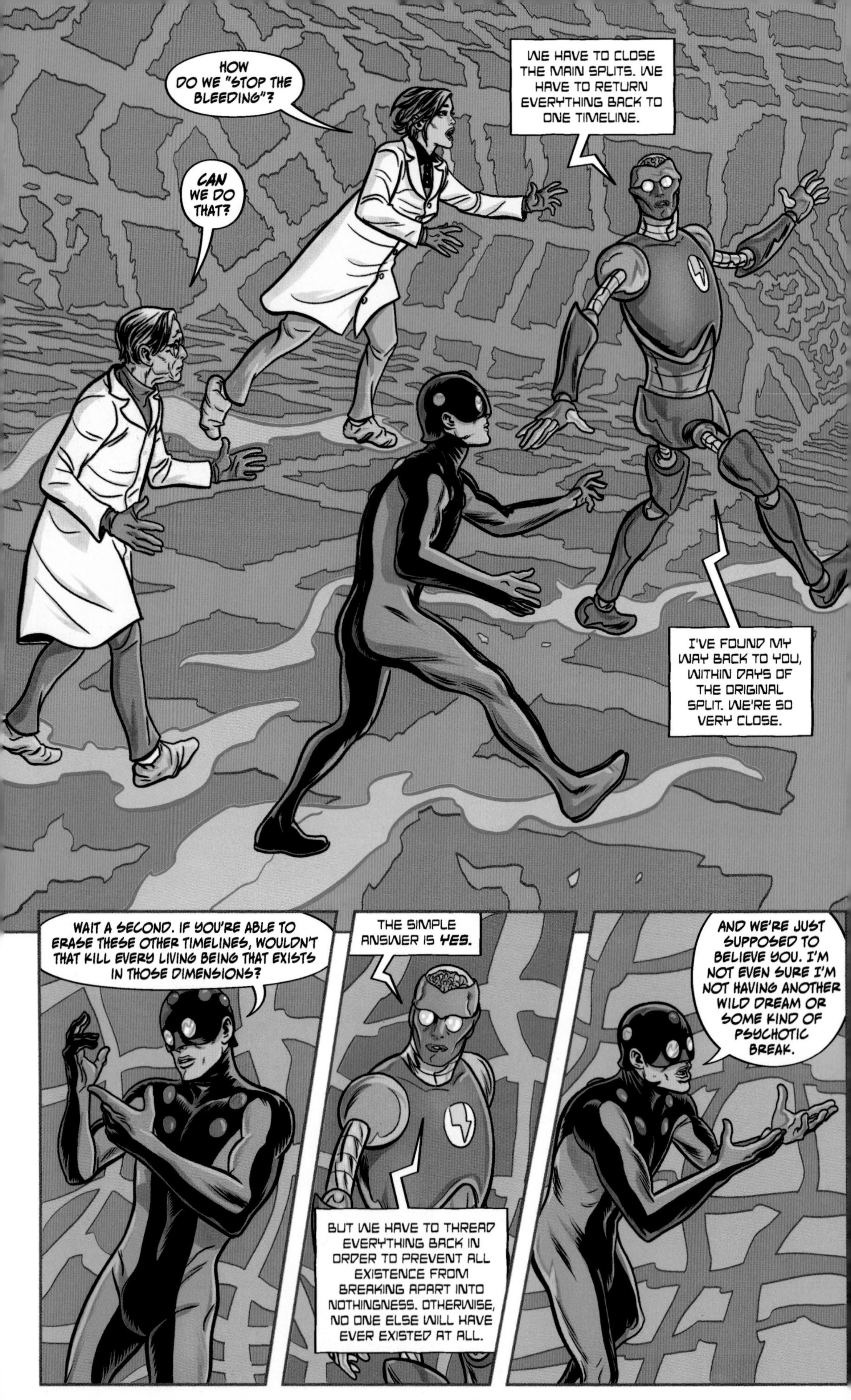
HOW DO WE "STOP THE BLEEDING"?
CAN WE DO THAT?
WE HAVE TO CLOSE THE MAIN SPLITS. WE HAVE TO RETURN EVERYTHING BACK TO ONE TIMELINE.
I'VE FOUND MY WAY BACK TO YOU, WITHIN DAYS OF THE ORIGINAL SPLIT. WE'RE SO VERY CLOSE.
WAIT A SECOND. IF YOU'RE ABLE TO ERASE THESE OTHER TIMELINES, WOULDN'T THAT KILL EVERY LIVING BEING THAT EXISTS IN THOSE DIMENSIONS?
THE SIMPLE ANSWER IS YES.
BUT WE HAVE TO THREAD EVERYTHING BACK IN ORDER TO PREVENT ALL EXISTENCE FROM BREAKING APART INTO NOTHINGNESS. OTHERWISE, NO ONE ELSE WILL HAVE EVER EXISTED AT ALL.
AND WE'RE JUST SUPPOSED TO BELIEVE YOU. I'M NOT EVEN SURE I'M NOT HAVING ANOTHER WILD DREAM OR SOME KIND OF PSYCHOTIC BREAK.

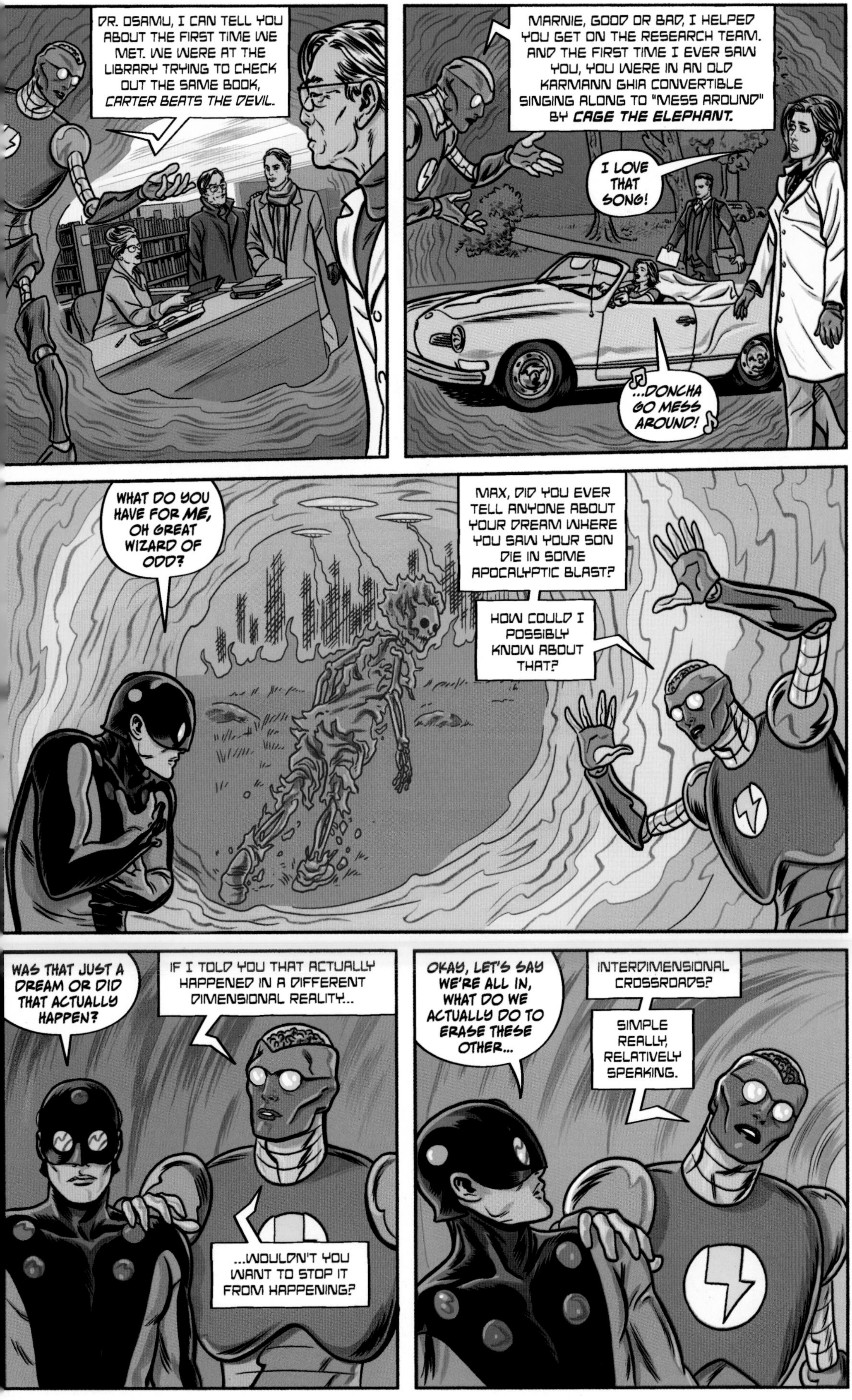
DR. OSAMU, I CAN TELL YOU ABOUT THE FIRST TIME WE MET. WE WERE AT THE LIBRARY TRYING TO CHECK OUT THE SAME BOOK, *CARTER BEATS THE DEVIL.*
MARNIE, GOOD OR BAD, I HELPED YOU GET ON THE RESEARCH TEAM. AND THE FIRST TIME I EVER SAW YOU, YOU WERE IN AN OLD KARMANN GHIA CONVERTIBLE SINGING ALONG TO "MESS AROUND" BY ***CAGE THE ELEPHANT.***
I LOVE THAT SONG!
...DONCHA GO MESS AROUND!
WHAT DO YOU HAVE FOR *ME*, OH GREAT WIZARD OF ODD?
MAX, DID YOU EVER TELL ANYONE ABOUT YOUR DREAM WHERE YOU SAW YOUR SON DIE IN SOME APOCALYPTIC BLAST?
HOW COULD I POSSIBLY KNOW ABOUT THAT?
WAS THAT JUST A *DREAM OR DID* THAT ACTUALLY HAPPEN?
IF I TOLD YOU THAT ACTUALLY HAPPENED IN A DIFFERENT DIMENSIONAL REALITY...
...WOULDN'T YOU WANT TO STOP IT FROM HAPPENING?
OKAY, LET'S SAY WE'RE ALL IN, WHAT DO WE ACTUALLY DO TO ERASE THESE OTHER...
INTERDIMENSIONAL CROSSROADS?
SIMPLE REALLY, RELATIVELY SPEAKING.

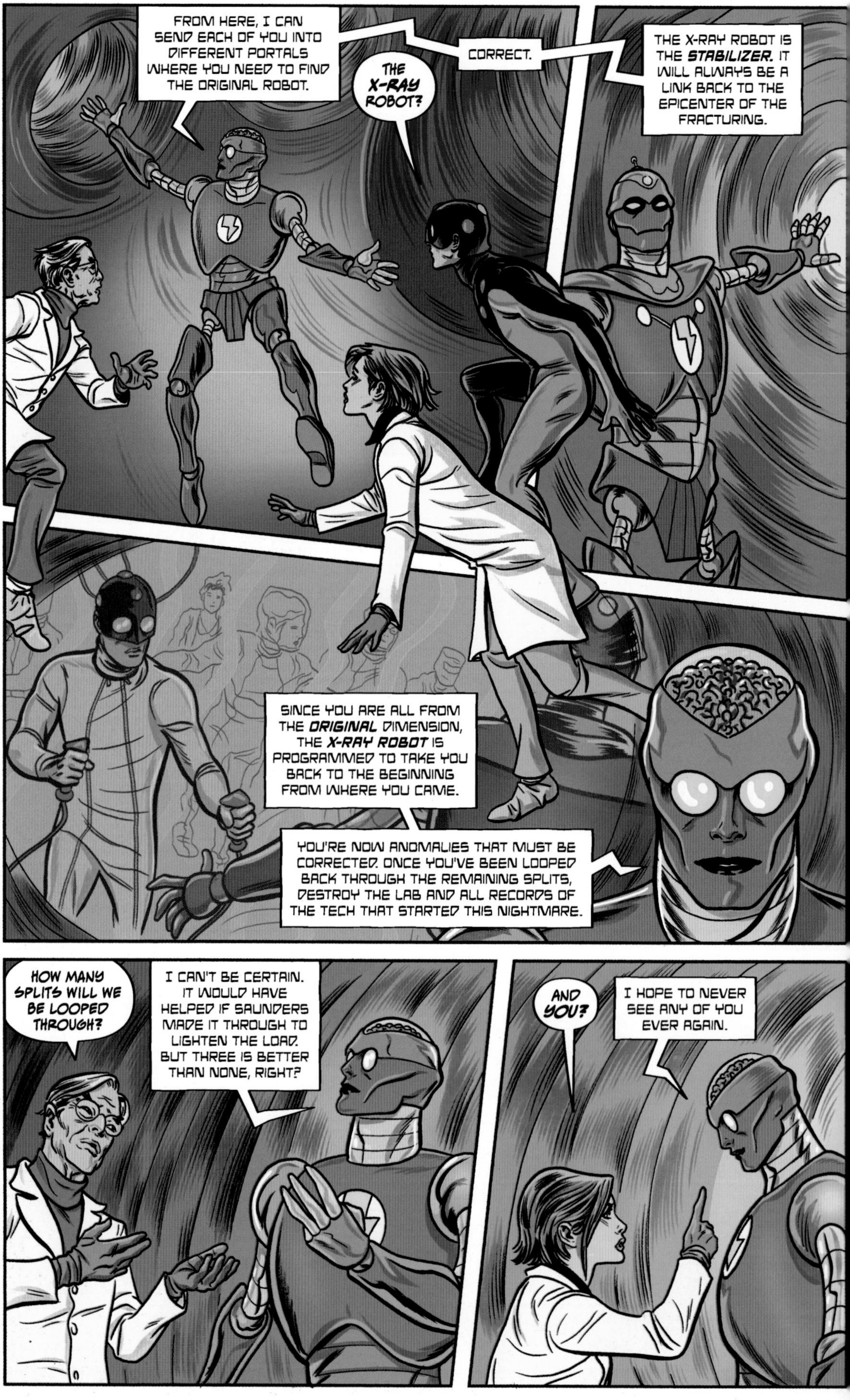
FROM HERE, I CAN SEND EACH OF YOU INTO DIFFERENT PORTALS WHERE YOU NEED TO FIND THE ORIGINAL ROBOT.
THE X-RAY ROBOT?
CORRECT.
THE X-RAY ROBOT IS THE STABILIZER. IT WILL ALWAYS BE A LINK BACK TO THE EPICENTER OF THE FRACTURING.
SINCE YOU ARE ALL FROM THE ORIGINAL DIMENSION, THE X-RAY ROBOT IS PROGRAMMED TO TAKE YOU BACK TO THE BEGINNING FROM WHERE YOU CAME.
YOU'RE NOW ANOMALIES THAT MUST BE CORRECTED. ONCE YOU'VE BEEN LOOPED BACK THROUGH THE REMAINING SPLITS, DESTROY THE LAB AND ALL RECORDS OF THE TECH THAT STARTED THIS NIGHTMARE.
HOW MANY SPLITS WILL WE BE LOOPED THROUGH?
I CAN'T BE CERTAIN. IT WOULD HAVE HELPED IF SAUNDERS MADE IT THROUGH TO LIGHTEN THE LOAD. BUT THREE IS BETTER THAN NONE, RIGHT?
AND YOU?
I HOPE TO NEVER SEE ANY OF YOU EVER AGAIN.

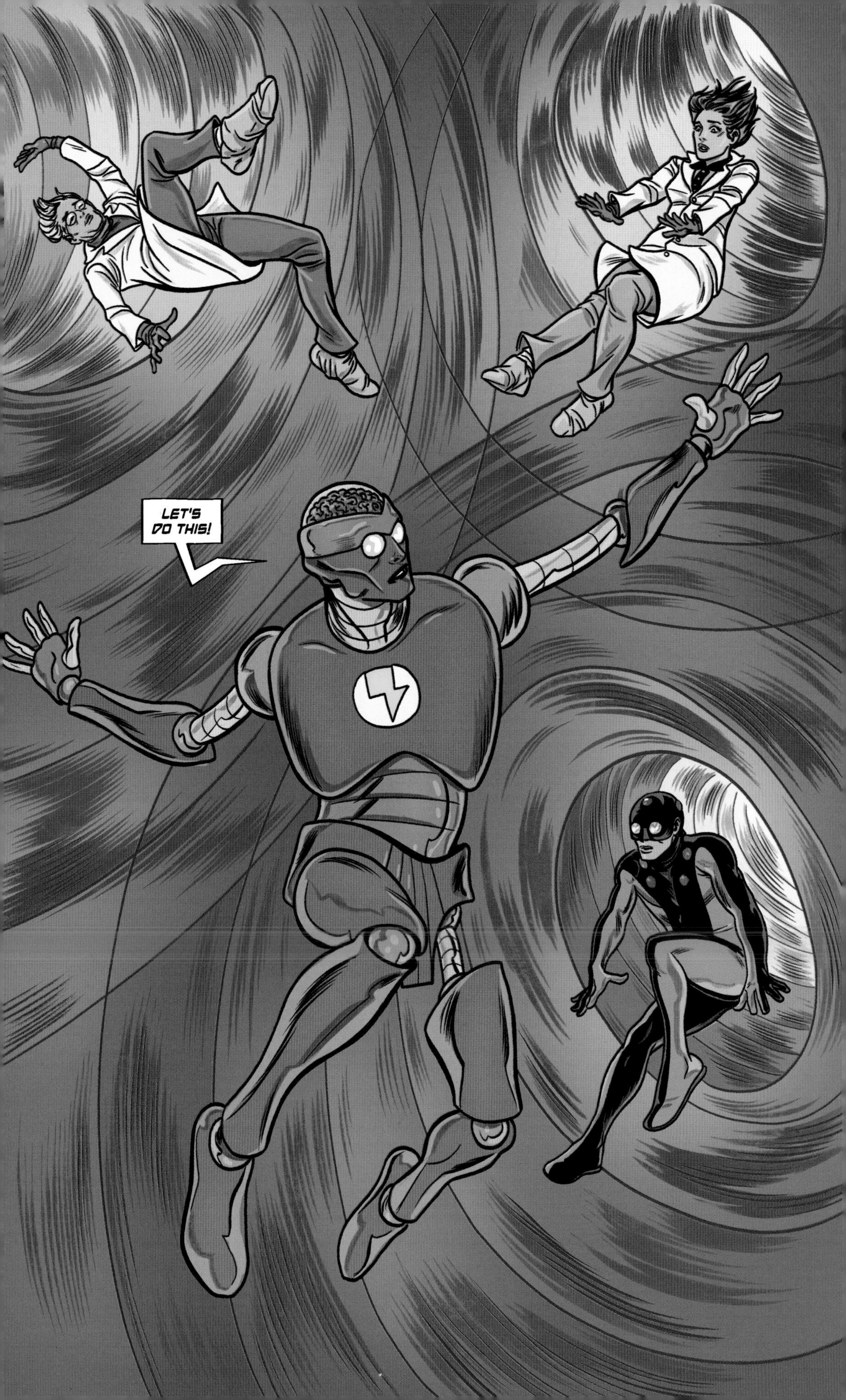
LET'S DO THIS!

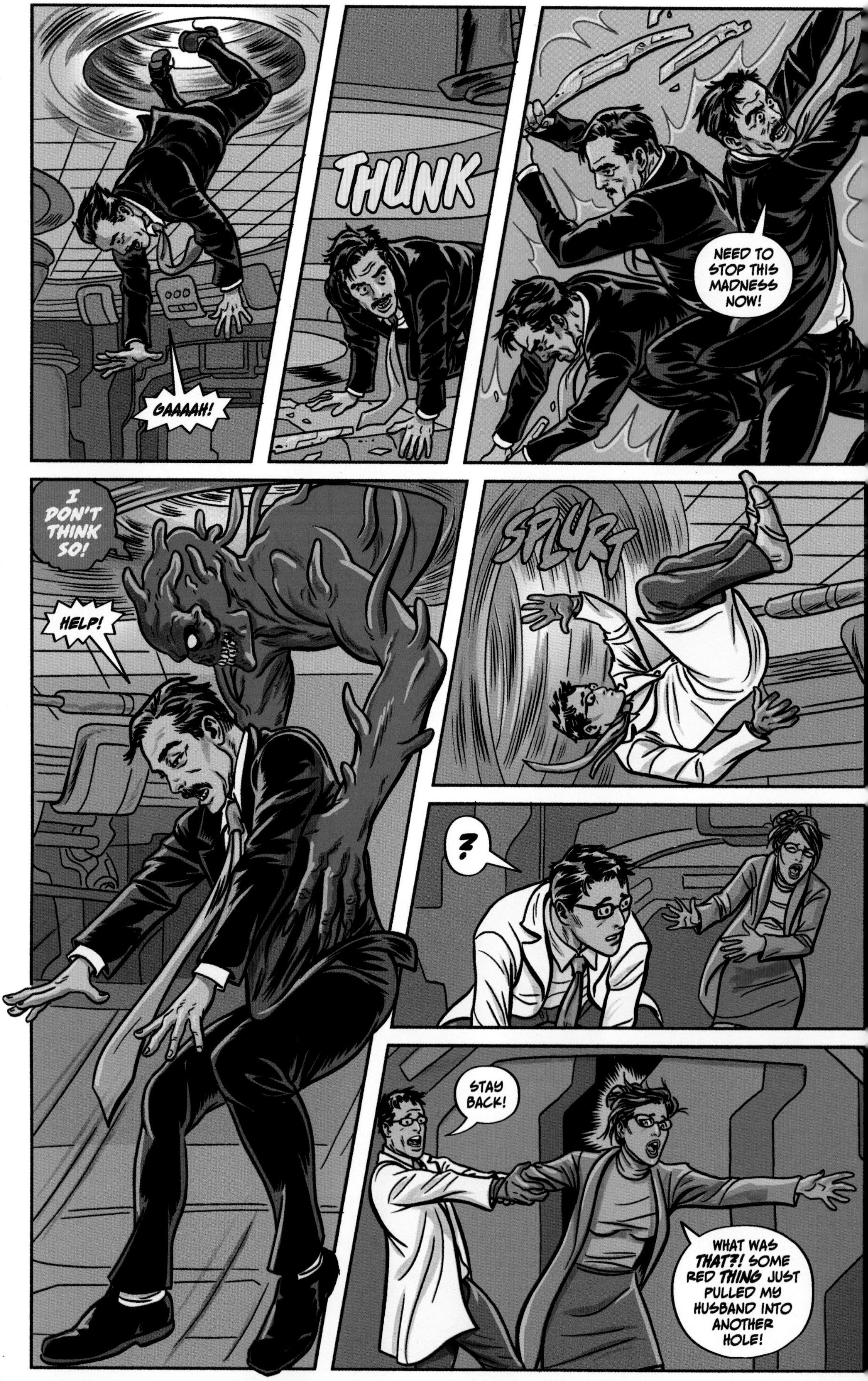
GAAAAH!
THUNK
NEED TO STOP THIS MADNESS NOW!
I DON'T THINK SO!
HELP!
SPLURT
?
STAY BACK!
WHAT WAS THAT?! SOME RED THING JUST PULLED MY HUSBAND INTO ANOTHER HOLE!

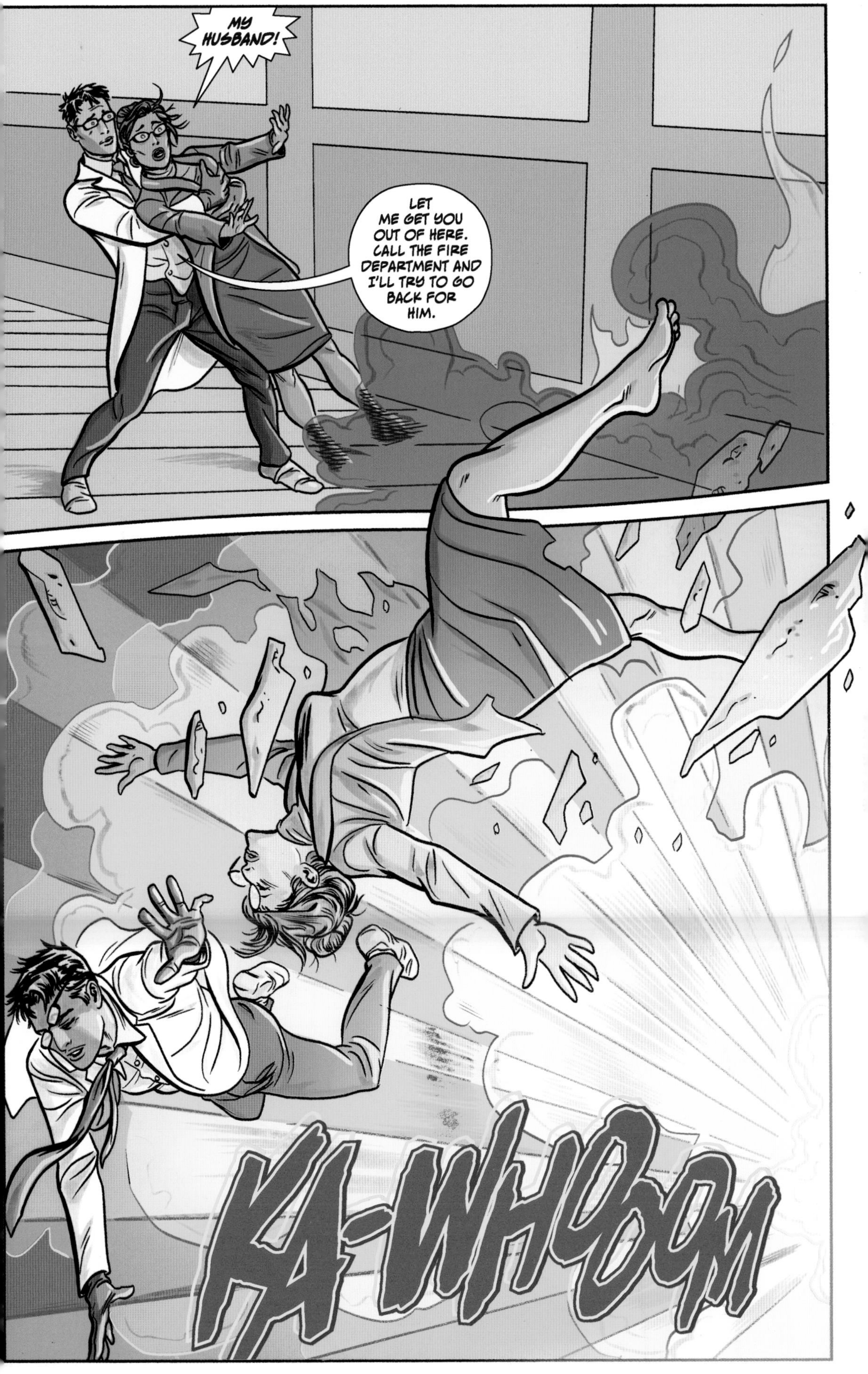
MY HUSBAND!
LET ME GET YOU OUT OF HERE. CALL THE FIRE DEPARTMENT AND I'LL TRY TO GO BACK FOR HIM.
KA-WHOOM

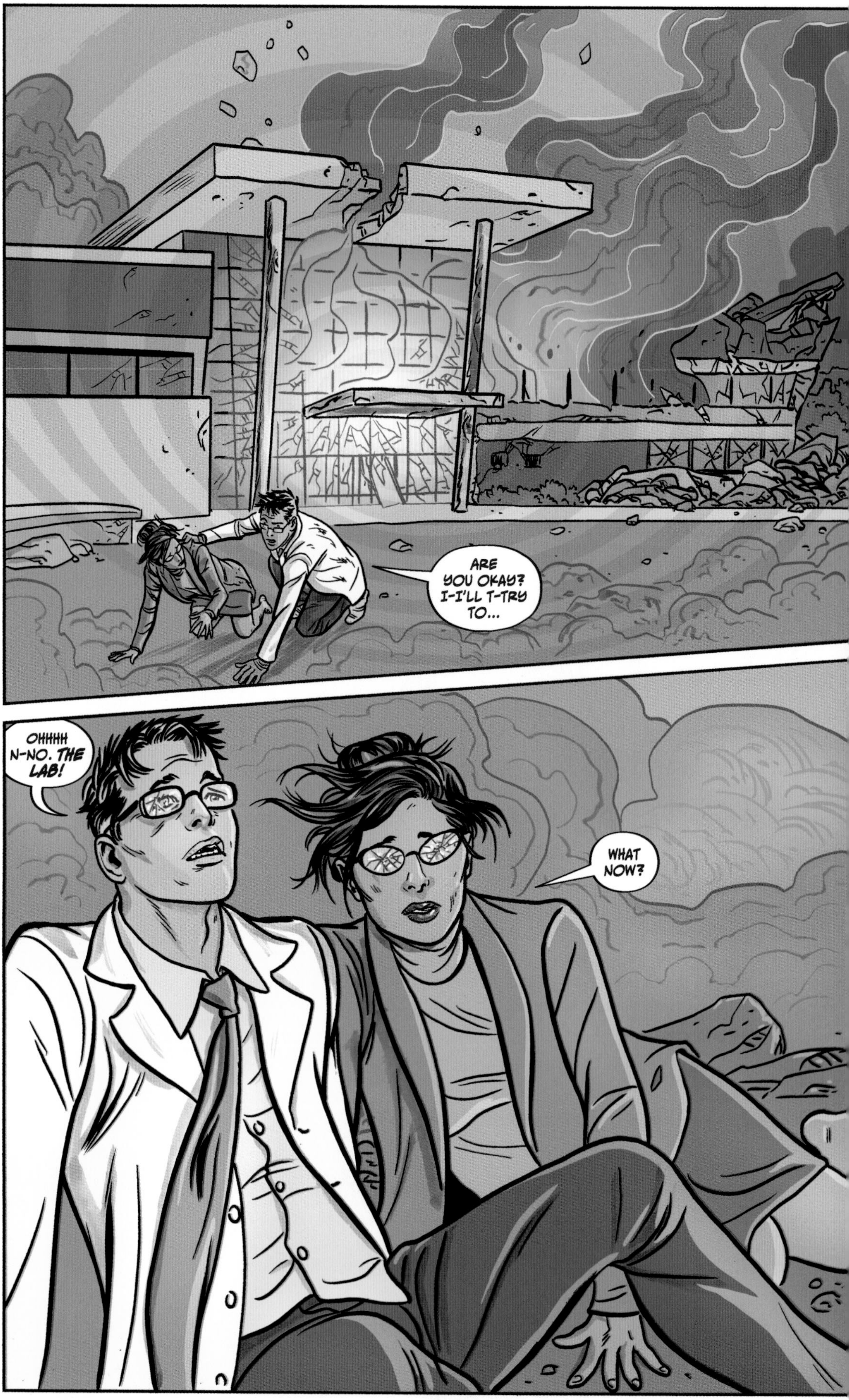
ARE YOU OKAY? I-I'LL T-TRY TO...
OHHHH N-NO. *THE LAB!*
WHAT NOW?

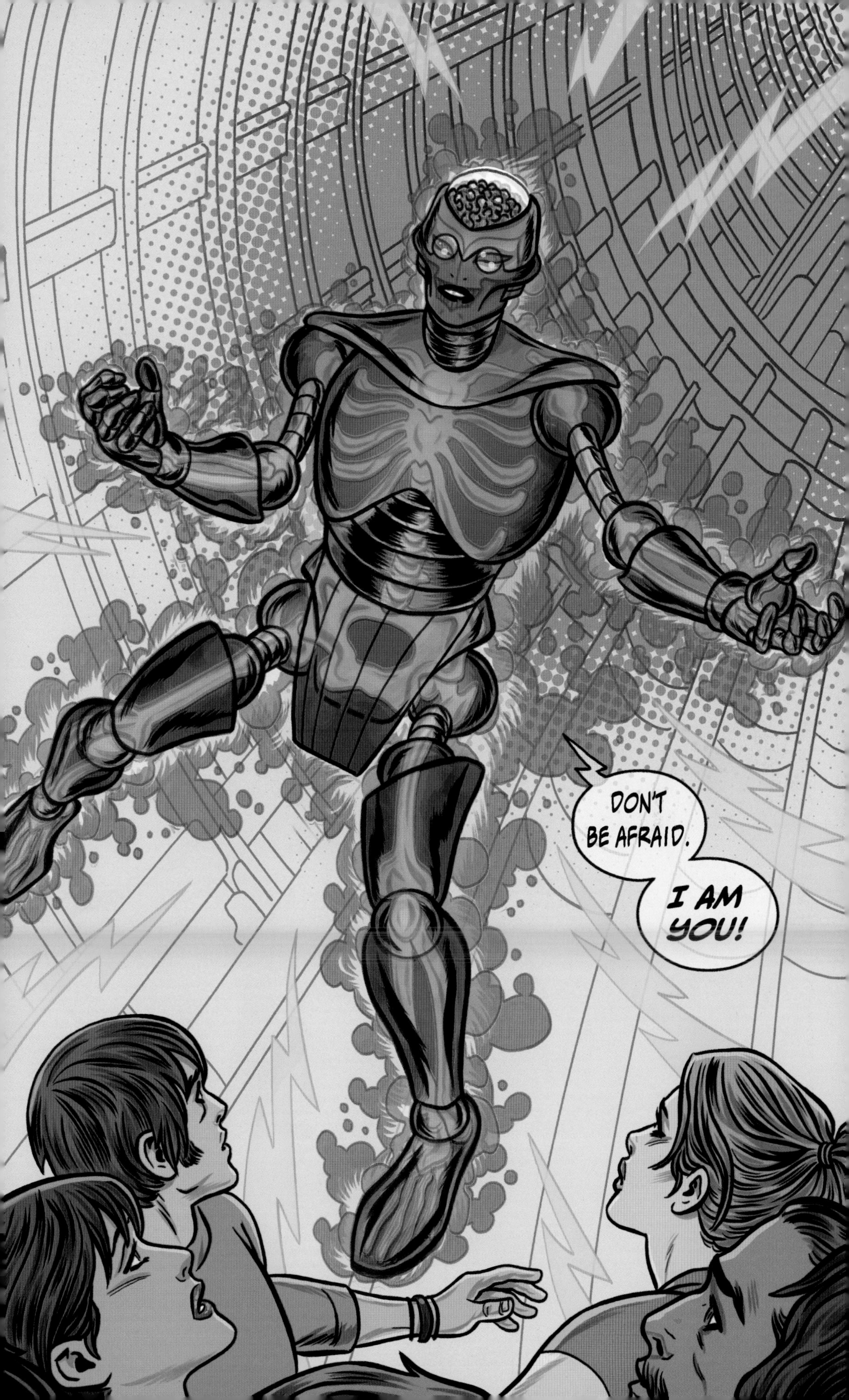
DON'T BE AFRAID.
I AM YOU!

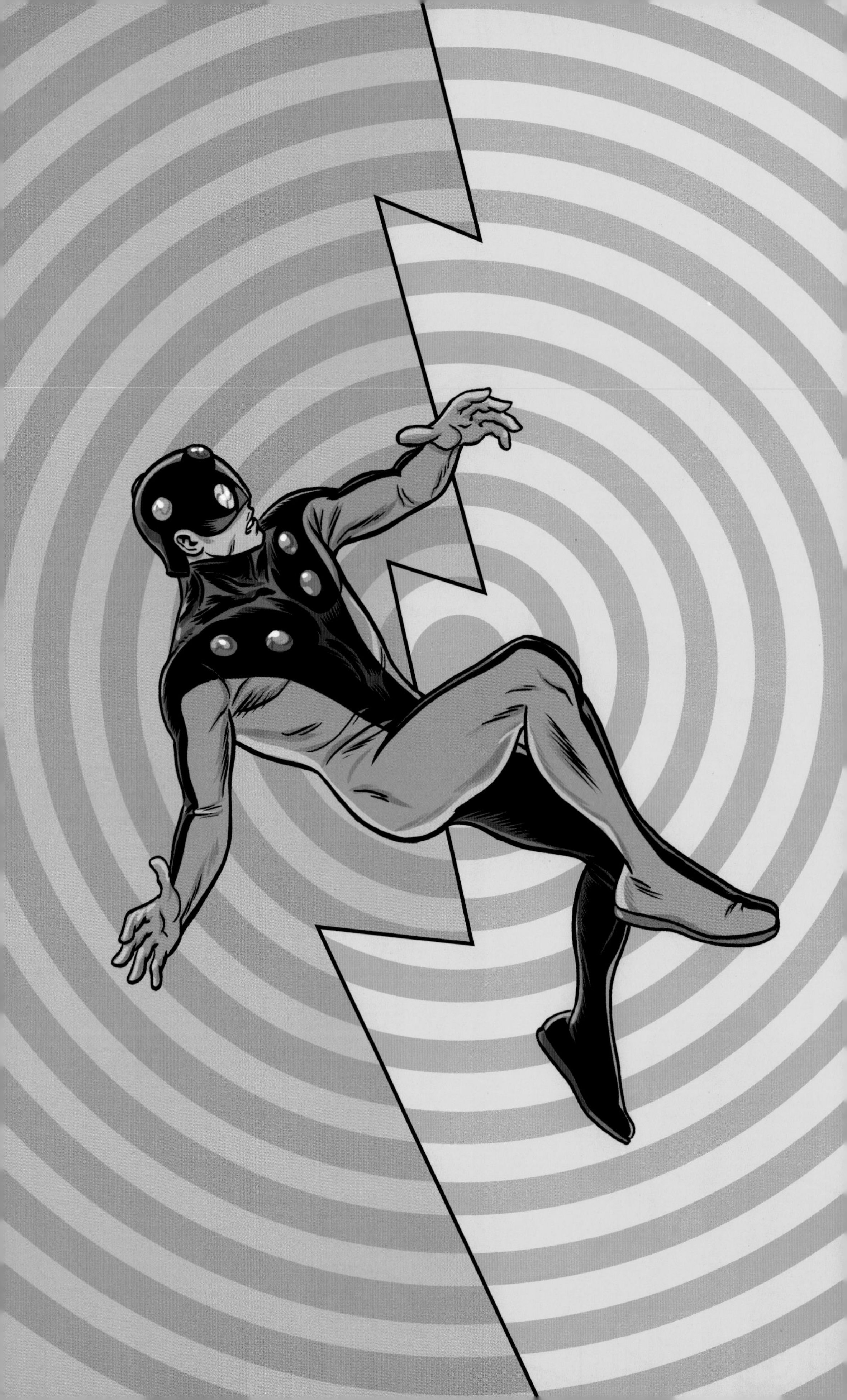

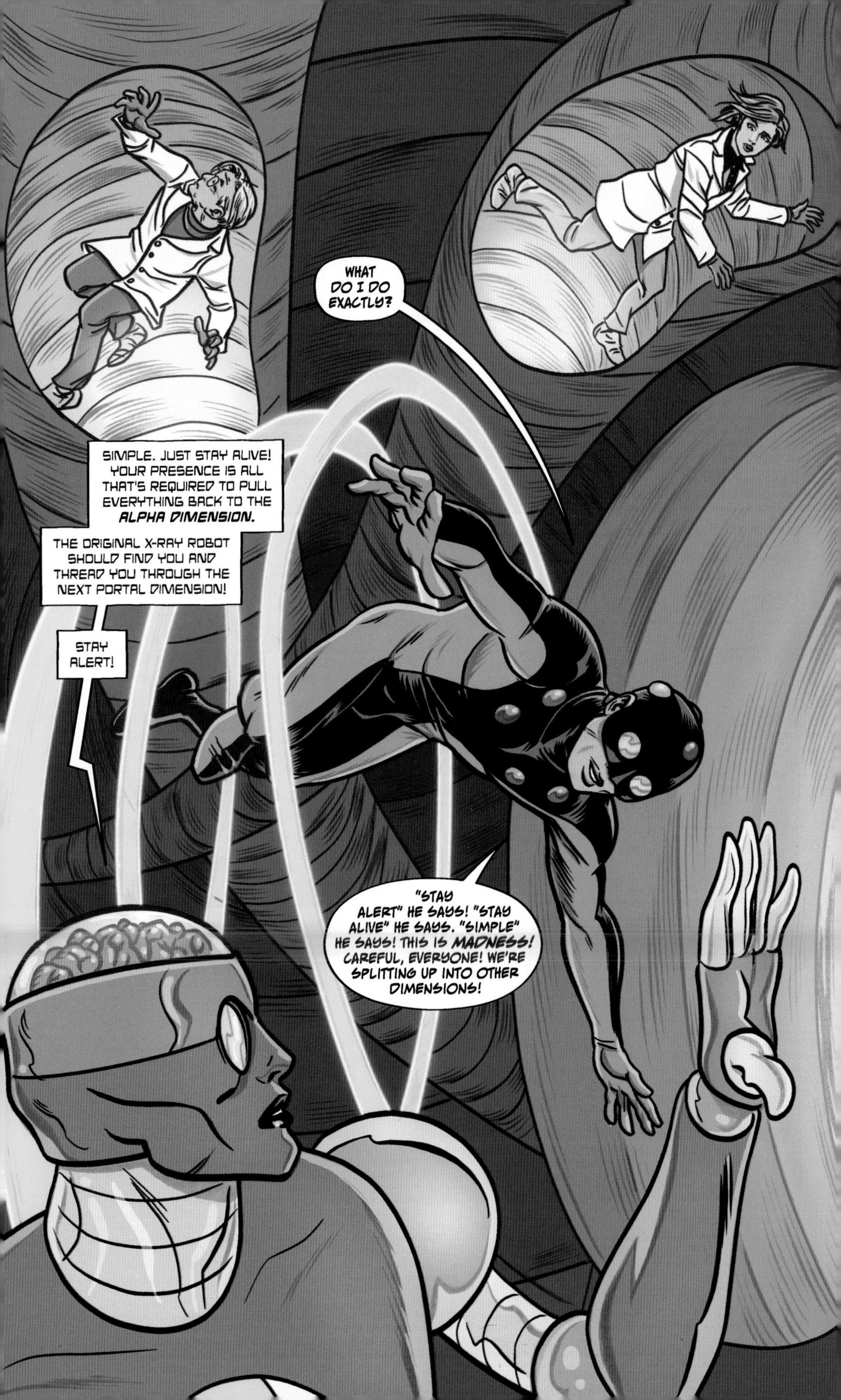
WHAT DO I DO EXACTLY?
SIMPLE. JUST STAY ALIVE! YOUR PRESENCE IS ALL THAT'S REQUIRED TO PULL EVERYTHING BACK TO THE *ALPHA DIMENSION.*
THE ORIGINAL X-RAY ROBOT SHOULD FIND YOU AND THREAD YOU THROUGH THE NEXT PORTAL DIMENSION!
STAY ALERT!
"STAY ALERT" HE SAYS! "STAY ALIVE" HE SAYS. "SIMPLE" HE SAYS! THIS IS *MADNESS!* CAREFUL, EVERYONE! WE'RE SPLITTING UP INTO OTHER DIMENSIONS!

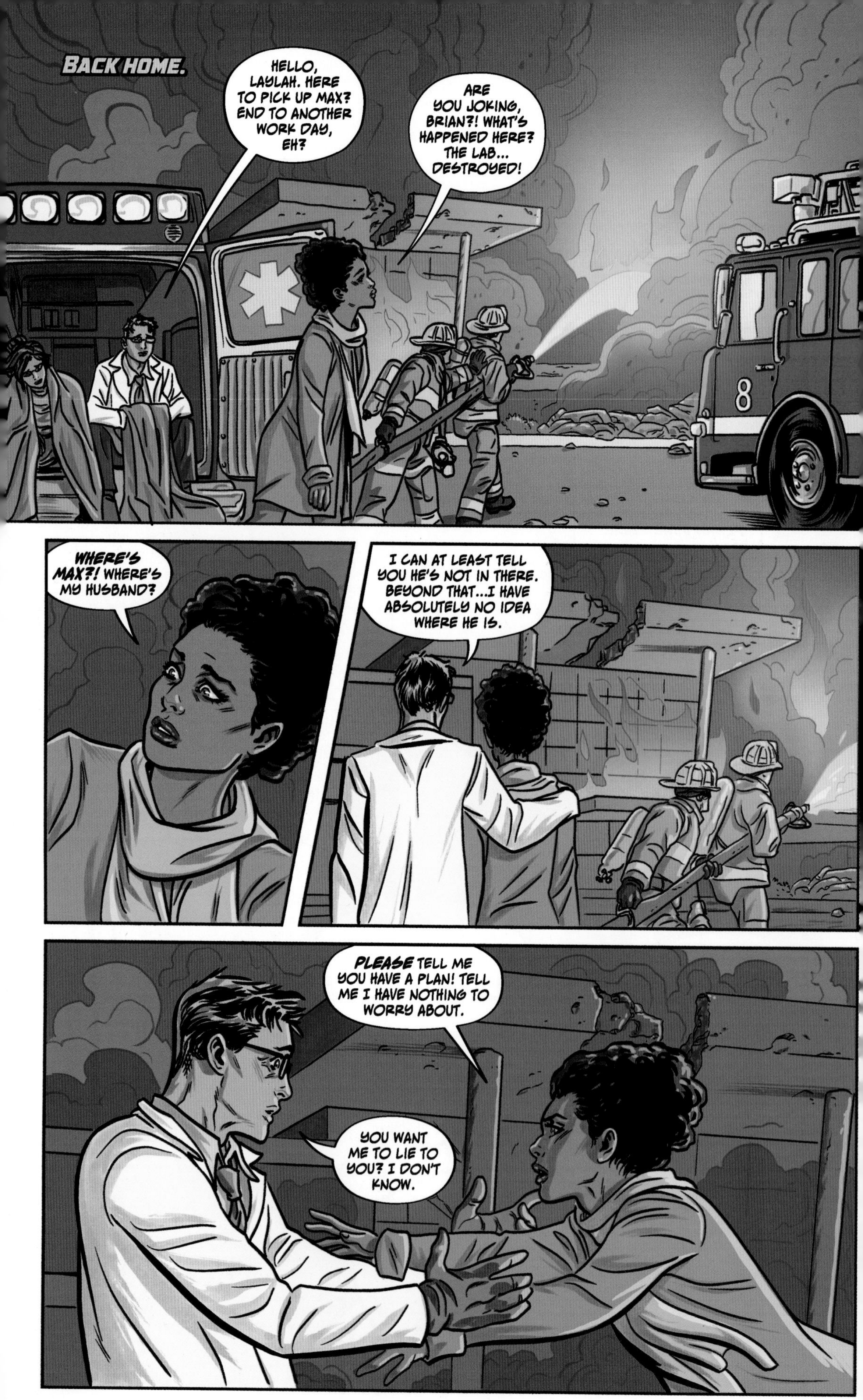
BACK HOME.
HELLO, LAYLAH. HERE TO PICK UP MAX? END TO ANOTHER WORK DAY, EH?
ARE YOU JOKING, BRIAN?! WHAT'S HAPPENED HERE? THE LAB... DESTROYED!
8
WHERE'S MAX?! WHERE'S MY HUSBAND?
I CAN AT LEAST TELL YOU HE'S NOT IN THERE. BEYOND THAT...I HAVE ABSOLUTELY NO IDEA WHERE HE IS.
PLEASE TELL ME YOU HAVE A PLAN! TELL ME I HAVE NOTHING TO WORRY ABOUT.
YOU WANT ME TO LIE TO YOU? I DON'T KNOW.

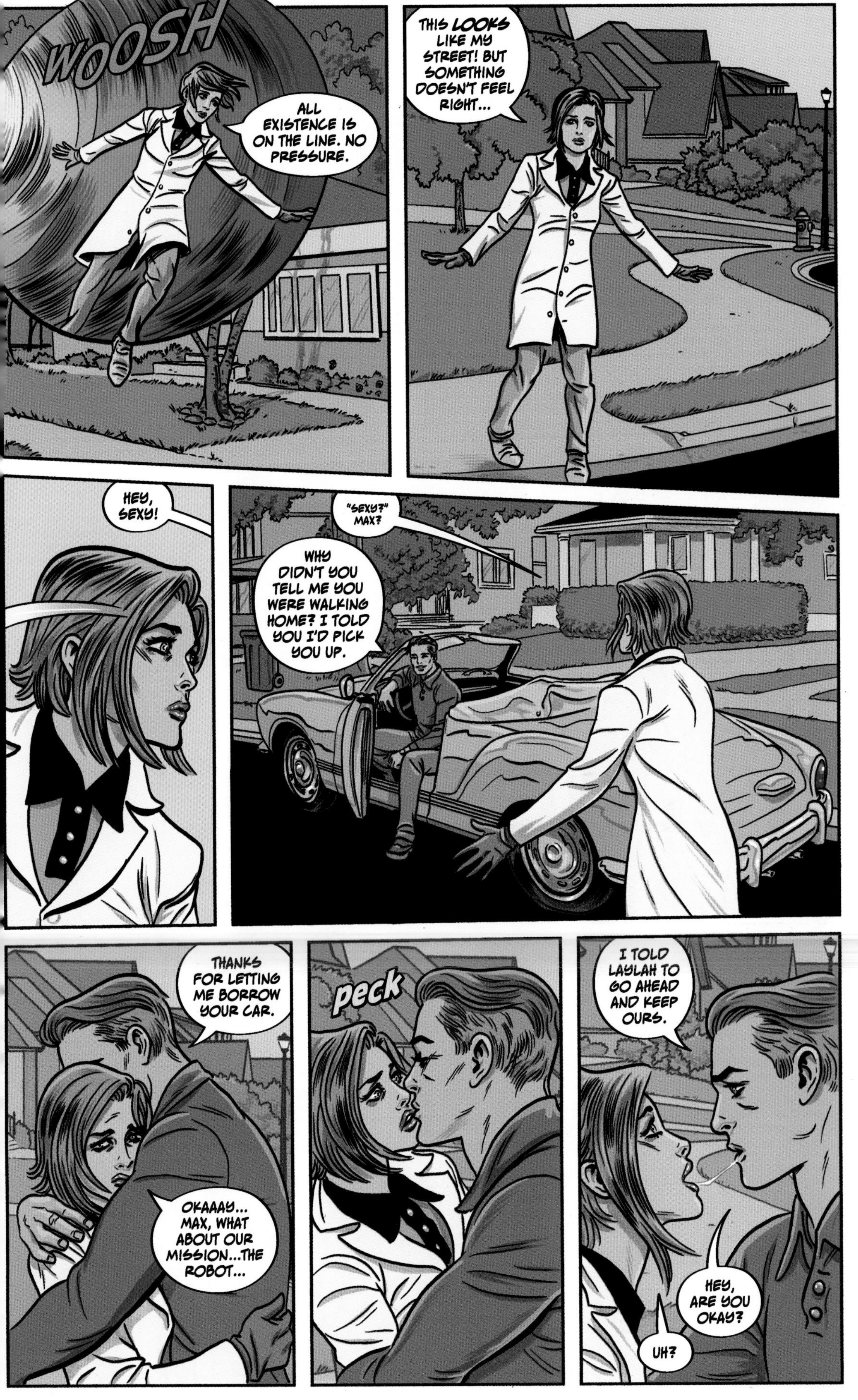
WOOSH
ALL EXISTENCE IS ON THE LINE. NO PRESSURE.
THIS LOOKS LIKE MY STREET! BUT SOMETHING DOESN'T FEEL RIGHT...
HEY, SEXY!
"SEXY?" MAX?
WHY DIDN'T YOU TELL ME YOU WERE WALKING HOME? I TOLD YOU I'D PICK YOU UP.
THANKS FOR LETTING ME BORROW YOUR CAR.
OKAAAY... MAX, WHAT ABOUT OUR MISSION...THE ROBOT...
peck
I TOLD LAYLAH TO GO AHEAD AND KEEP OURS.
HEY, ARE YOU OKAY?
UH?

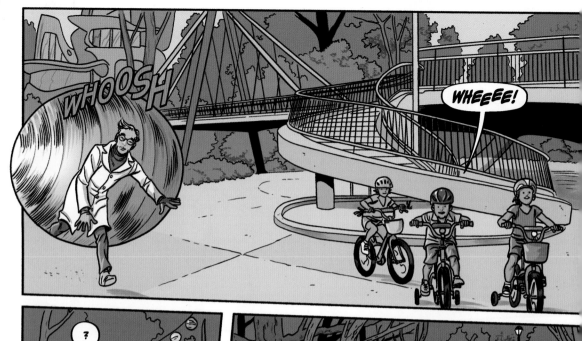

WHOOSH

WHEEEE!

?

LOOK AT THAT MAN!

MOMMY LOOK! WHAT'S WRONG WITH THAT MAN?

WHAT'S WRONG WITH HIM?! WHY IS HE DRESSED LIKE THAT?!

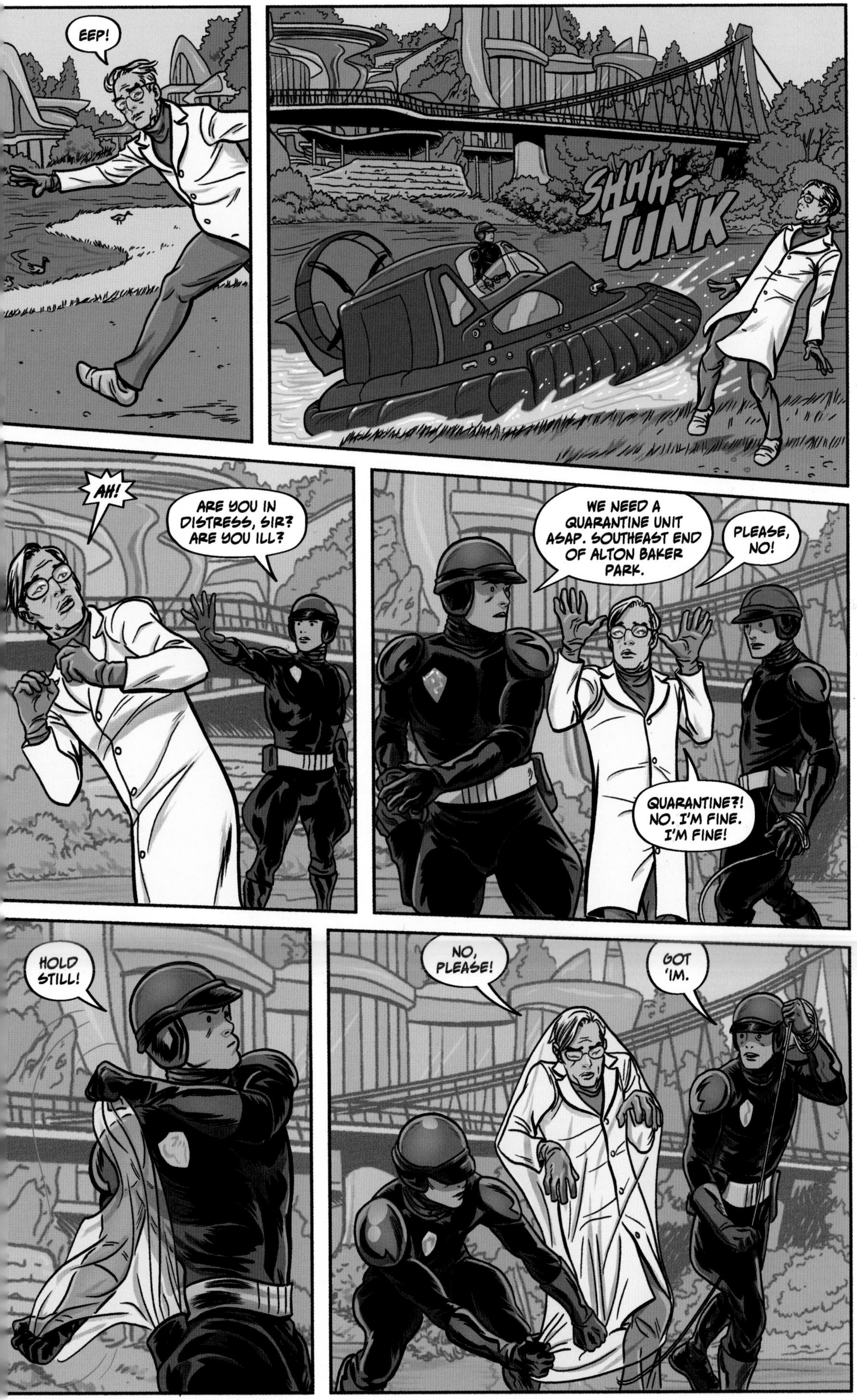
EEP!
SHHH-TUNK
AH!
ARE YOU IN DISTRESS, SIR? ARE YOU ILL?
WE NEED A QUARANTINE UNIT ASAP. SOUTHEAST END OF ALTON BAKER PARK.
PLEASE, NO!
QUARANTINE?! NO. I'M FINE. I'M FINE!
HOLD STILL!
NO, PLEASE!
GOT 'IM.

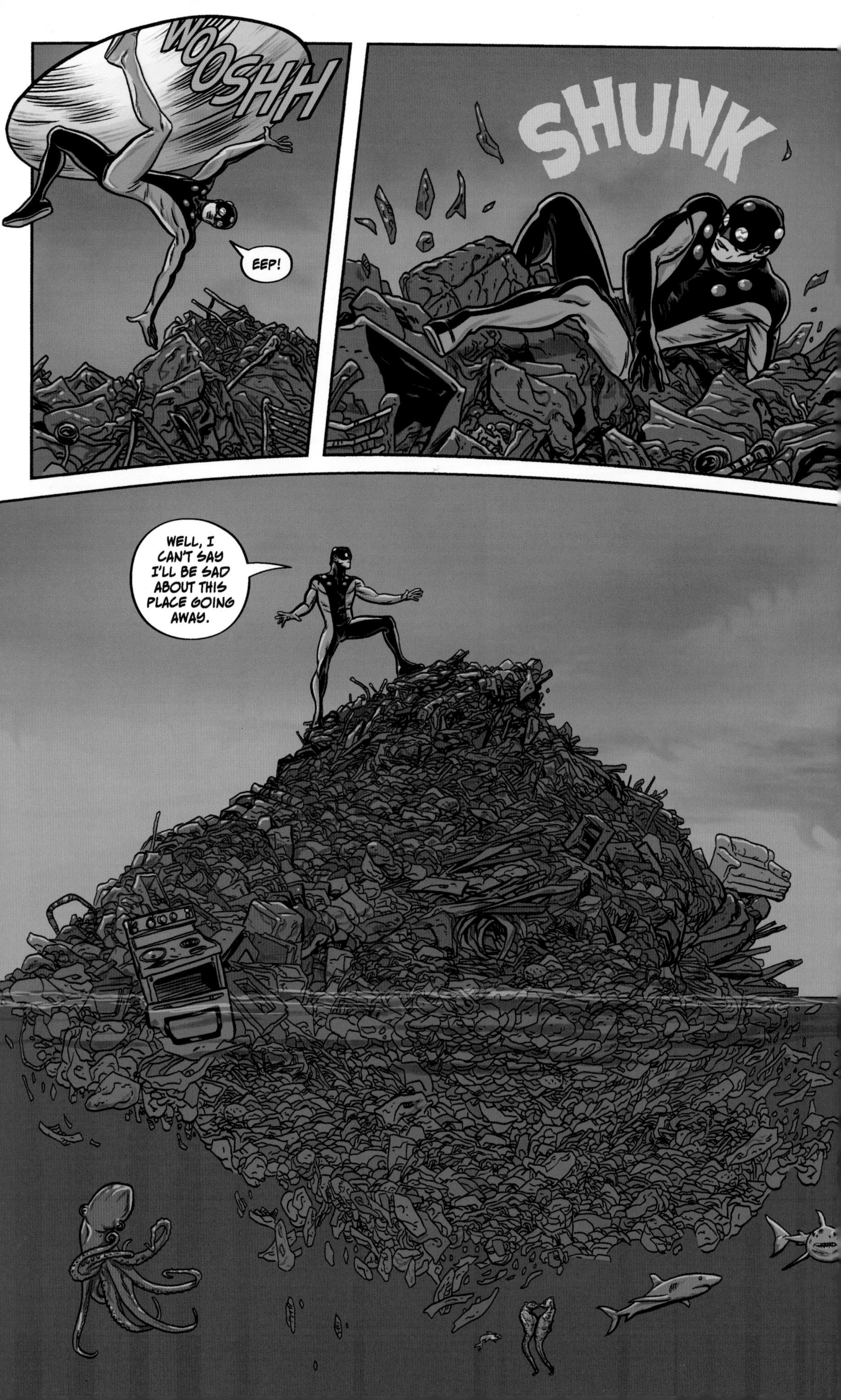
WOOOSHH
EEP!
SHUNK
WELL, I CAN'T SAY I'LL BE SAD ABOUT THIS PLACE GOING AWAY.

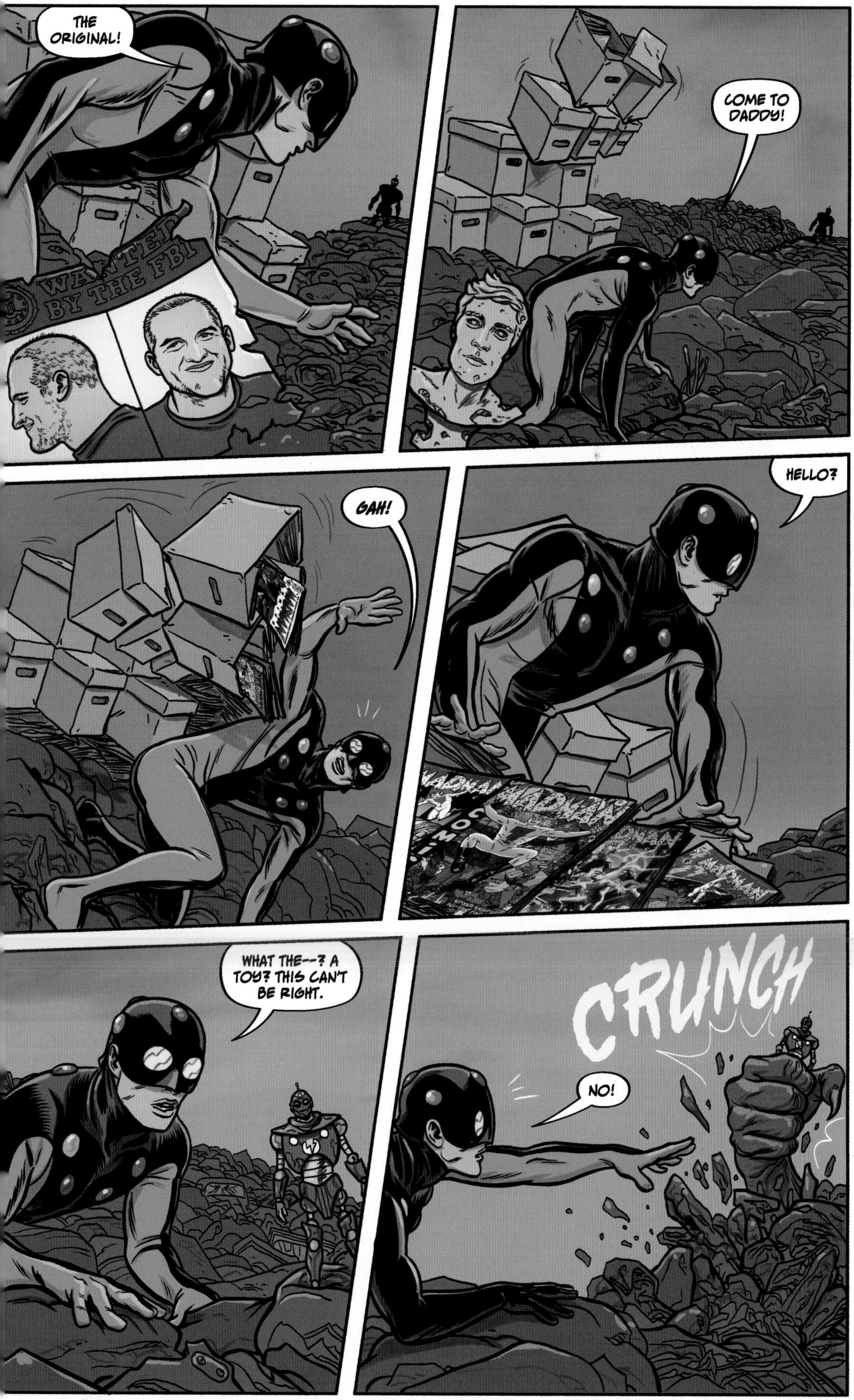
THE ORIGINAL!
WANTED BY THE FBI
COME TO DADDY!
GAH!
HELLO?
WHAT THE--? A TOY? THIS CAN'T BE RIGHT.
CRUNCH
NO!

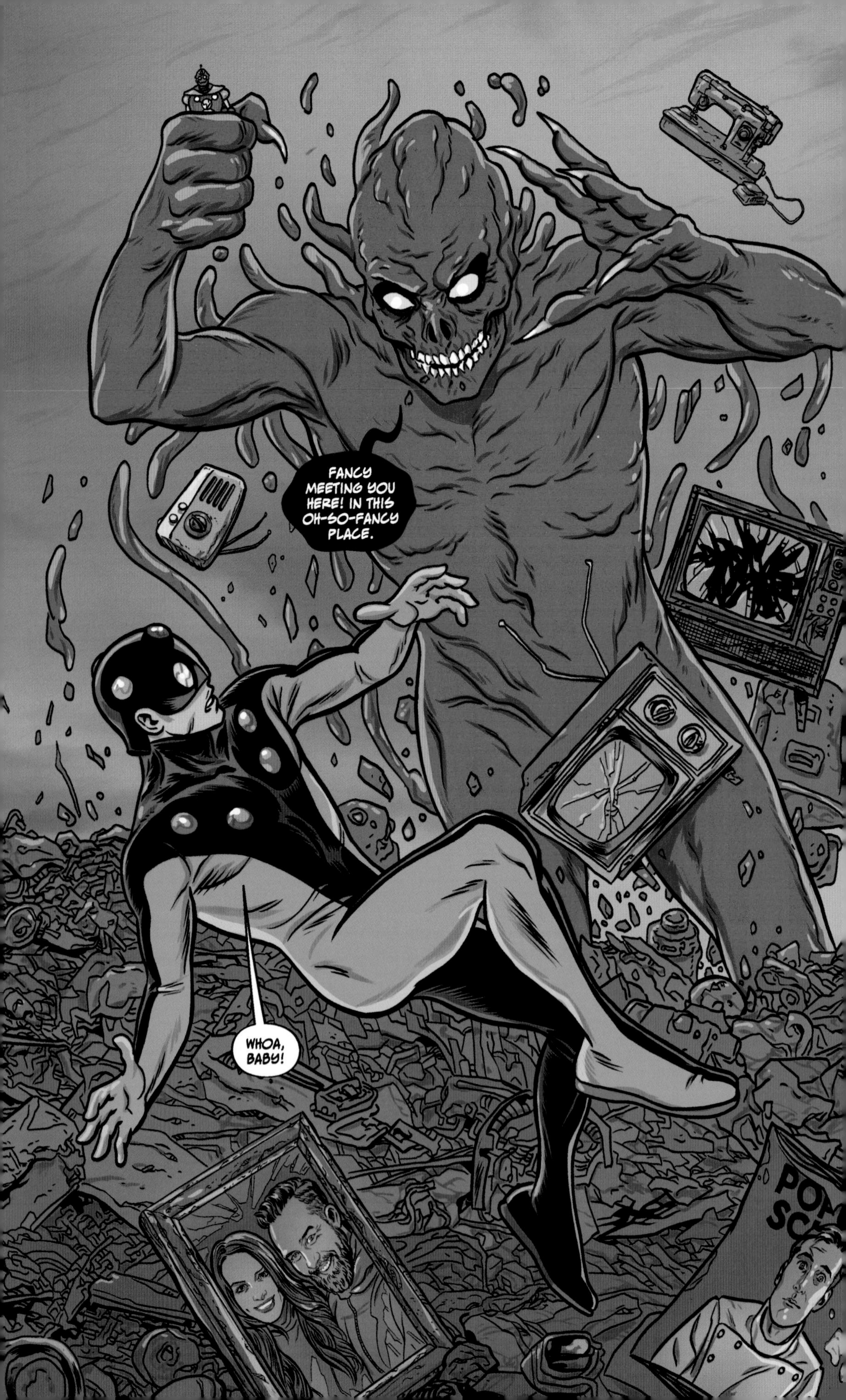
FANCY MEETING YOU HERE! IN THIS OH-SO-FANCY PLACE.
WHOA, BABY!

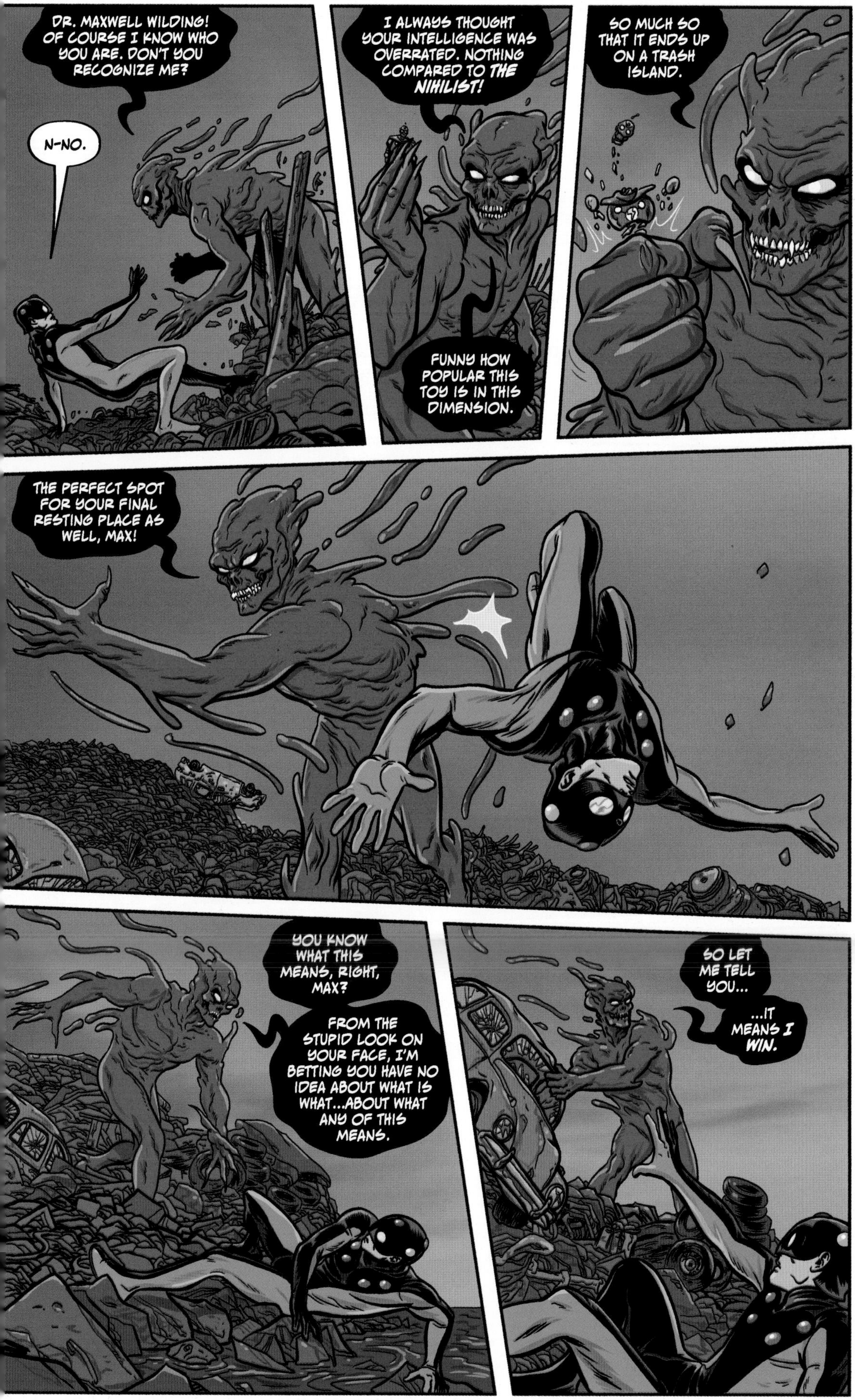
DR. MAXWELL WILDING! OF COURSE I KNOW WHO YOU ARE. DON'T YOU RECOGNIZE ME?
N-NO.
I ALWAYS THOUGHT YOUR INTELLIGENCE WAS OVERRATED. NOTHING COMPARED TO THE NIHILIST!
FUNNY HOW POPULAR THIS TOY IS IN THIS DIMENSION.
SO MUCH SO THAT IT ENDS UP ON A TRASH ISLAND.
THE PERFECT SPOT FOR YOUR FINAL RESTING PLACE AS WELL, MAX!
YOU KNOW WHAT THIS MEANS, RIGHT, MAX?
FROM THE STUPID LOOK ON YOUR FACE, I'M BETTING YOU HAVE NO IDEA ABOUT WHAT IS WHAT...ABOUT WHAT ANY OF THIS MEANS.
SO LET ME TELL YOU...
...IT MEANS I WIN.

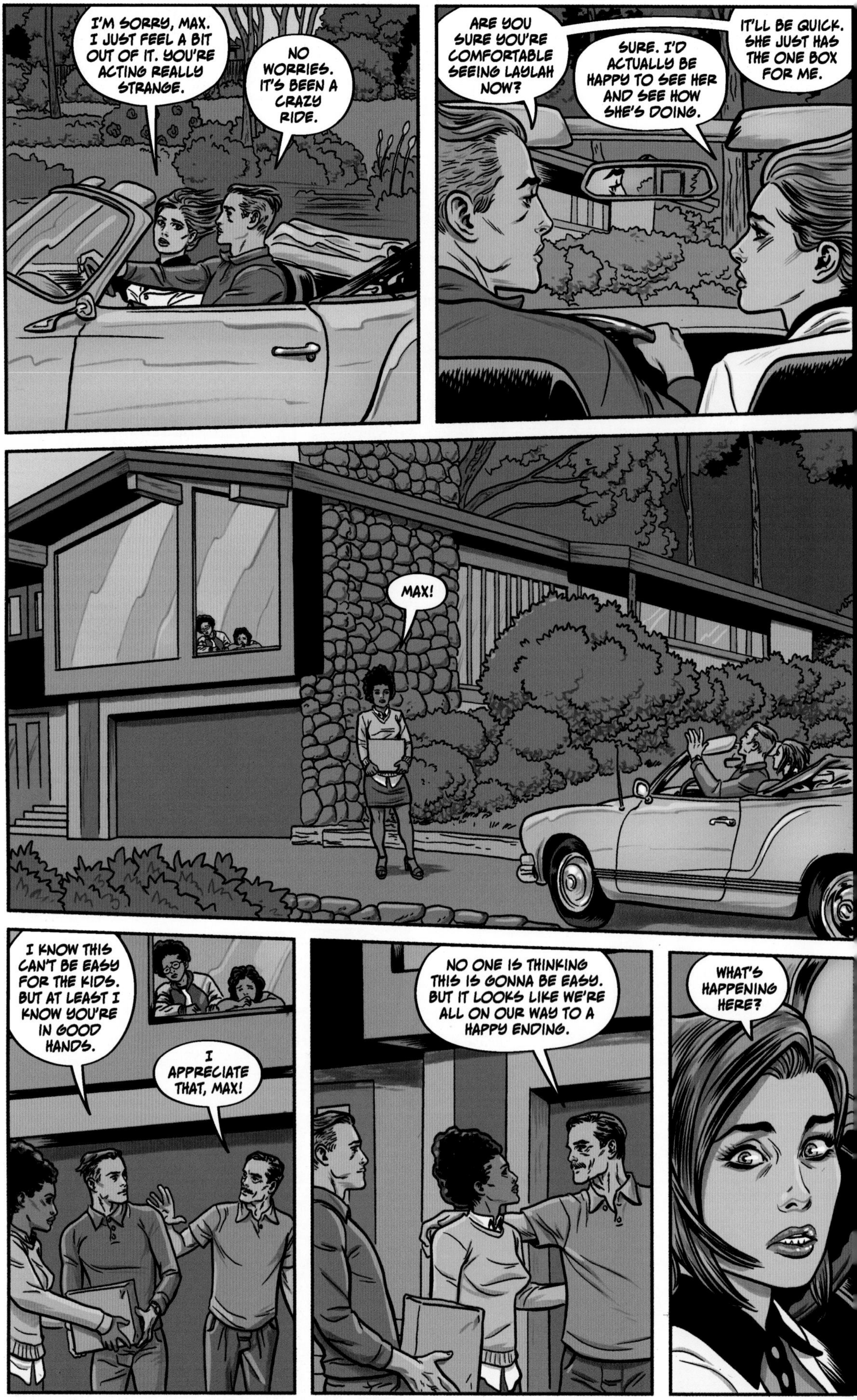
I'M SORRY, MAX. I JUST FEEL A BIT OUT OF IT. YOU'RE ACTING REALLY STRANGE.
NO WORRIES. IT'S BEEN A CRAZY RIDE.
ARE YOU SURE YOU'RE COMFORTABLE SEEING LAYLAH NOW?
SURE. I'D ACTUALLY BE HAPPY TO SEE HER AND SEE HOW SHE'S DOING.
IT'LL BE QUICK. SHE JUST HAS THE ONE BOX FOR ME.
MAX!
I KNOW THIS CAN'T BE EASY FOR THE KIDS. BUT AT LEAST I KNOW YOU'RE IN GOOD HANDS.
I APPRECIATE THAT, MAX!
NO ONE IS THINKING THIS IS GONNA BE EASY. BUT IT LOOKS LIKE WE'RE ALL ON OUR WAY TO A HAPPY ENDING.
WHAT'S HAPPENING HERE?

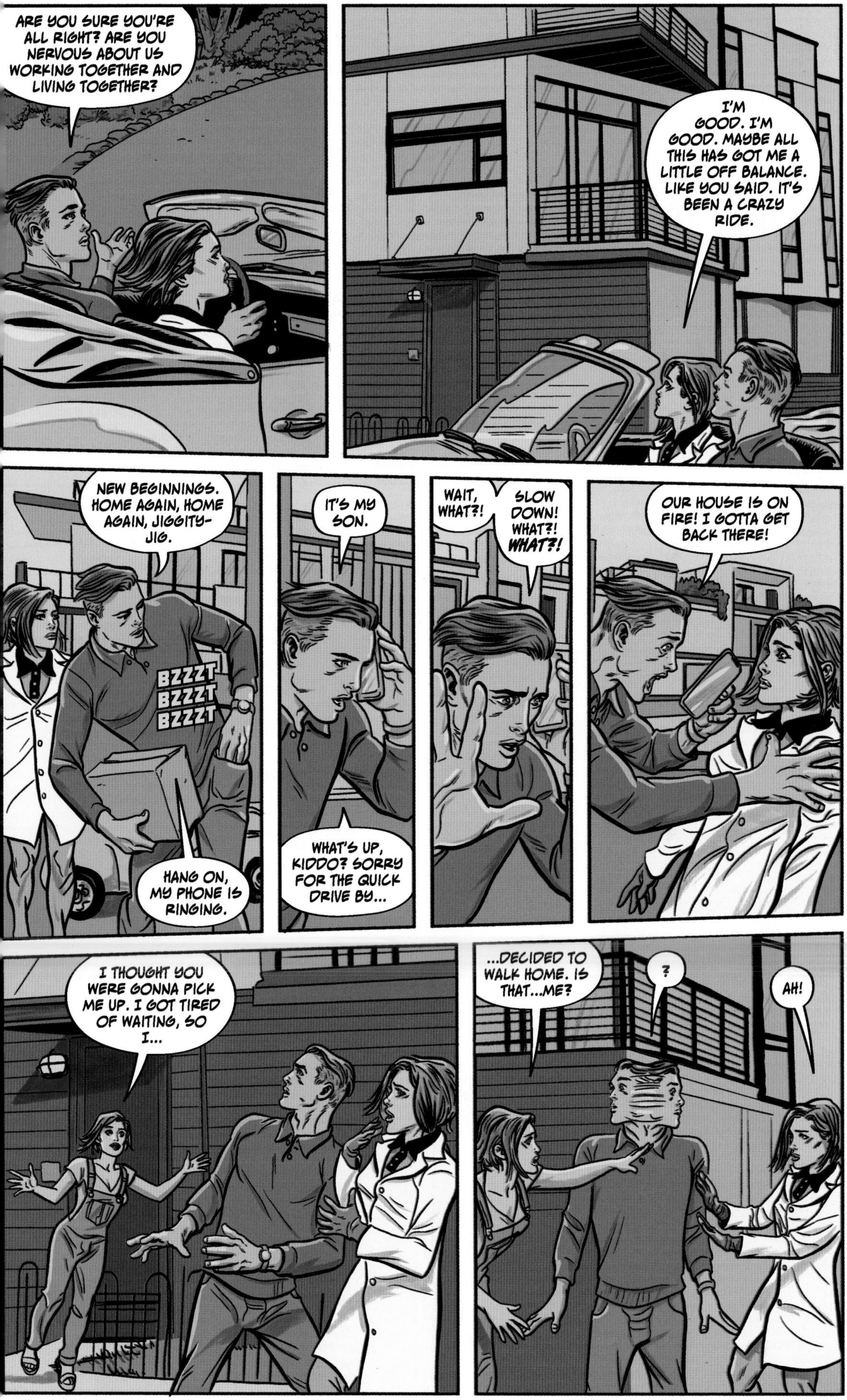
ARE YOU SURE YOU'RE ALL RIGHT? ARE YOU NERVOUS ABOUT US WORKING TOGETHER AND LIVING TOGETHER?
I'M GOOD. I'M GOOD. MAYBE ALL THIS HAS GOT ME A LITTLE OFF BALANCE. LIKE YOU SAID. IT'S BEEN A CRAZY RIDE.
NEW BEGINNINGS. HOME AGAIN, HOME AGAIN, JIGGITY-JIG.
BZZZT BZZZT BZZZT
HANG ON, MY PHONE IS RINGING.
IT'S MY SON.
WHAT'S UP, KIDDO? SORRY FOR THE QUICK DRIVE BY...
WAIT, WHAT?!
SLOW DOWN! WHAT?! WHAT?!
OUR HOUSE IS ON FIRE! I GOTTA GET BACK THERE!
I THOUGHT YOU WERE GONNA PICK ME UP. I GOT TIRED OF WAITING, SO I...
...DECIDED TO WALK HOME. IS THAT...ME?
?
AH!

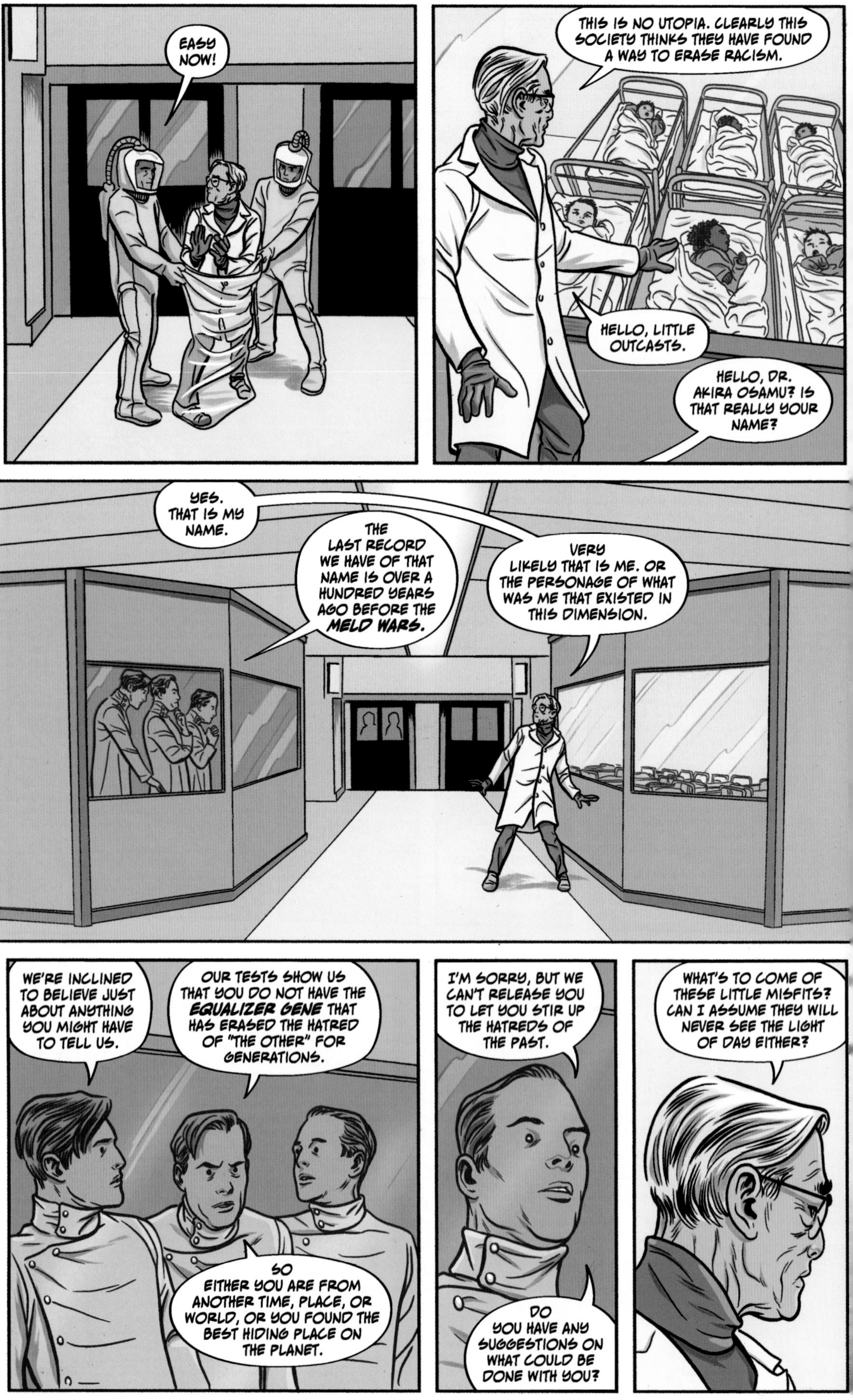
EASY NOW!
THIS IS NO UTOPIA. CLEARLY THIS SOCIETY THINKS THEY HAVE FOUND A WAY TO ERASE RACISM.
HELLO, LITTLE OUTCASTS.
HELLO, DR. AKIRA OSAMU? IS THAT REALLY YOUR NAME?
YES. THAT IS MY NAME.
THE LAST RECORD WE HAVE OF THAT NAME IS OVER A HUNDRED YEARS AGO BEFORE THE MELD WARS.
VERY LIKELY THAT IS ME. OR THE PERSONAGE OF WHAT WAS ME THAT EXISTED IN THIS DIMENSION.
WE'RE INCLINED TO BELIEVE JUST ABOUT ANYTHING YOU MIGHT HAVE TO TELL US.
OUR TESTS SHOW US THAT YOU DO NOT HAVE THE EQUALIZER GENE THAT HAS ERASED THE HATRED OF "THE OTHER" FOR GENERATIONS.
SO EITHER YOU ARE FROM ANOTHER TIME, PLACE, OR WORLD, OR YOU FOUND THE BEST HIDING PLACE ON THE PLANET.
I'M SORRY, BUT WE CAN'T RELEASE YOU TO LET YOU STIR UP THE HATREDS OF THE PAST.
DO YOU HAVE ANY SUGGESTIONS ON WHAT COULD BE DONE WITH YOU?
WHAT'S TO COME OF THESE LITTLE MISFITS? CAN I ASSUME THEY WILL NEVER SEE THE LIGHT OF DAY EITHER?

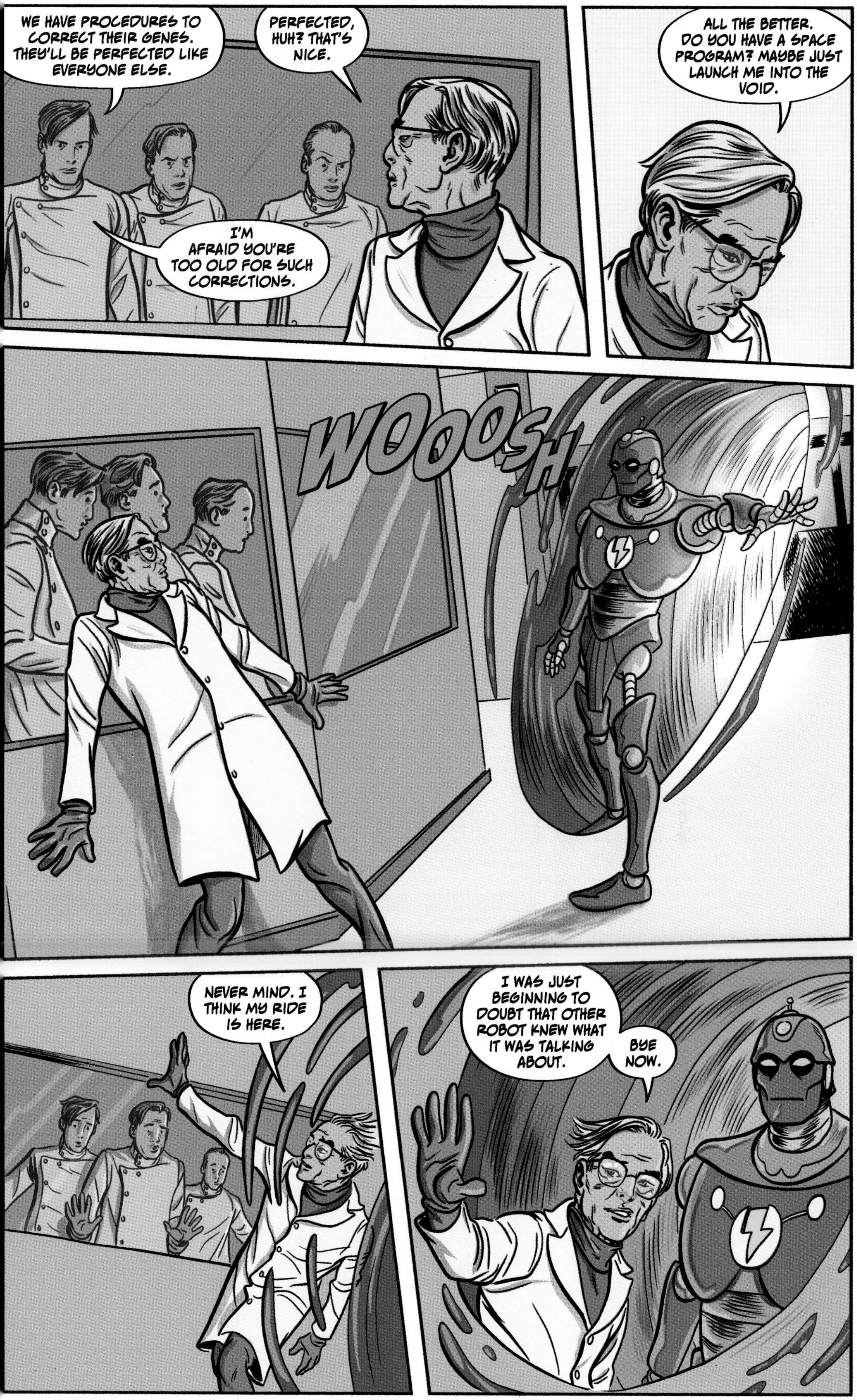
WE HAVE PROCEDURES TO CORRECT THEIR GENES. THEY'LL BE PERFECTED LIKE EVERYONE ELSE.
PERFECTED, HUH? THAT'S NICE.
I'M AFRAID YOU'RE TOO OLD FOR SUCH CORRECTIONS.
ALL THE BETTER. DO YOU HAVE A SPACE PROGRAM? MAYBE JUST LAUNCH ME INTO THE VOID.
WOOOSH
NEVER MIND. I THINK MY RIDE IS HERE.
I WAS JUST BEGINNING TO DOUBT THAT OTHER ROBOT KNEW WHAT IT WAS TALKING ABOUT.
BYE NOW.

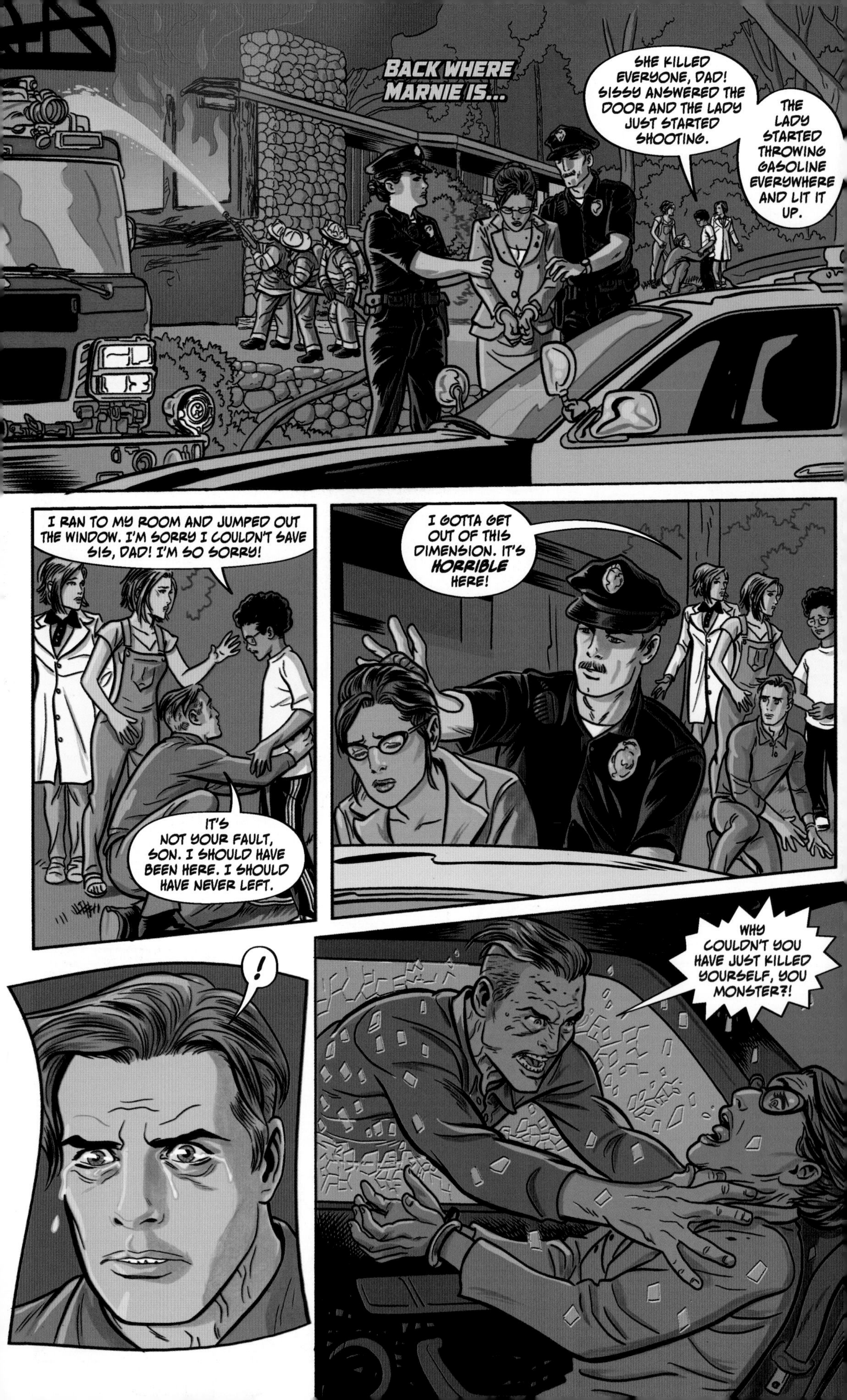
BACK WHERE MARNIE IS...
SHE KILLED EVERYONE, DAD! SISSY ANSWERED THE DOOR AND THE LADY JUST STARTED SHOOTING.
THE LADY STARTED THROWING GASOLINE EVERYWHERE AND LIT IT UP.
I RAN TO MY ROOM AND JUMPED OUT THE WINDOW. I'M SORRY I COULDN'T SAVE SIS, DAD! I'M SO SORRY!
IT'S NOT YOUR FAULT, SON. I SHOULD HAVE BEEN HERE. I SHOULD HAVE NEVER LEFT.
I GOTTA GET OUT OF THIS DIMENSION. IT'S HORRIBLE HERE!
!
WHY COULDN'T YOU HAVE JUST KILLED YOURSELF, YOU MONSTER?!

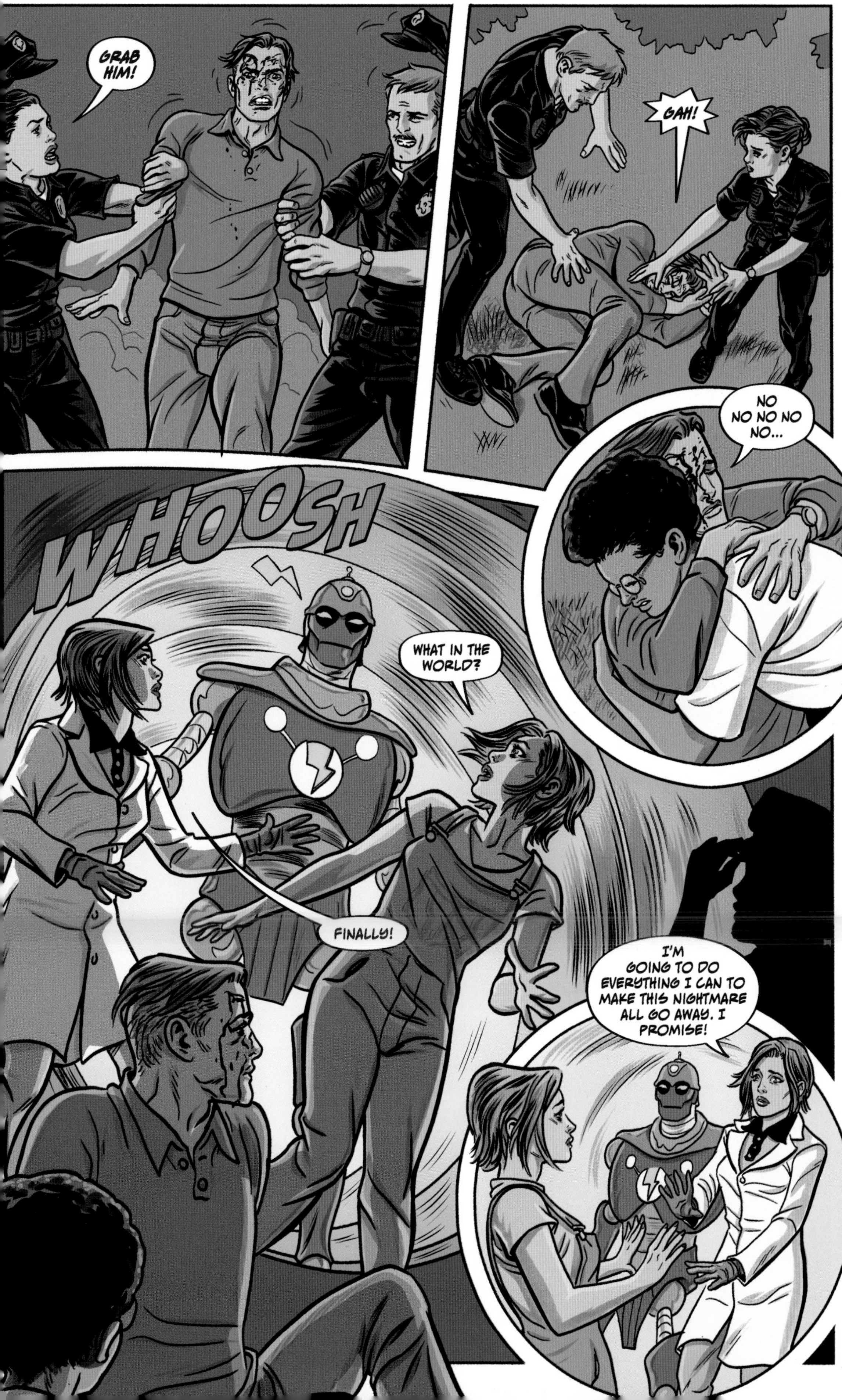
GRAB HIM!
GAH!
NO NO NO NO NO...
WHOOSH
WHAT IN THE WORLD?
FINALLY!
I'M GOING TO DO EVERYTHING I CAN TO MAKE THIS NIGHTMARE ALL GO AWAY. I PROMISE!

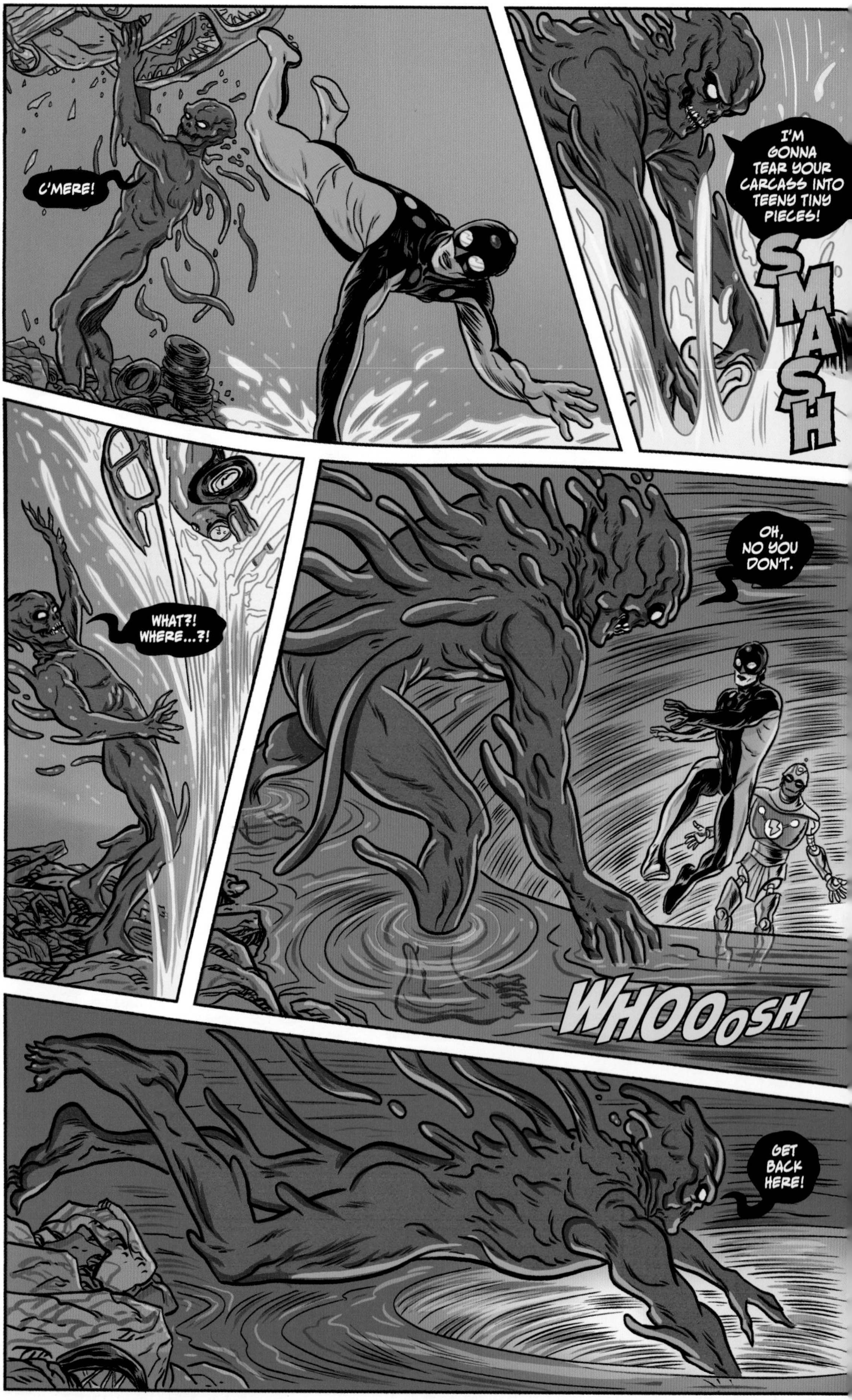

C'MERE!
I'M GONNA TEAR YOUR CARCASS INTO TEENY TINY PIECES!
SMASH
WHAT?! WHERE...?!
OH, NO YOU DON'T.
WHOOOSH
GET BACK HERE!

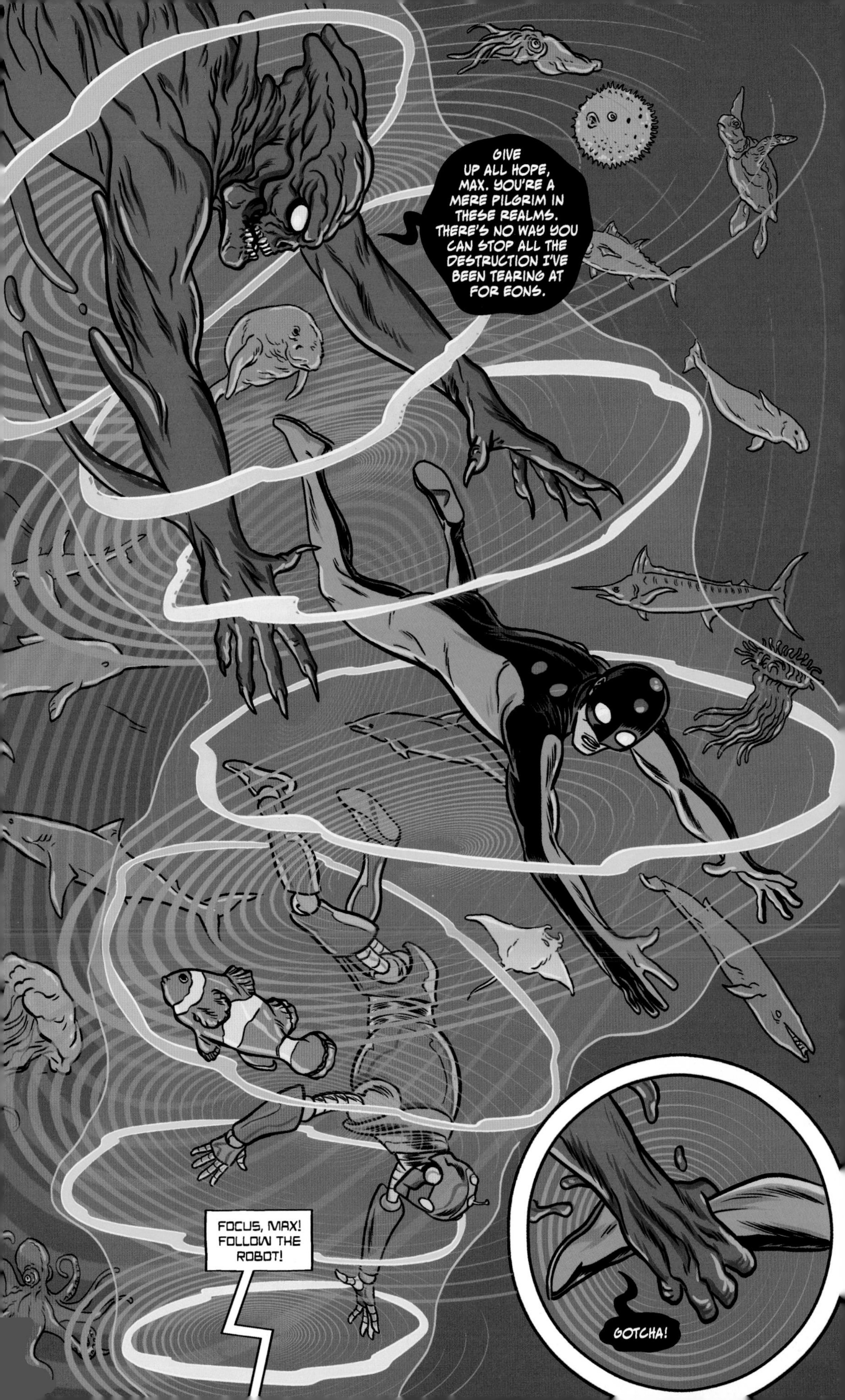
GIVE UP ALL HOPE, MAX. YOU'RE A MERE PILGRIM IN THESE REALMS. THERE'S NO WAY YOU CAN STOP ALL THE DESTRUCTION I'VE BEEN TEARING AT FOR EONS.
FOCUS, MAX! FOLLOW THE ROBOT!
GOTCHA!

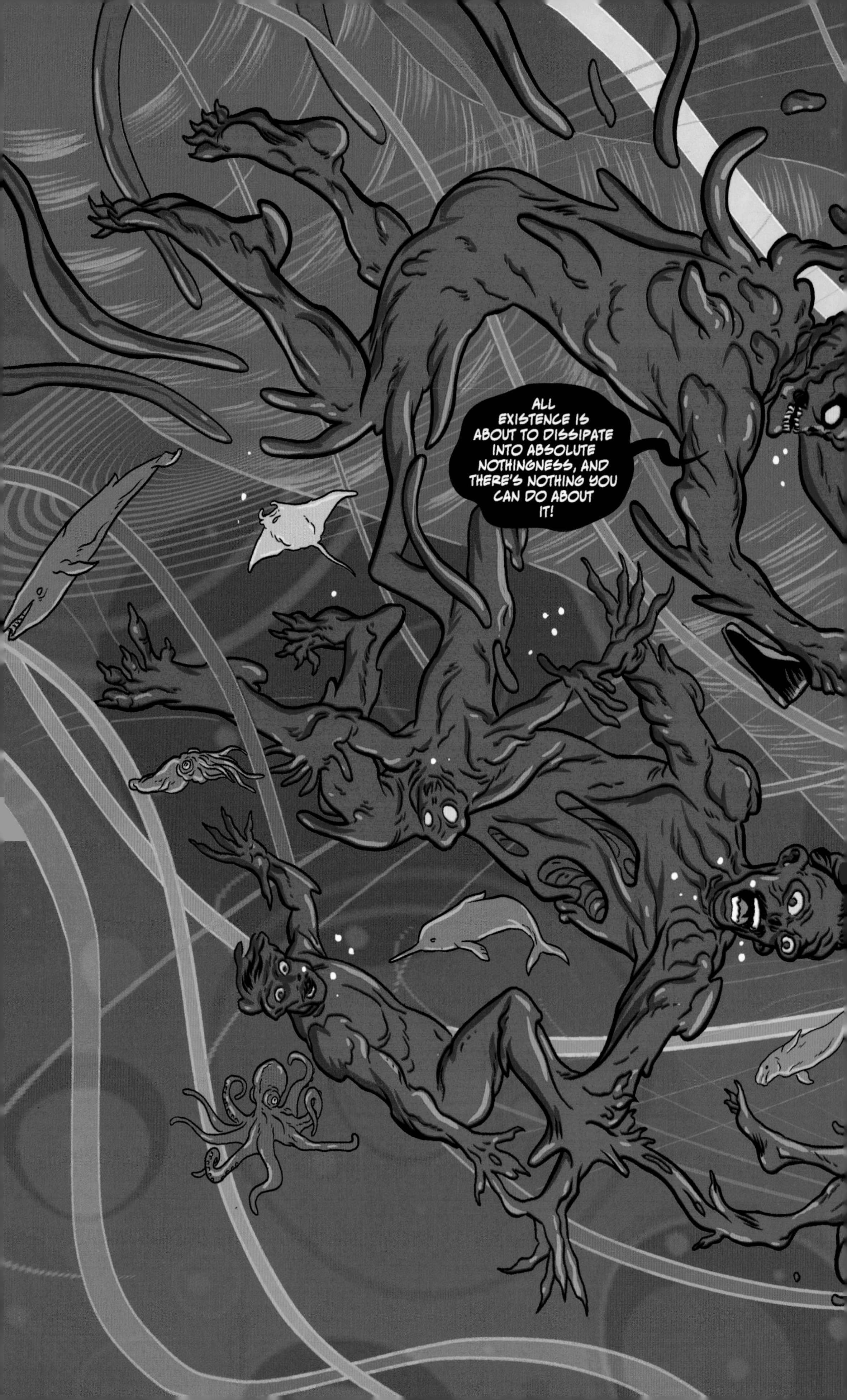
ALL EXISTENCE IS ABOUT TO DISSIPATE INTO ABSOLUTE NOTHINGNESS, AND THERE'S NOTHING YOU CAN DO ABOUT IT!

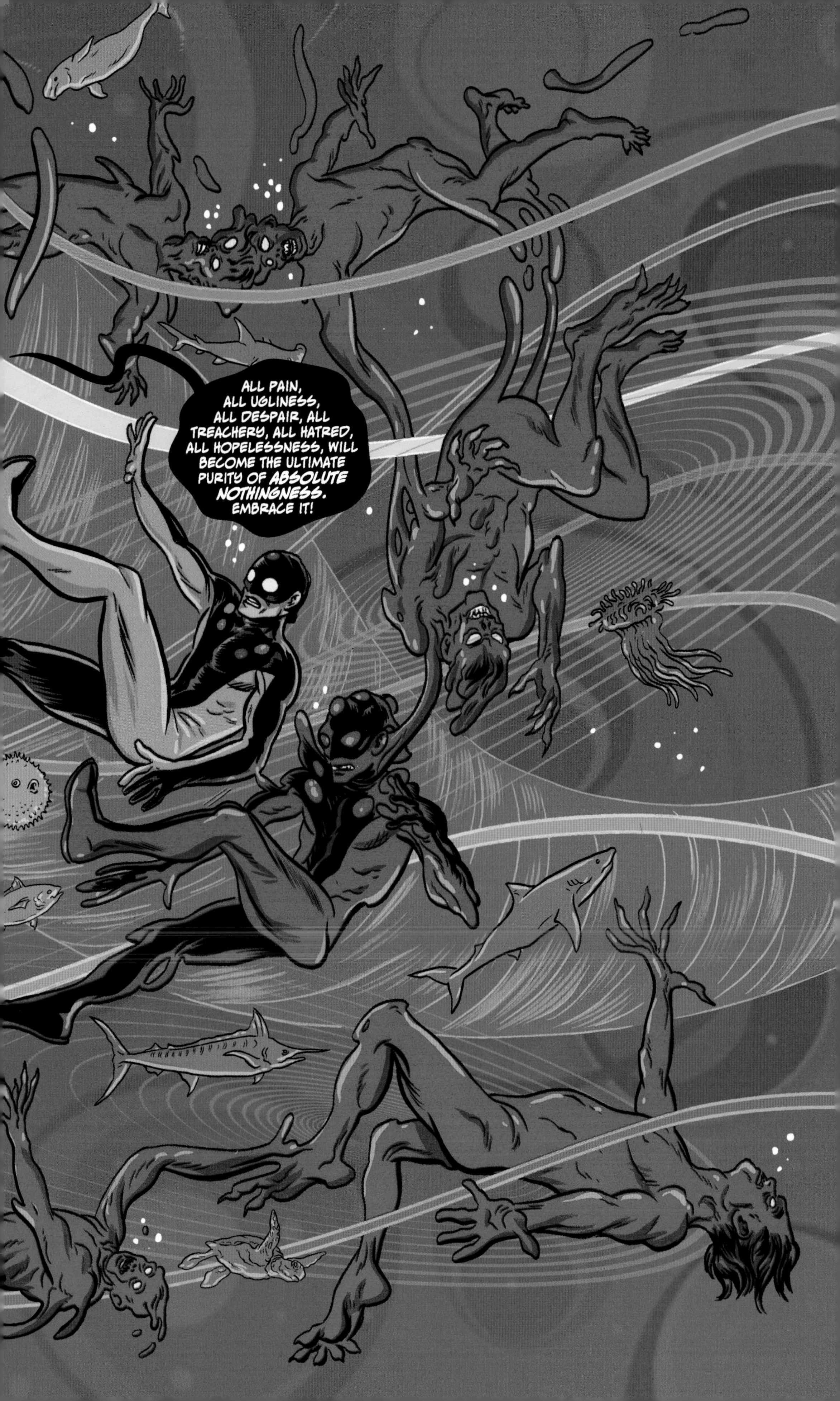
ALL PAIN, ALL UGLINESS, ALL DESPAIR, ALL TREACHERY, ALL HATRED, ALL HOPELESSNESS, WILL BECOME THE ULTIMATE PURITY OF ABSOLUTE NOTHINGNESS. EMBRACE IT!

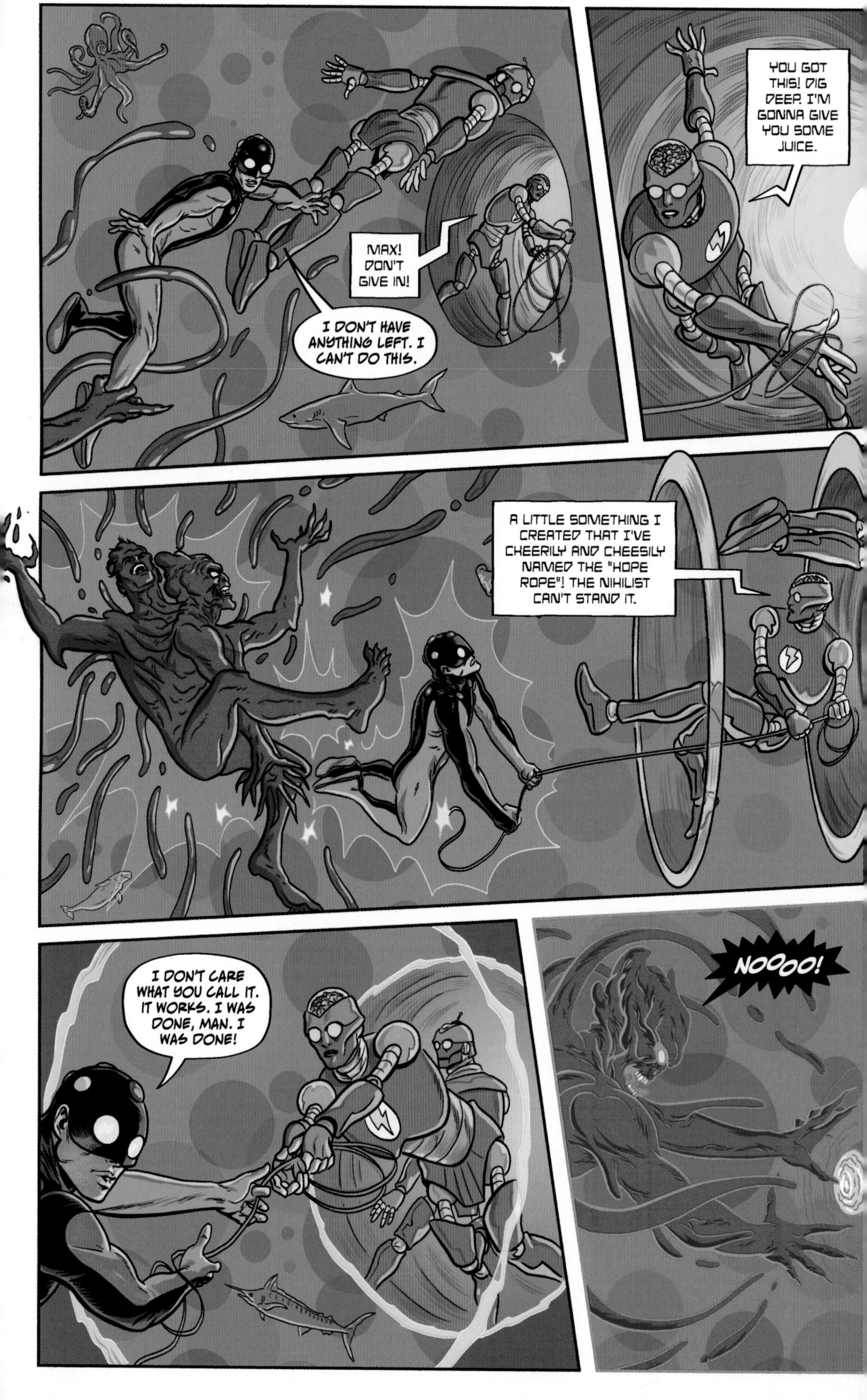
MAX! DON'T GIVE IN!
I DON'T HAVE ANYTHING LEFT. I CAN'T DO THIS.
YOU GOT THIS! DIG DEEP. I'M GONNA GIVE YOU SOME JUICE.
A LITTLE SOMETHING I CREATED THAT I'VE CHEERILY AND CHEESILY NAMED THE "HOPE ROPE"! THE NIHILIST CAN'T STAND IT.
I DON'T CARE WHAT YOU CALL IT. IT WORKS. I WAS DONE, MAN. I WAS DONE!
NOOOO!

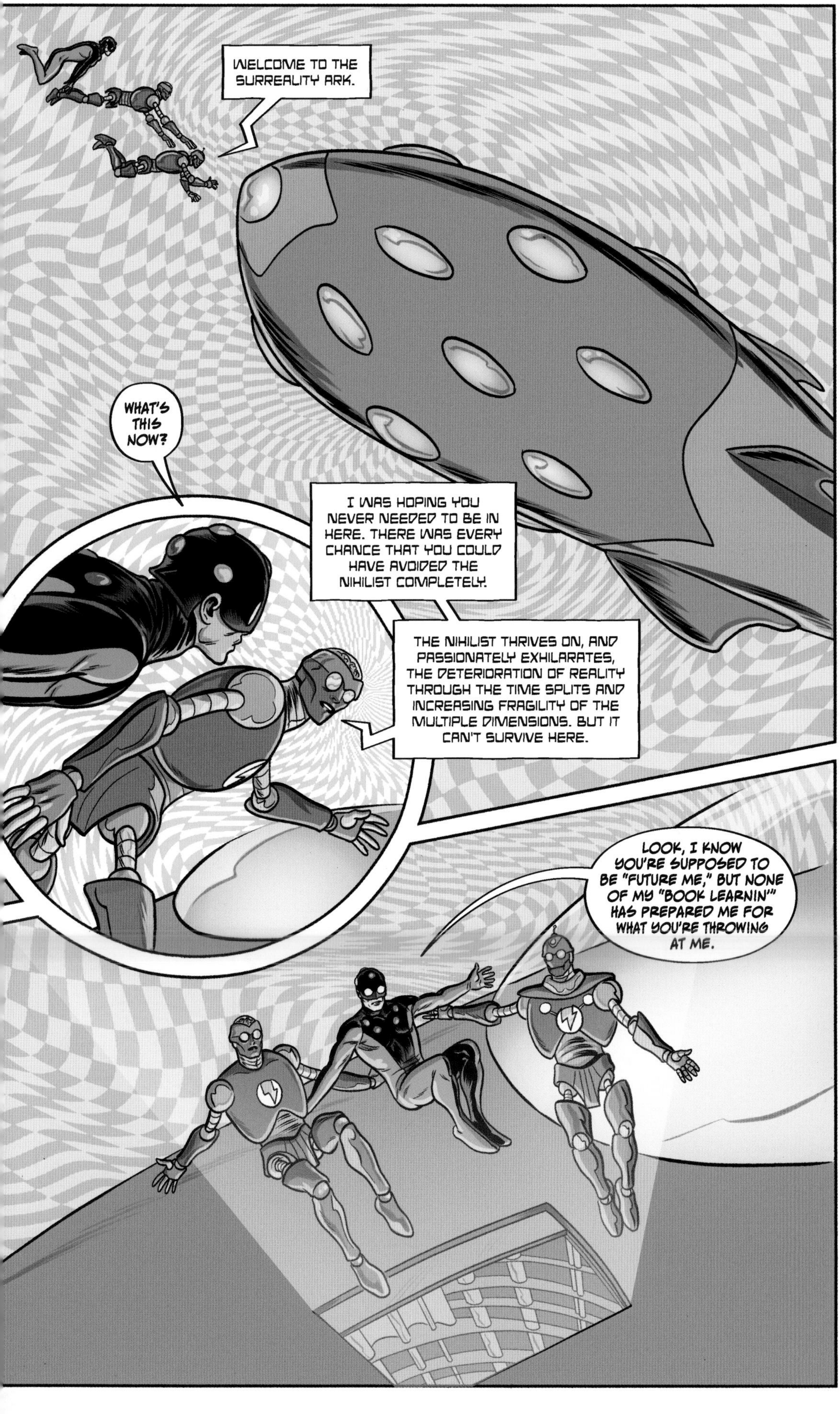
WELCOME TO THE SURREALITY ARK.
WHAT'S THIS NOW?
I WAS HOPING YOU NEVER NEEDED TO BE IN HERE. THERE WAS EVERY CHANCE THAT YOU COULD HAVE AVOIDED THE NIHILIST COMPLETELY.
THE NIHILIST THRIVES ON, AND PASSIONATELY EXHILARATES, THE DETERIORATION OF REALITY THROUGH THE TIME SPLITS AND INCREASING FRAGILITY OF THE MULTIPLE DIMENSIONS. BUT IT CAN'T SURVIVE HERE.
LOOK, I KNOW YOU'RE SUPPOSED TO BE "FUTURE ME," BUT NONE OF MY "BOOK LEARNIN'" HAS PREPARED ME FOR WHAT YOU'RE THROWING AT ME.

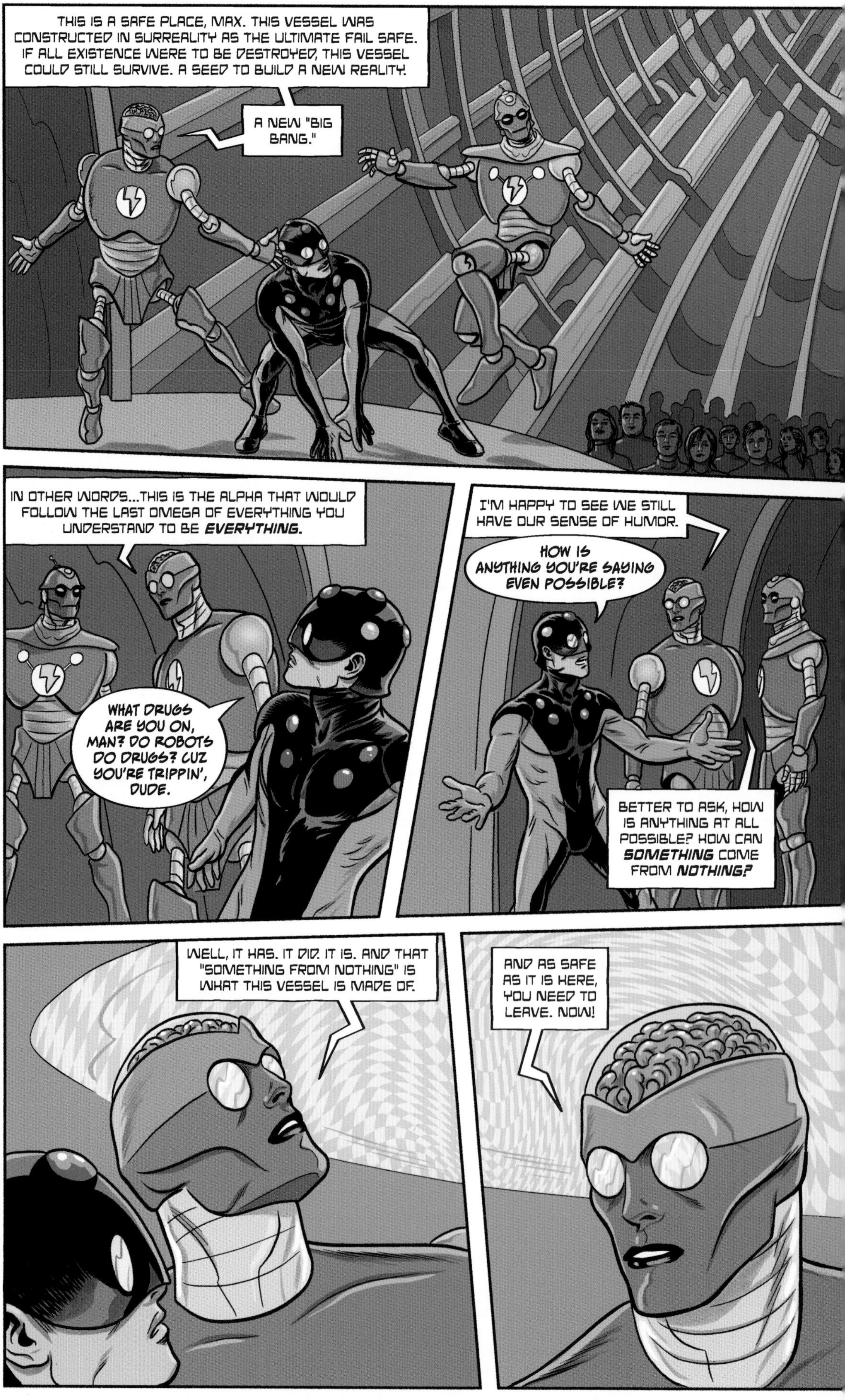
THIS IS A SAFE PLACE, MAX. THIS VESSEL WAS CONSTRUCTED IN SURREALITY AS THE ULTIMATE FAIL SAFE. IF ALL EXISTENCE WERE TO BE DESTROYED, THIS VESSEL COULD STILL SURVIVE. A SEED TO BUILD A NEW REALITY.
A NEW "BIG BANG."
IN OTHER WORDS...THIS IS THE ALPHA THAT WOULD FOLLOW THE LAST OMEGA OF EVERYTHING YOU UNDERSTAND TO BE ***EVERYTHING.***
WHAT DRUGS ARE YOU ON, MAN? DO ROBOTS DO DRUGS? CUZ YOU'RE TRIPPIN', DUDE.
I'M HAPPY TO SEE WE STILL HAVE OUR SENSE OF HUMOR.
HOW IS ANYTHING YOU'RE SAYING EVEN POSSIBLE?
BETTER TO ASK, HOW IS ANYTHING AT ALL POSSIBLE? HOW CAN ***SOMETHING*** COME FROM ***NOTHING?***
WELL, IT HAS. IT DID. IT IS. AND THAT "SOMETHING FROM NOTHING" IS WHAT THIS VESSEL IS MADE OF.
AND AS SAFE AS IT IS HERE, YOU NEED TO LEAVE. NOW!

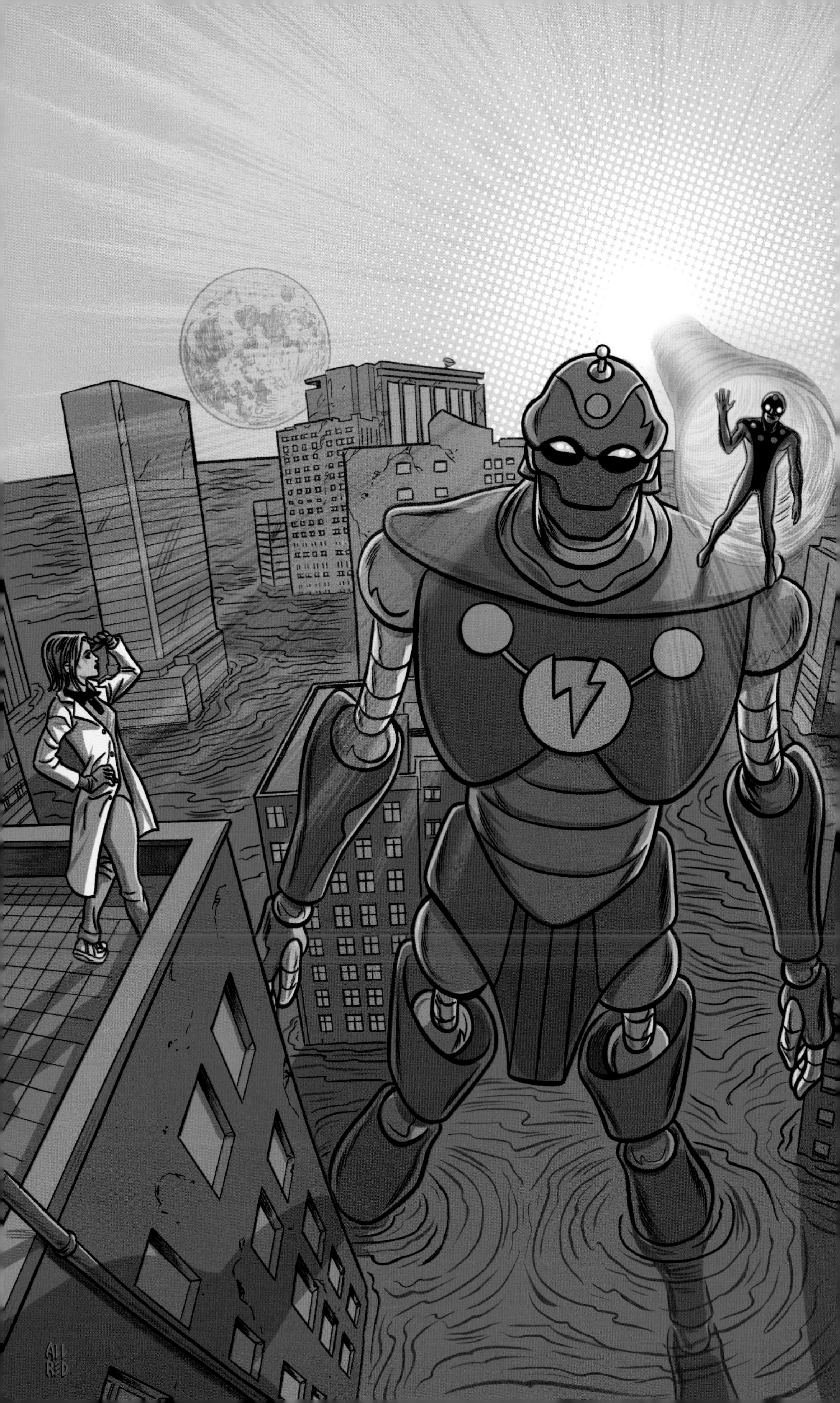

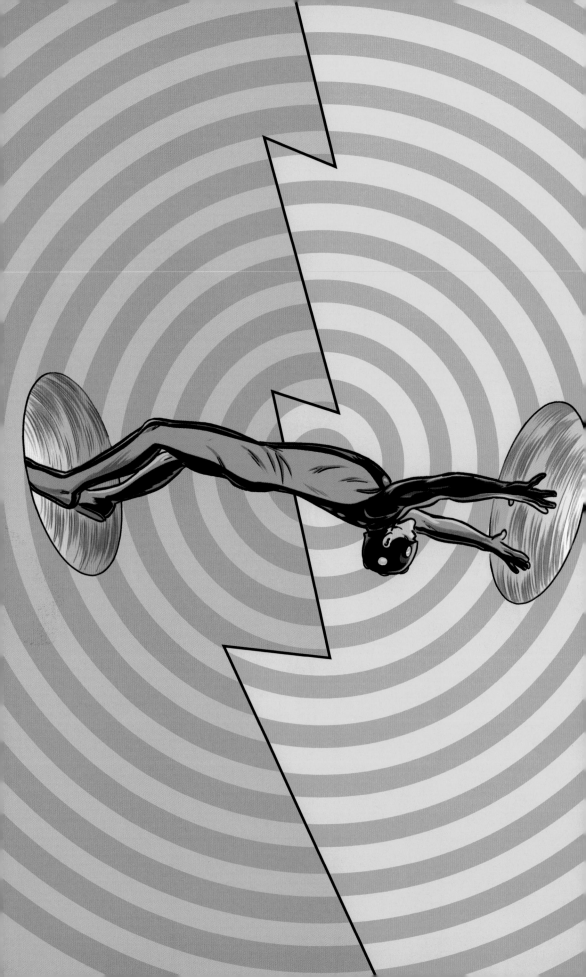

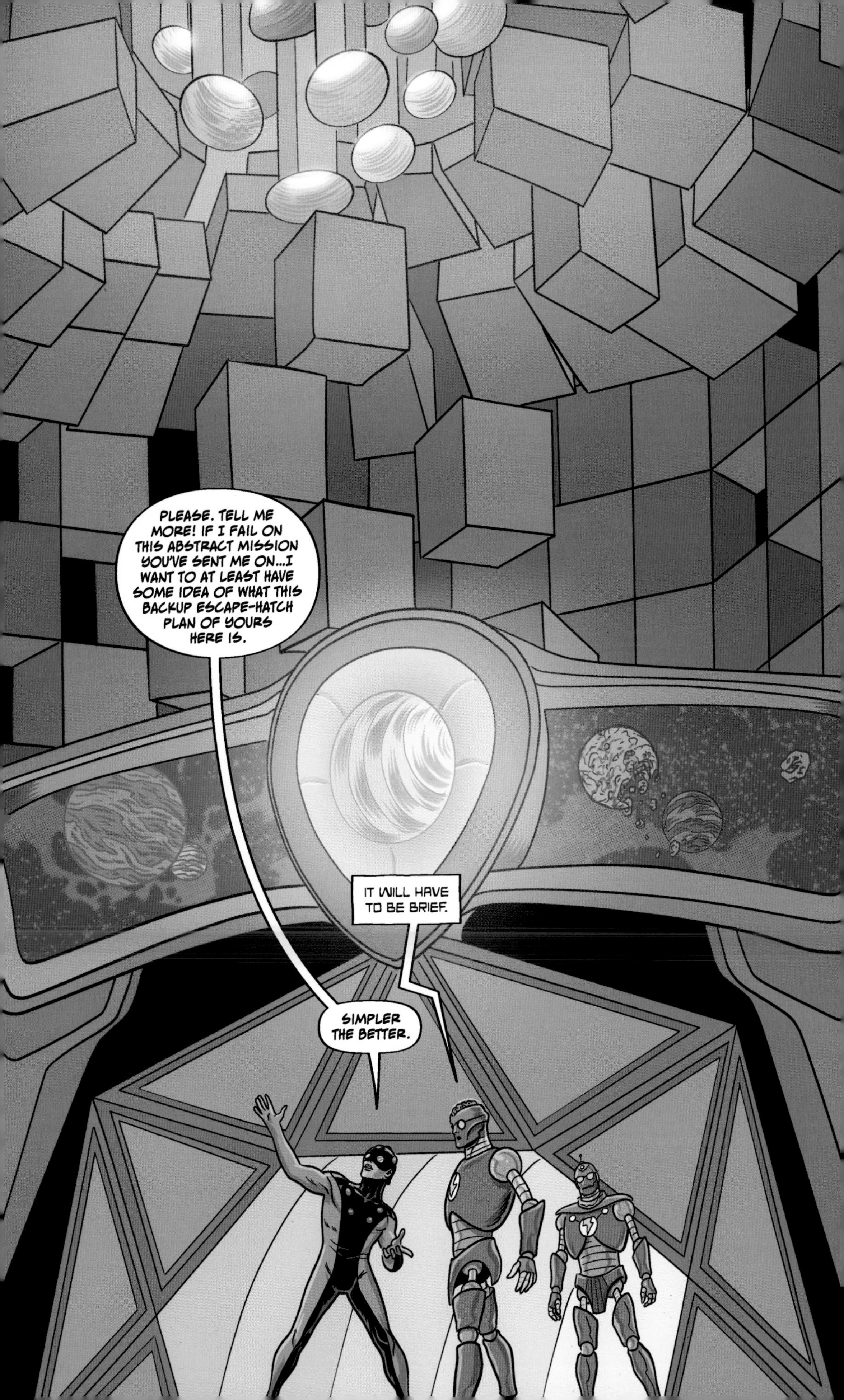
PLEASE. TELL ME MORE! IF I FAIL ON THIS ABSTRACT MISSION YOU'VE SENT ME ON...I WANT TO AT LEAST HAVE SOME IDEA OF WHAT THIS BACKUP ESCAPE-HATCH PLAN OF YOURS HERE IS.
IT WILL HAVE TO BE BRIEF.
SIMPLER THE BETTER.

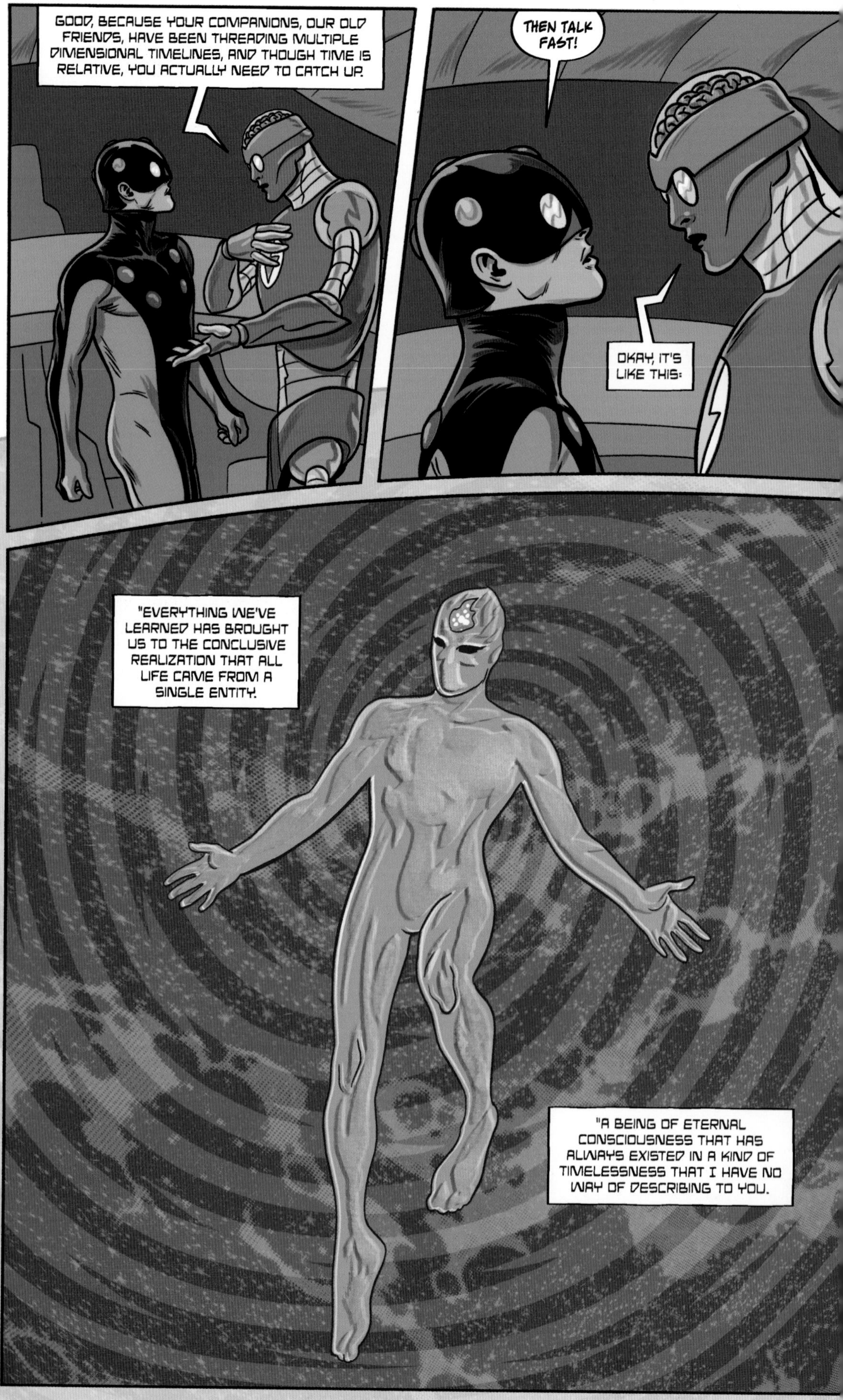
GOOD, BECAUSE YOUR COMPANIONS, OUR OLD FRIENDS, HAVE BEEN THREADING MULTIPLE DIMENSIONAL TIMELINES, AND THOUGH TIME IS RELATIVE, YOU ACTUALLY NEED TO CATCH UP.
THEN TALK FAST!
OKAY, IT'S LIKE THIS:
"EVERYTHING WE'VE LEARNED HAS BROUGHT US TO THE CONCLUSIVE REALIZATION THAT ALL LIFE CAME FROM A SINGLE ENTITY.
"A BEING OF ETERNAL CONSCIOUSNESS THAT HAS ALWAYS EXISTED IN A KIND OF TIMELESSNESS THAT I HAVE NO WAY OF DESCRIBING TO YOU.

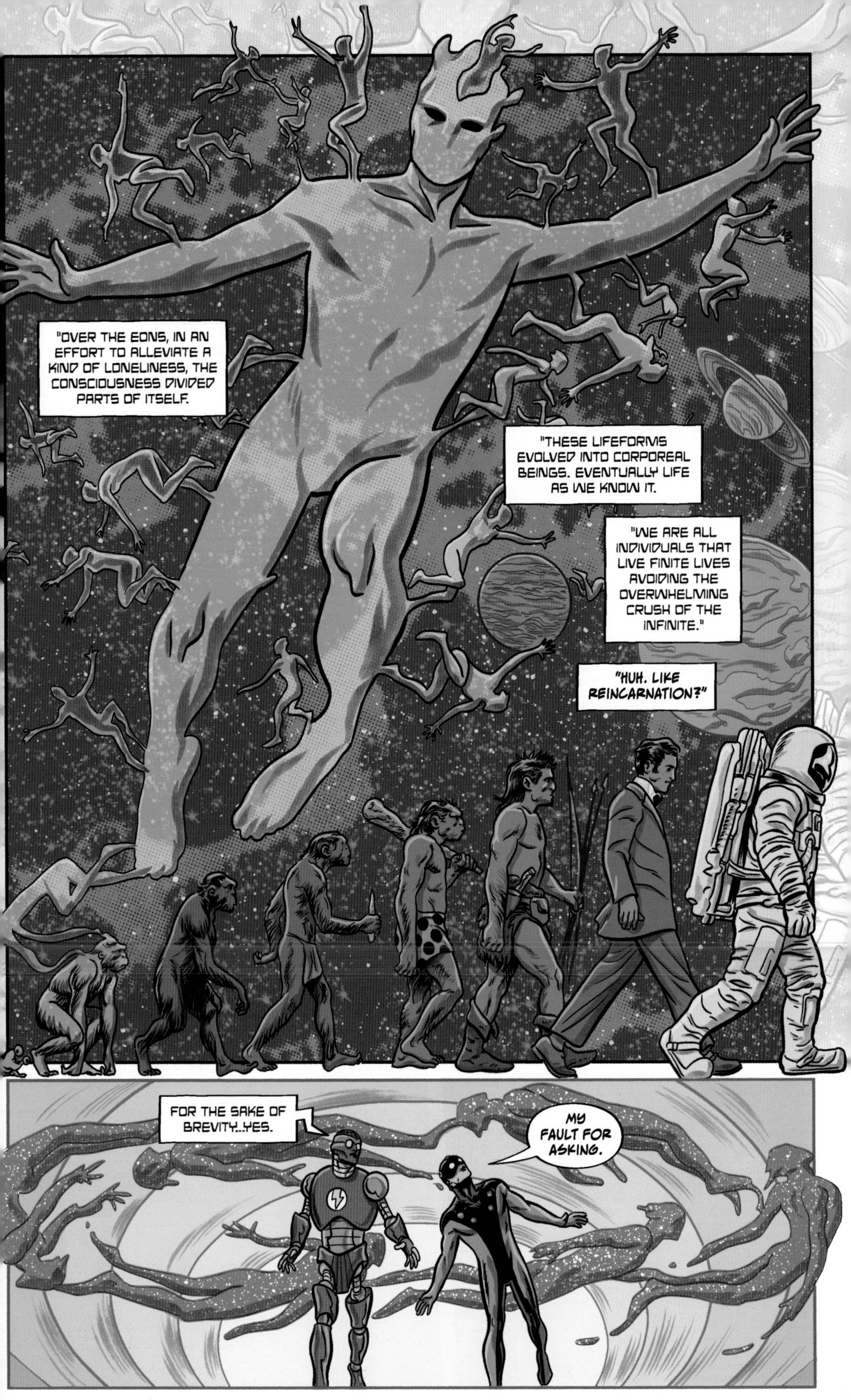

"OVER THE EONS, IN AN EFFORT TO ALLEVIATE A KIND OF LONELINESS, THE CONSCIOUSNESS DIVIDED PARTS OF ITSELF.
"THESE LIFEFORMS EVOLVED INTO CORPOREAL BEINGS. EVENTUALLY LIFE AS WE KNOW IT.
"WE ARE ALL INDIVIDUALS THAT LIVE FINITE LIVES AVOIDING THE OVERWHELMING CRUSH OF THE INFINITE."
"HUH. LIKE REINCARNATION?"
FOR THE SAKE OF BREVITY...YES.
MY FAULT FOR ASKING.

THE LONGER I EXIST, THE MORE I FEEL THE CLARITY OF ALL THINGS. IT'S AN ACCUMULATIVE SIMULTANEOUS FEELING OF ENLIGHTENMENT AND TERROR.

I THINK THAT'S EXPLANATION ENOUGH. THIS IS WHERE WE UTILIZE THE EXPRESSION "TIME IS OF THE ESSENCE" IN THE MOST CRITICAL USAGE EVER.

AND THESE PEOPLE?

THINK OF THEM AS THE LAST HOPE OF CREATION.

I'VE COLLECTED THEM OVER TIME. PEOPLE OF EMPATHY, COMMON SENSE, INTELLIGENCE, CREATIVITY, AND GOOD WILL.

IF ALL ELSE FAILS, AT LEAST THIS PLACE OF IMPOSSIBILITY WILL HAVE SOME SMALL PIECE OF THE ORIGINAL CONSCIOUSNESS. ONE LAST SEED TO PROTECT SOMETHING FROM NOTHINGNESS.

ENOUGH FOR YOU?

I GUESS.

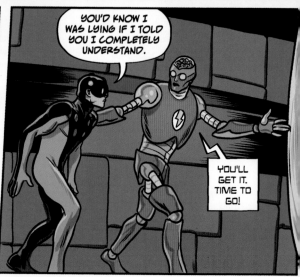

YOU'D KNOW I WAS LYING IF I TOLD YOU I COMPLETELY UNDERSTAND.

YOU'LL GET IT. TIME TO GO!

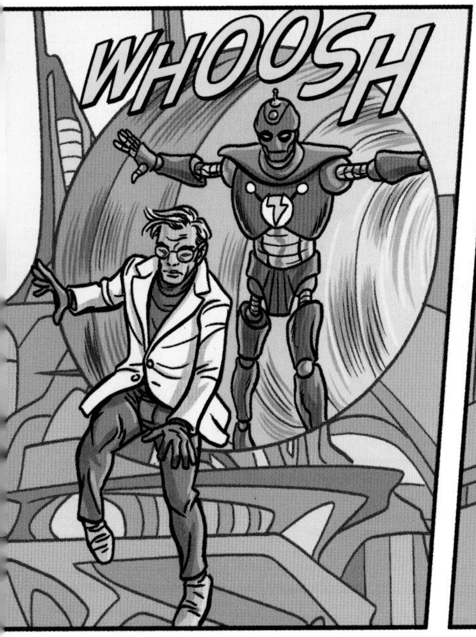
WHOOSH

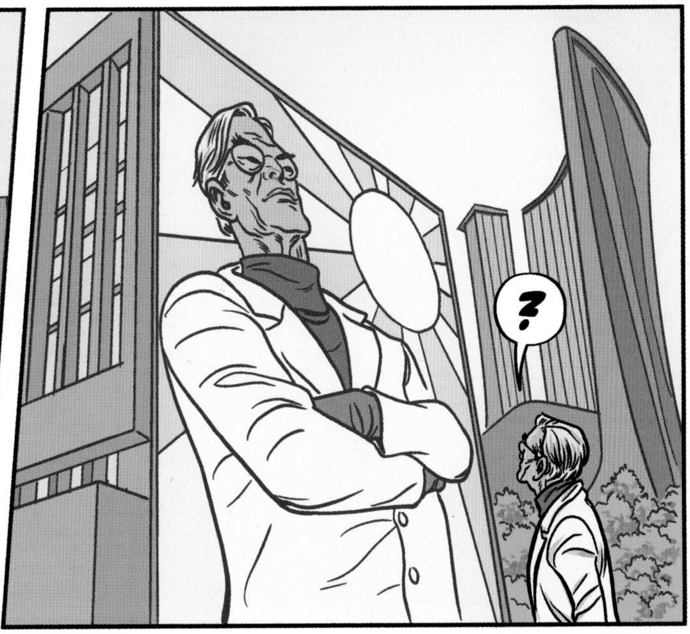
?

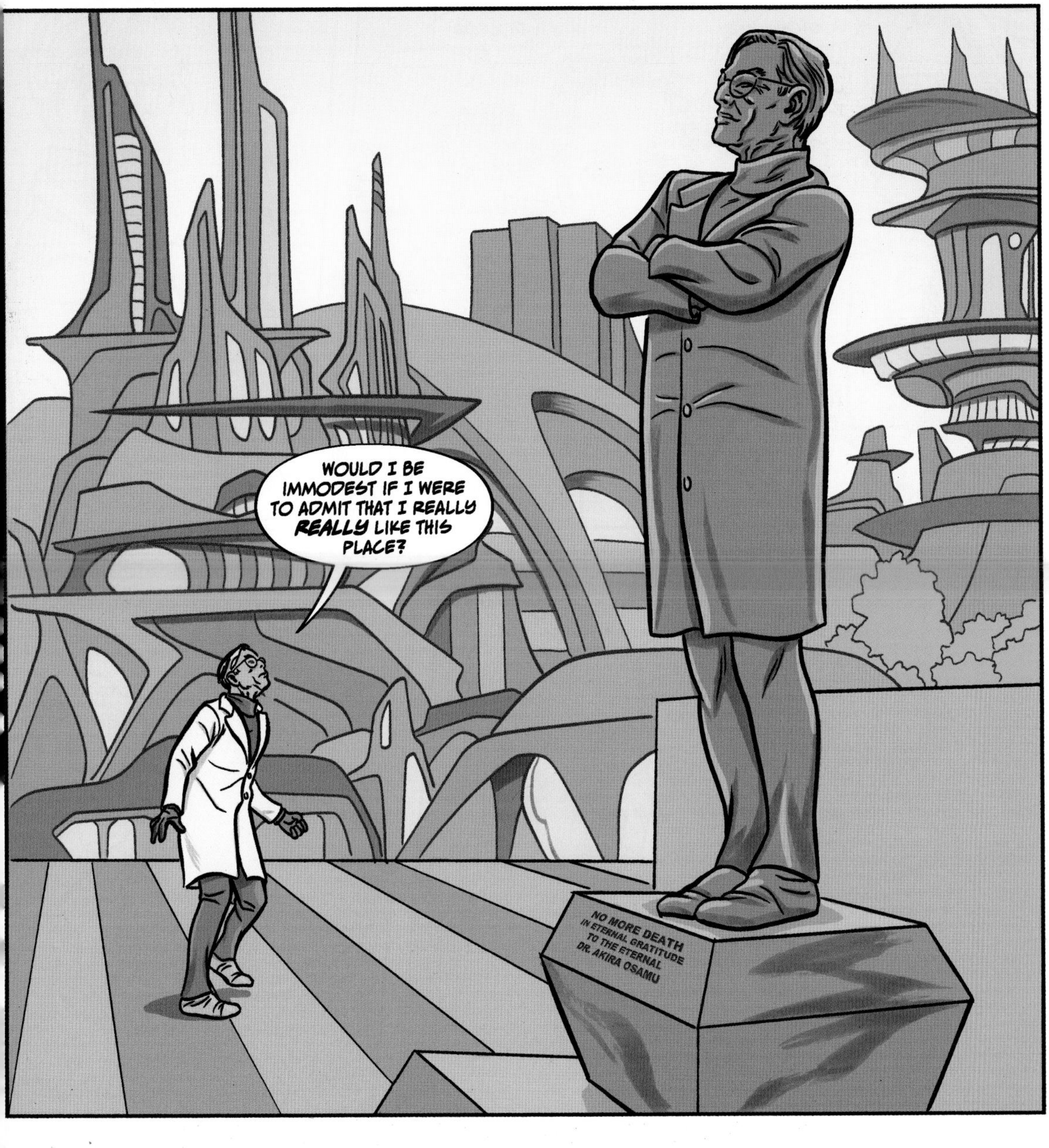
WOULD I BE IMMODEST IF I WERE TO ADMIT THAT I REALLY ***REALLY*** LIKE THIS PLACE?
NO MORE DEATH
IN ETERNAL GRATITUDE
TO THE ETERNAL
DR. AKIRA OSAMU

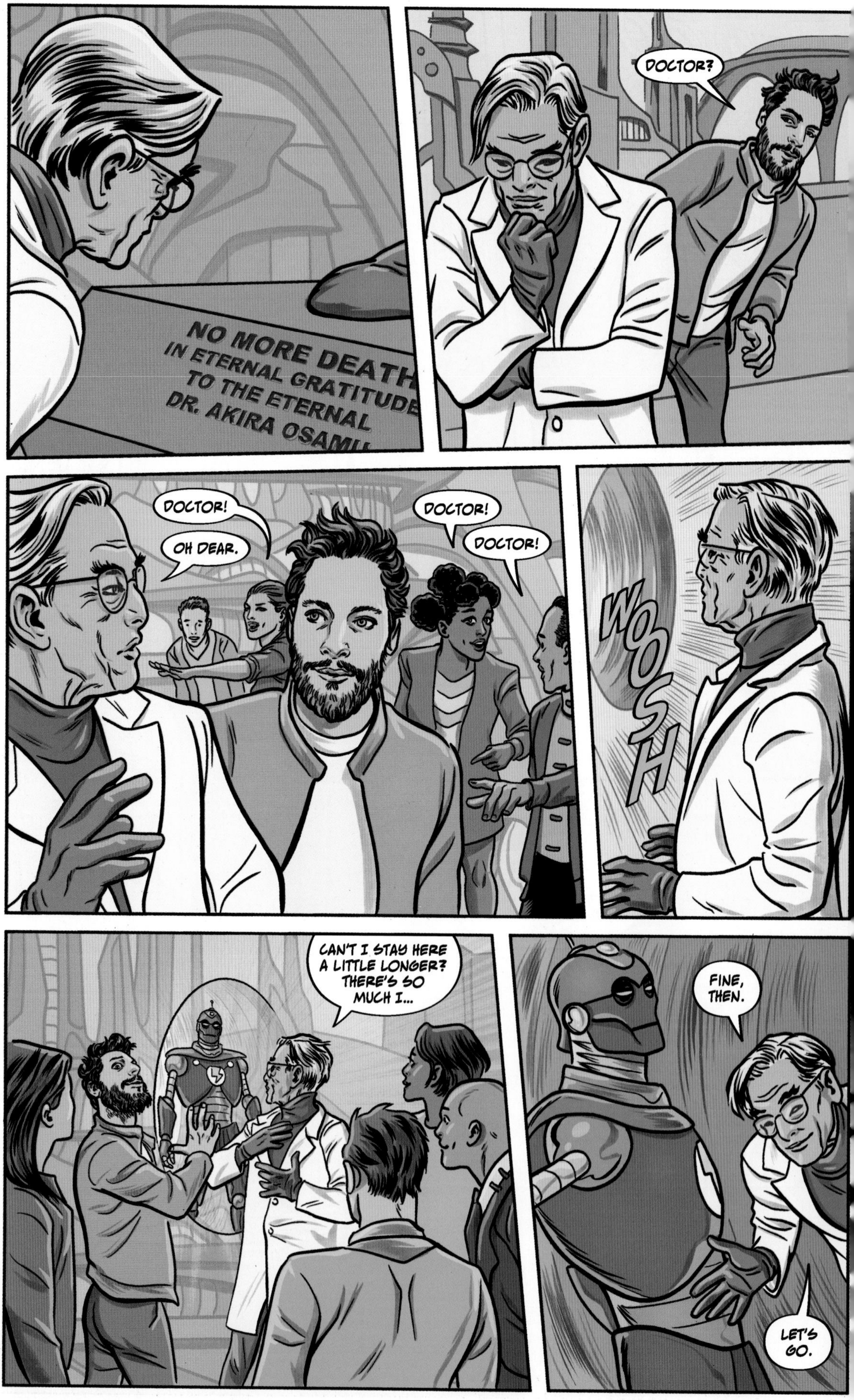
NO MORE DEATH
IN ETERNAL GRATITUDE
TO THE ETERNAL
DR. AKIRA OSAMU
DOCTOR?
DOCTOR!
OH DEAR.
DOCTOR!
DOCTOR!
WOOSH
CAN'T I STAY HERE A LITTLE LONGER? THERE'S SO MUCH I...
FINE, THEN.
LET'S GO.

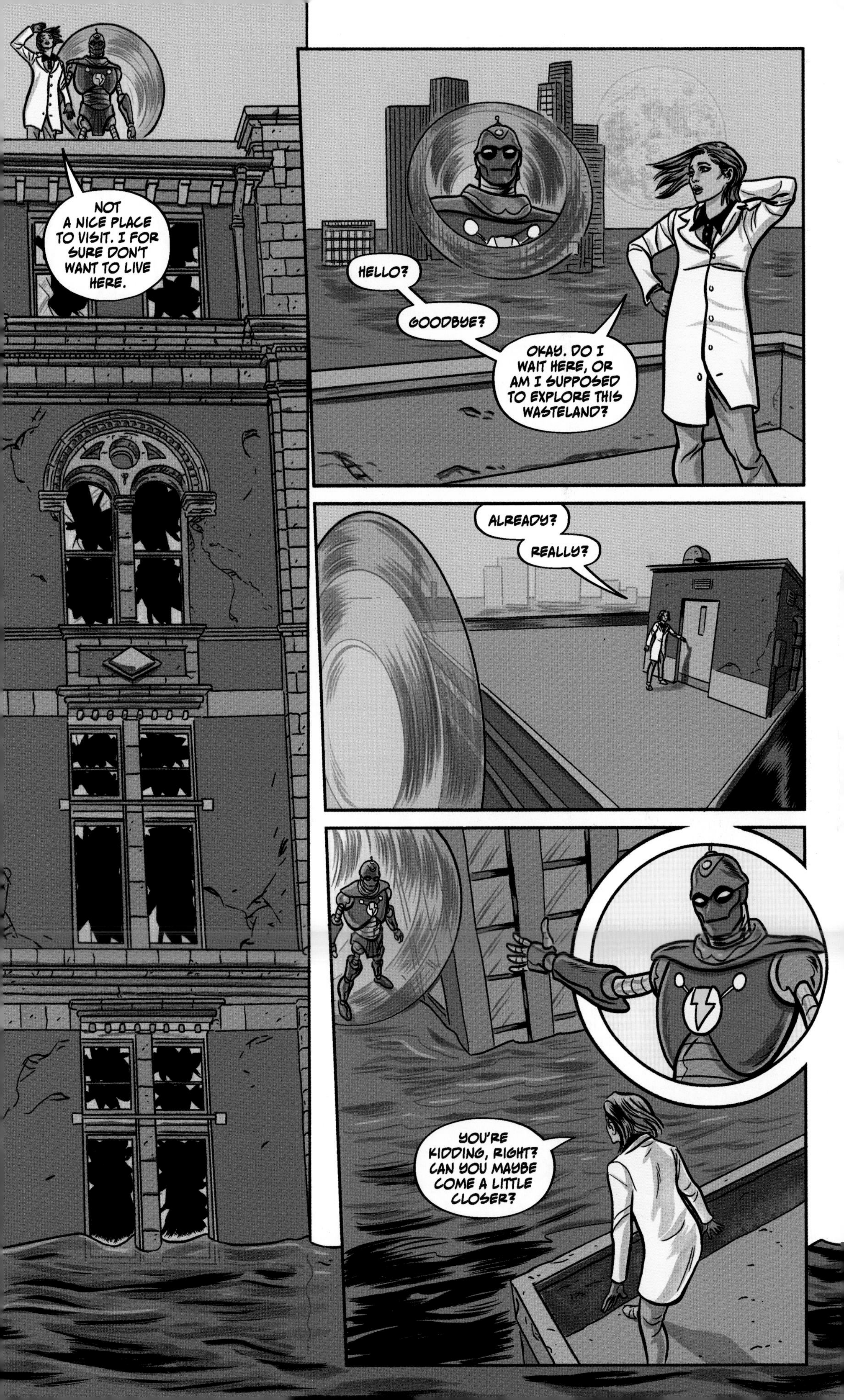
NOT A NICE PLACE TO VISIT. I FOR SURE DON'T WANT TO LIVE HERE.
HELLO?
GOODBYE?
OKAY. DO I WAIT HERE, OR AM I SUPPOSED TO EXPLORE THIS WASTELAND?
ALREADY?
REALLY?
YOU'RE KIDDING, RIGHT? CAN YOU MAYBE COME A LITTLE CLOSER?

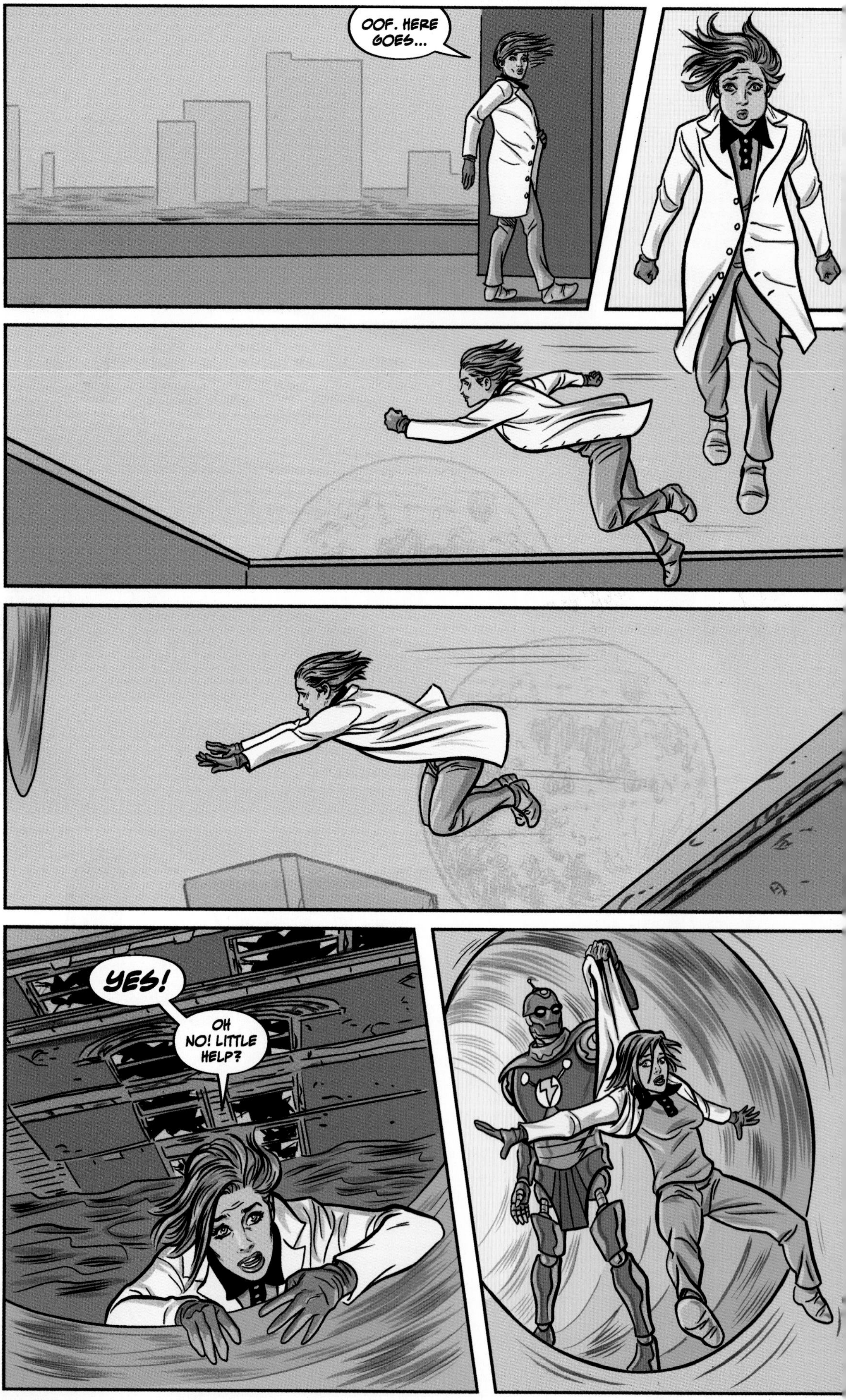
OOF. HERE GOES...
YES!
OH NO! LITTLE HELP?

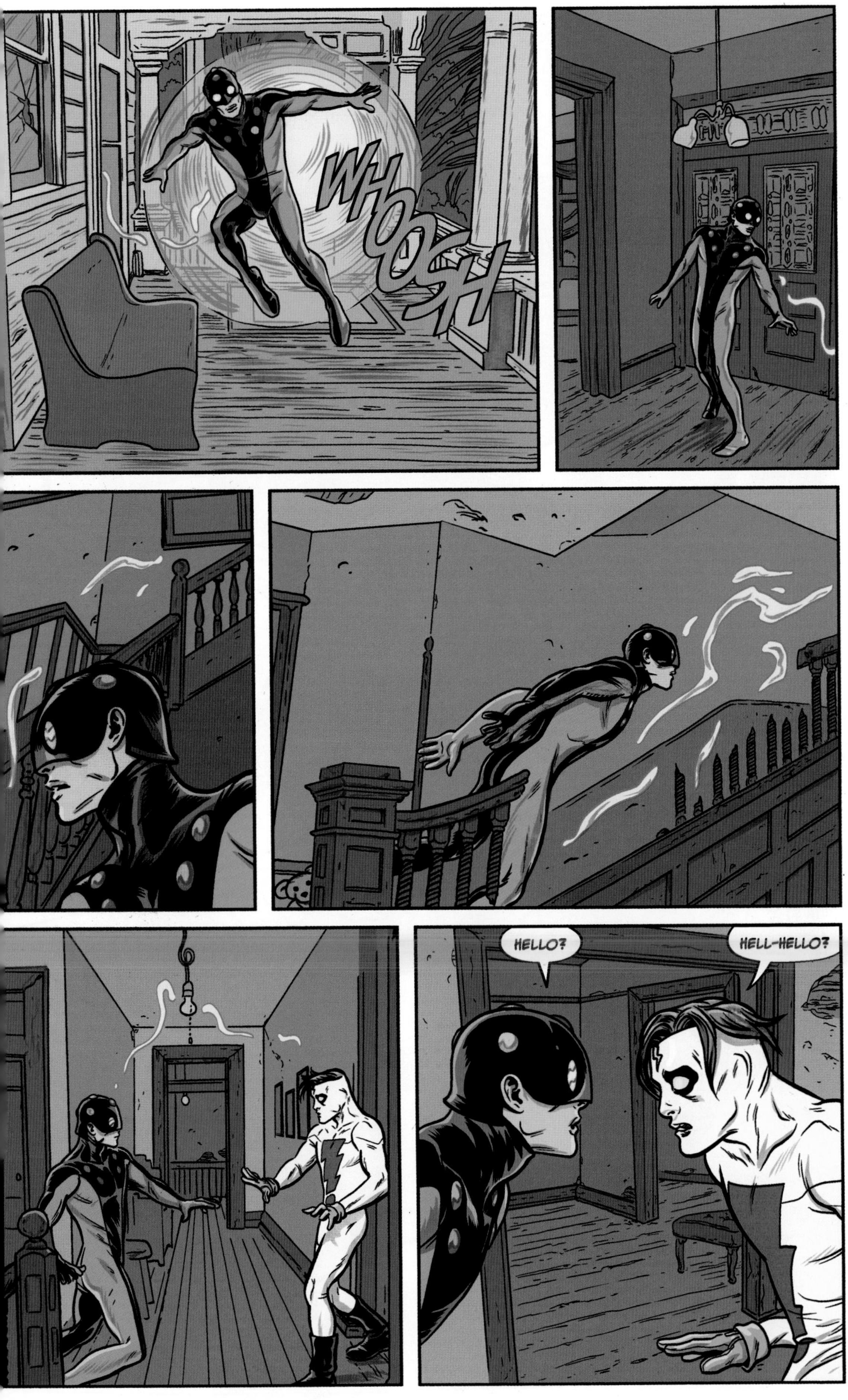
WHOOSH
HELLO?
HELL-HELLO?

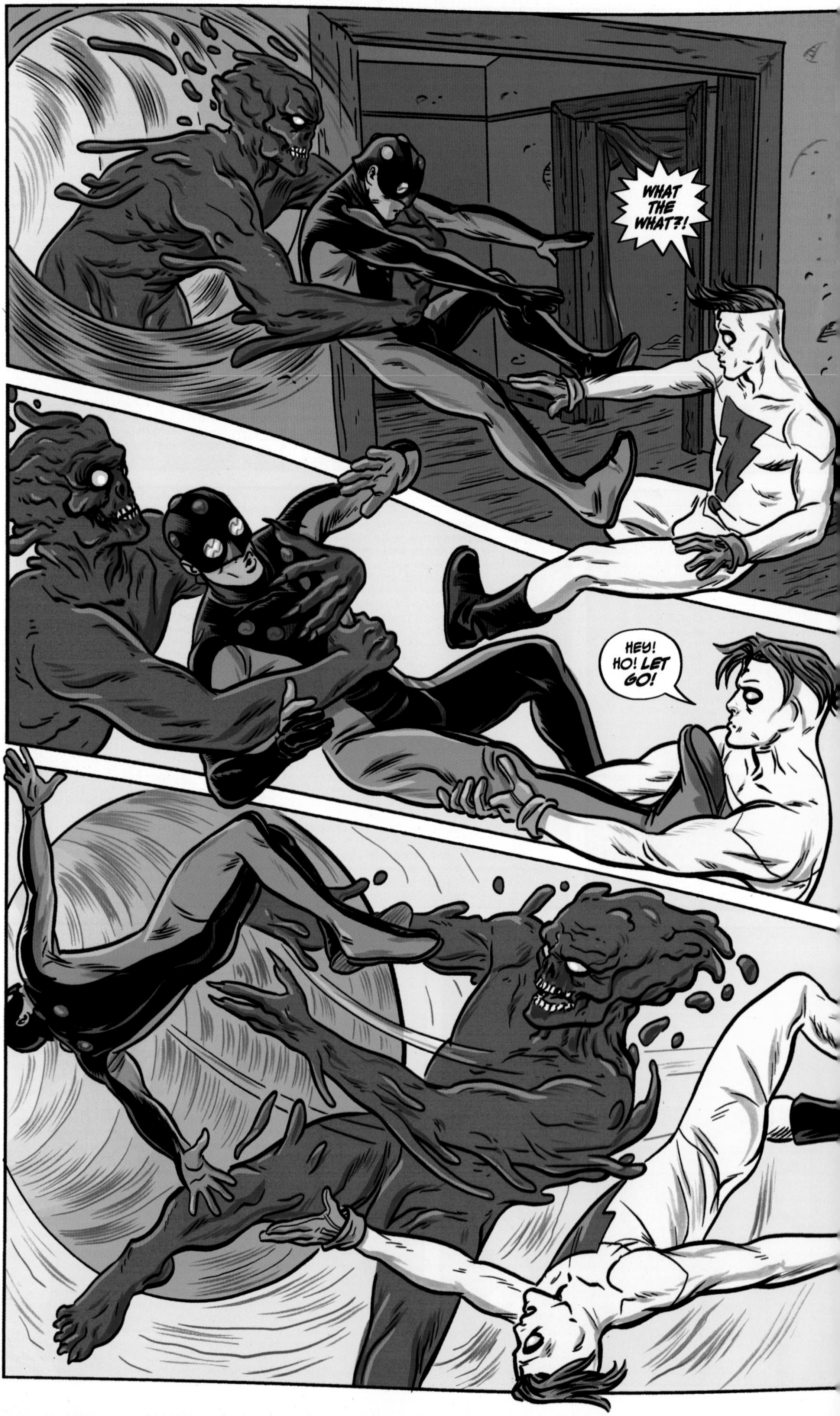
WHAT THE WHAT?!
HEY! HO! LET GO!

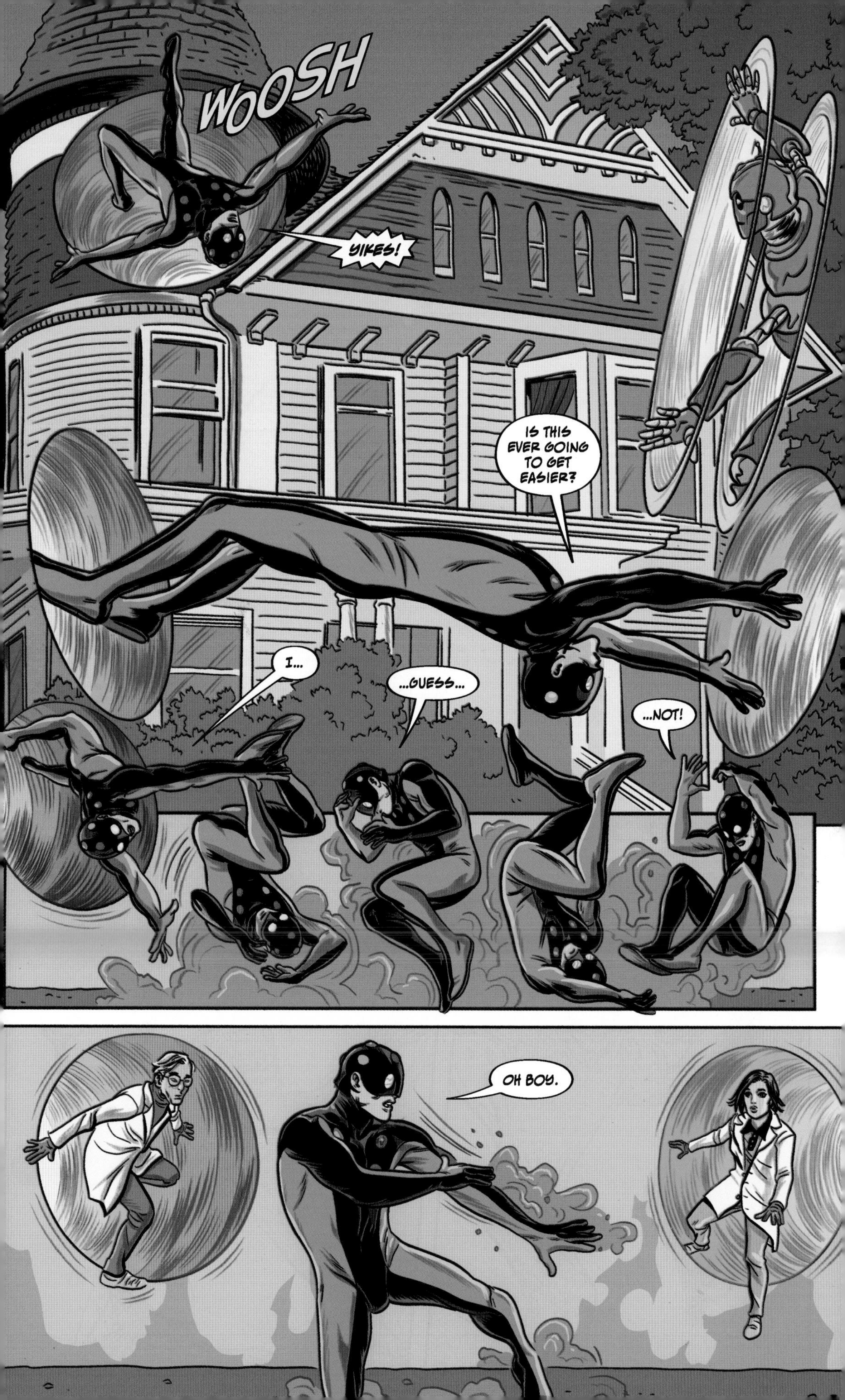
WOOSH
YIKES!
IS THIS EVER GOING TO GET EASIER?
I...
...GUESS...
...NOT!
OH BOY.

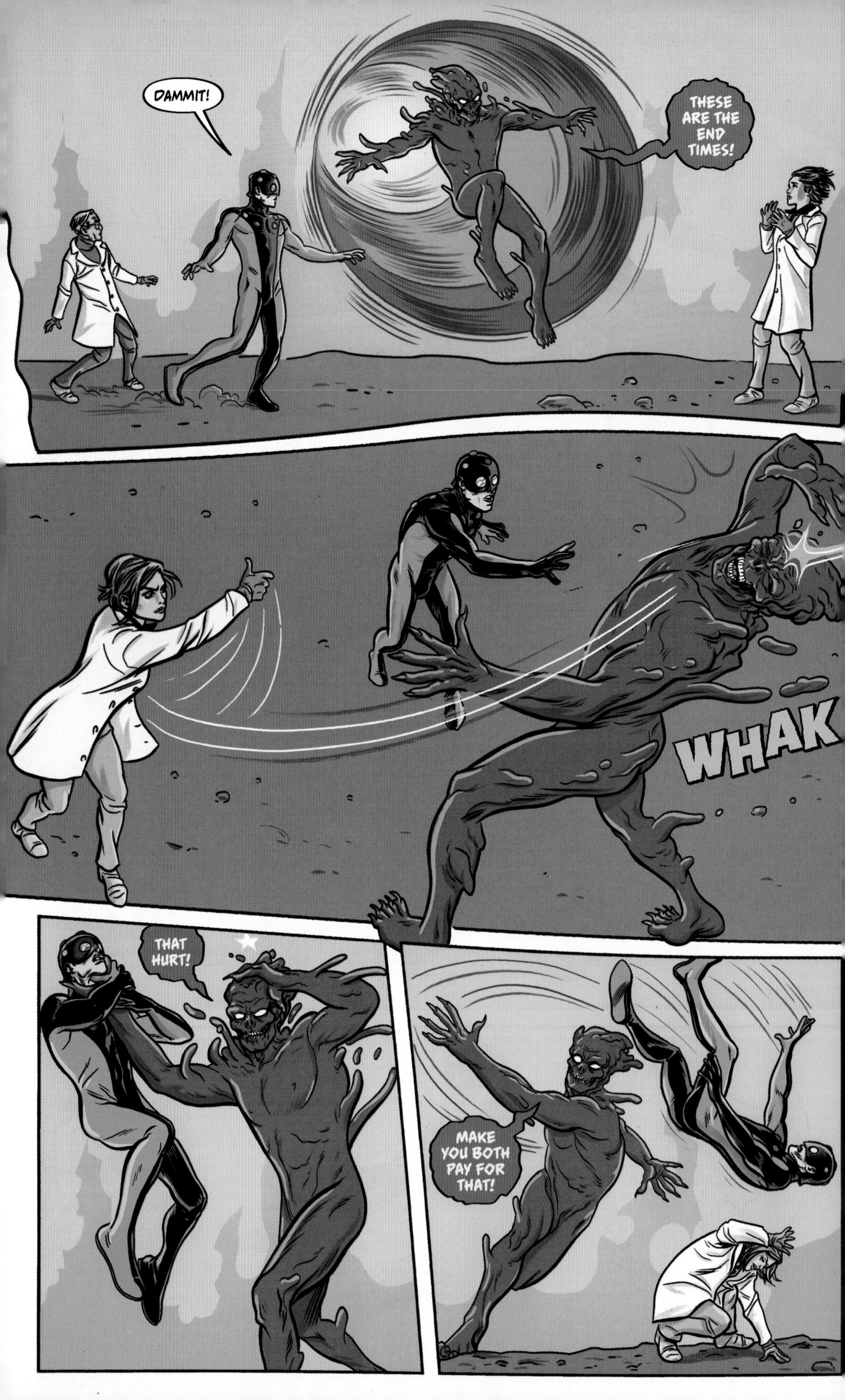

DAMMIT!
THESE ARE THE END TIMES!
WHAK
THAT HURT!
MAKE YOU BOTH PAY FOR THAT!

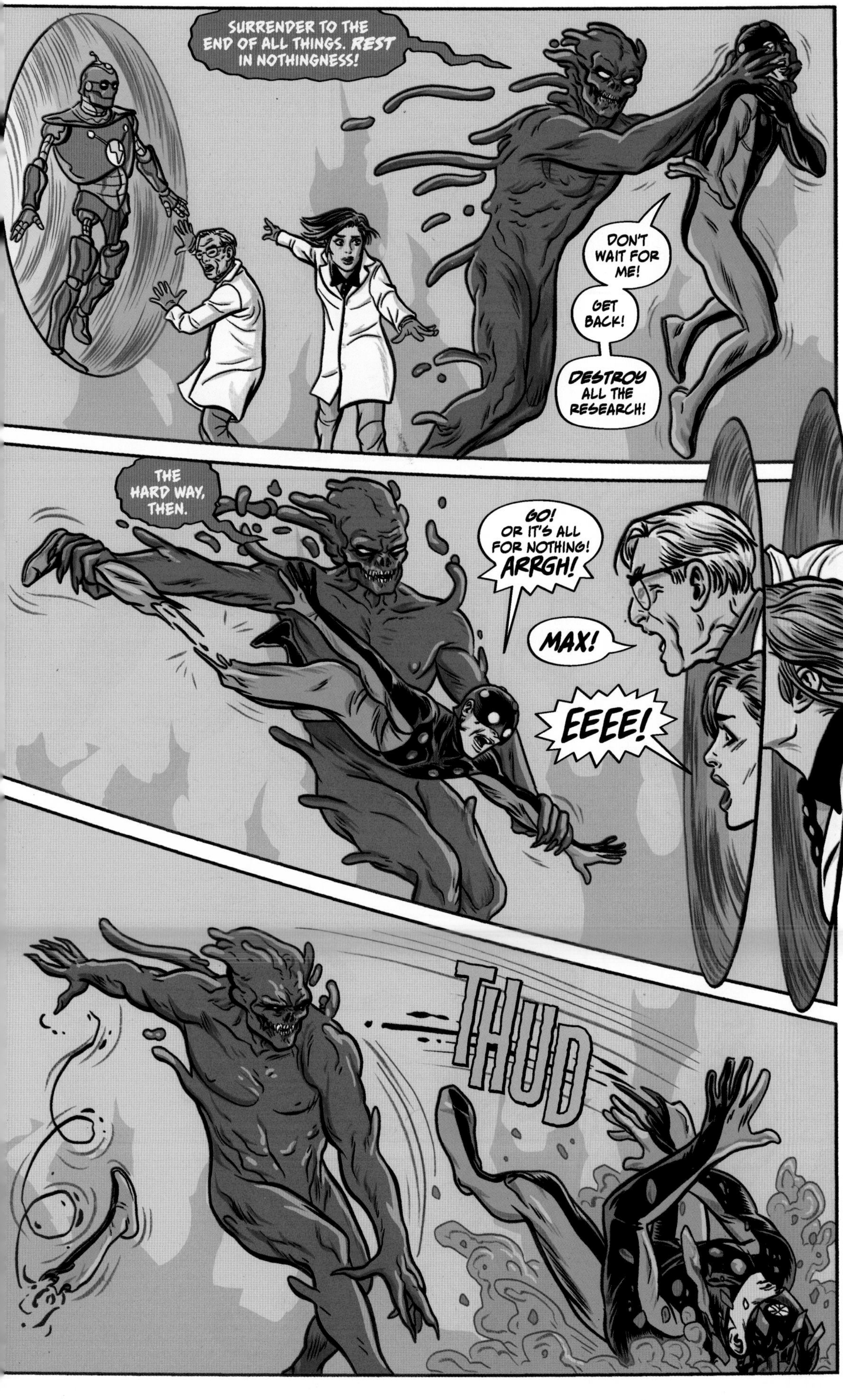

SURRENDER TO THE END OF ALL THINGS. REST IN NOTHINGNESS!
DON'T WAIT FOR ME!
GET BACK!
DESTROY ALL THE RESEARCH!
THE HARD WAY, THEN.
GO! OR IT'S ALL FOR NOTHING! ARRGH!
MAX!
EEEE!
THUD

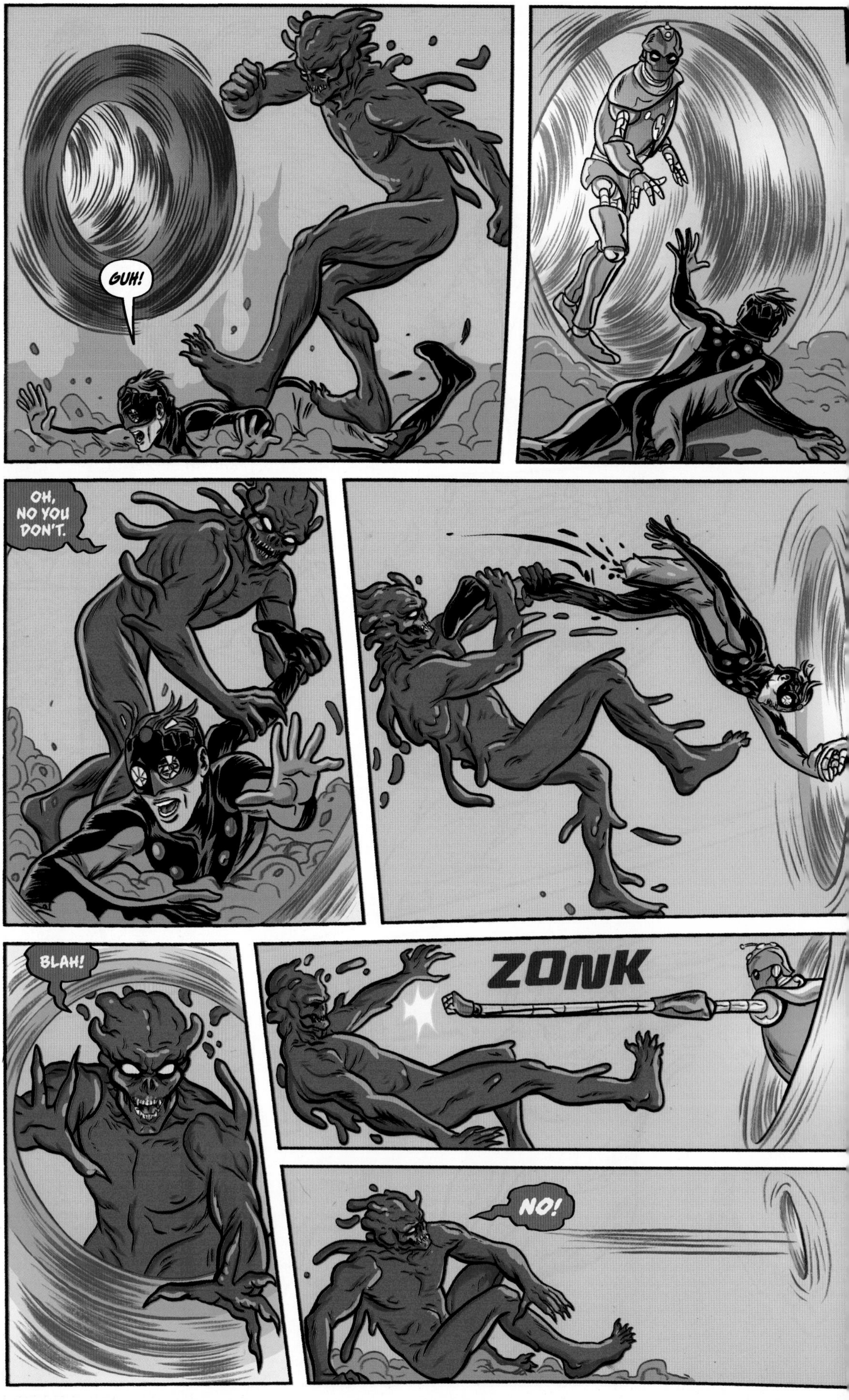
GUH!
OH, NO YOU DON'T.
BLAH!
ZONK
NO!

STOP! WE CAN'T DO THIS.

SHE'S RIGHT! WE NEED TO DESTROY EVERYTHING!

WHAT ARE YOU TWO GOING ON ABOUT?!

ARE YOU CRAZY? WE'VE BEEN PREPPING THIS FOR MONTHS!

WHAT'S THIS?!

MAX, WHAT IF I TOLD YOU YOUR FUTURE SELF TOLD US ABOUT YOUR RECURRING NIGHTMARE OF THE DEATH OF YOUR SON?

MY SON? I—I HAVEN'T TOLD ANYONE ABOUT THAT. NOT EVEN LAYLAH.

YOU PEOPLE ARE DELUSIONAL! I'M NOT ABANDONING ALL OUR RESEARCH.

WE DON'T HAVE TO. WE CAN RECYCLE ANY NUMBER OF AVENUES OF OUR RESEARCH. JUST NOT THIS PROJECT. NOT WHAT WE'RE DOING IN THIS LAB. INFINITE BREAKTHROUGHS IN AREAS OF MEDICINE AND COMMUNICATION.

BUT WE HAVE TO SHUT THIS DOWN AND DISASSEMBLE ALL THIS EQUIPMENT IMMEDIATELY.

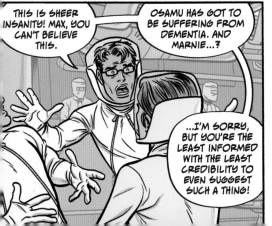

THIS IS SHEER INSANITY! MAX, YOU CAN'T BELIEVE THIS.

OSAMU HAS GOT TO BE SUFFERING FROM DEMENTIA. AND MARNIE...?

...I'M SORRY, BUT YOU'RE THE LEAST INFORMED WITH THE LEAST CREDIBILITY TO EVEN SUGGEST SUCH A THING!

WHAT ABOUT ME, BRIAN? WILL YOU BELIEVE ME?

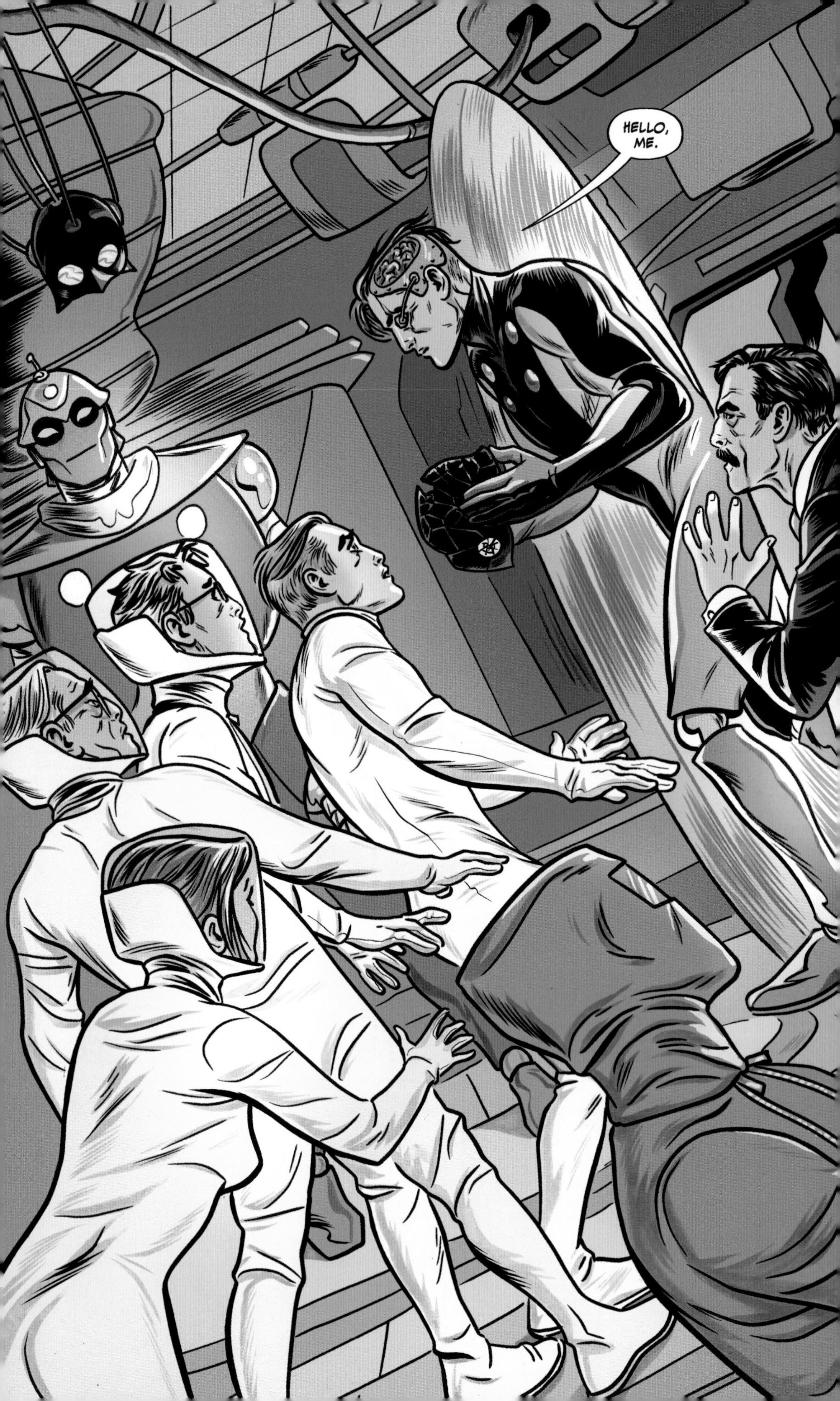
HELLO, ME.

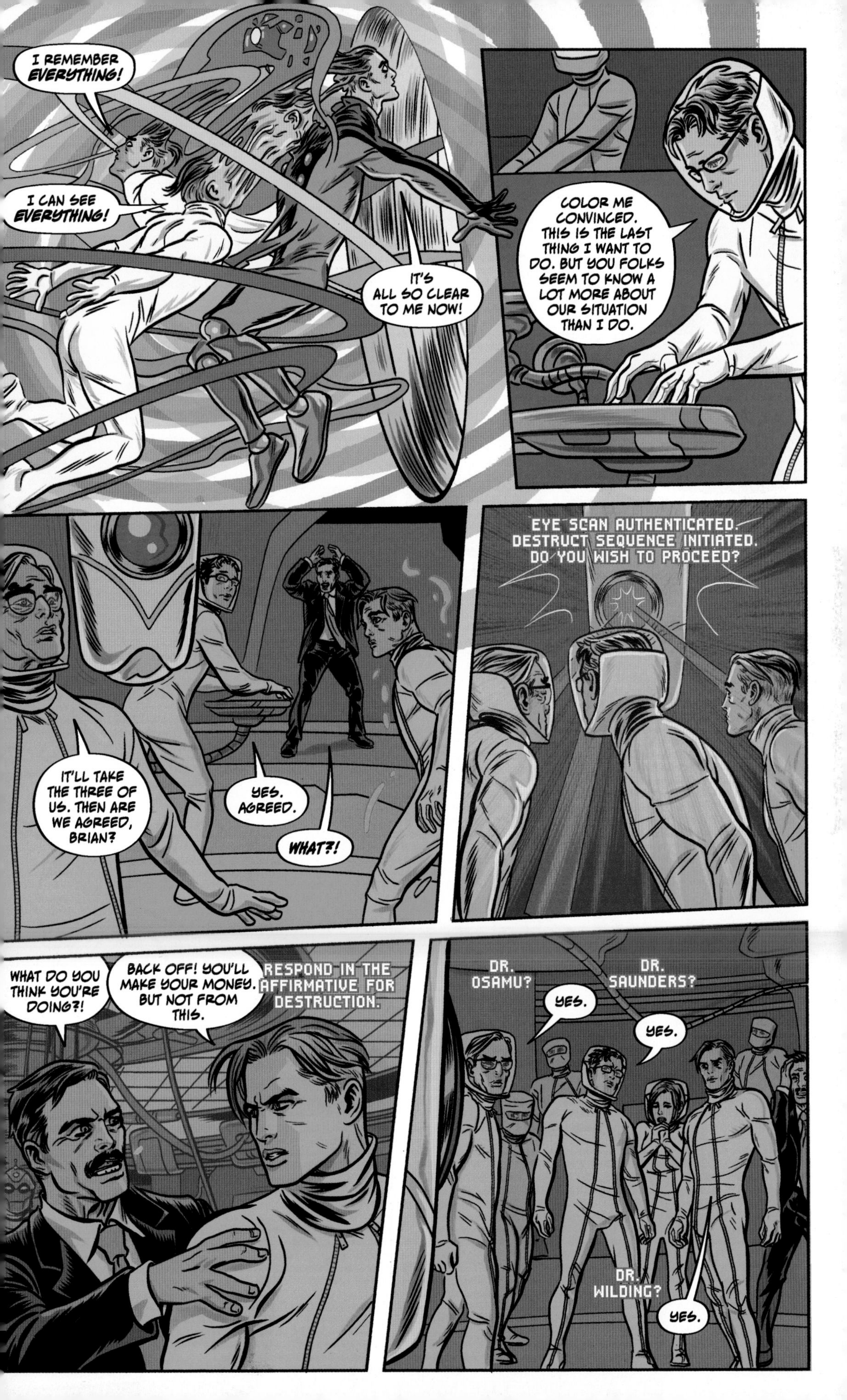
I REMEMBER EVERYTHING!
I CAN SEE EVERYTHING!
IT'S ALL SO CLEAR TO ME NOW!
COLOR ME CONVINCED. THIS IS THE LAST THING I WANT TO DO. BUT YOU FOLKS SEEM TO KNOW A LOT MORE ABOUT OUR SITUATION THAN I DO.
IT'LL TAKE THE THREE OF US. THEN ARE WE AGREED, BRIAN?
YES. AGREED.
WHAT?!
EYE SCAN AUTHENTICATED. DESTRUCT SEQUENCE INITIATED. DO YOU WISH TO PROCEED?
WHAT DO YOU THINK YOU'RE DOING?!
BACK OFF! YOU'LL MAKE YOUR MONEY. BUT NOT FROM THIS.
RESPOND IN THE AFFIRMATIVE FOR DESTRUCTION.
DR. OSAMU?
YES.
DR. SAUNDERS?
YES.
DR. WILDING?
YES.

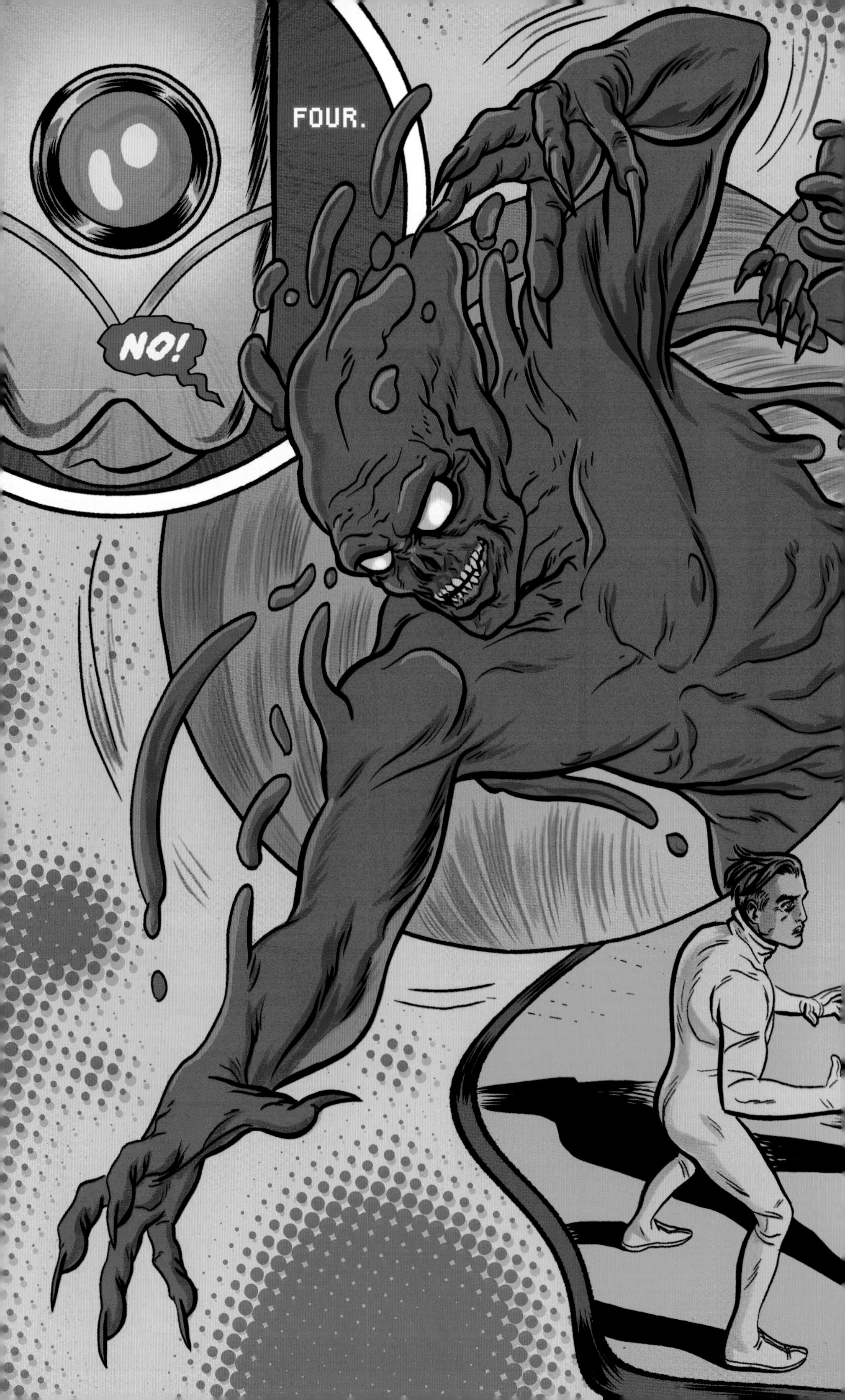
FOUR.
NO!

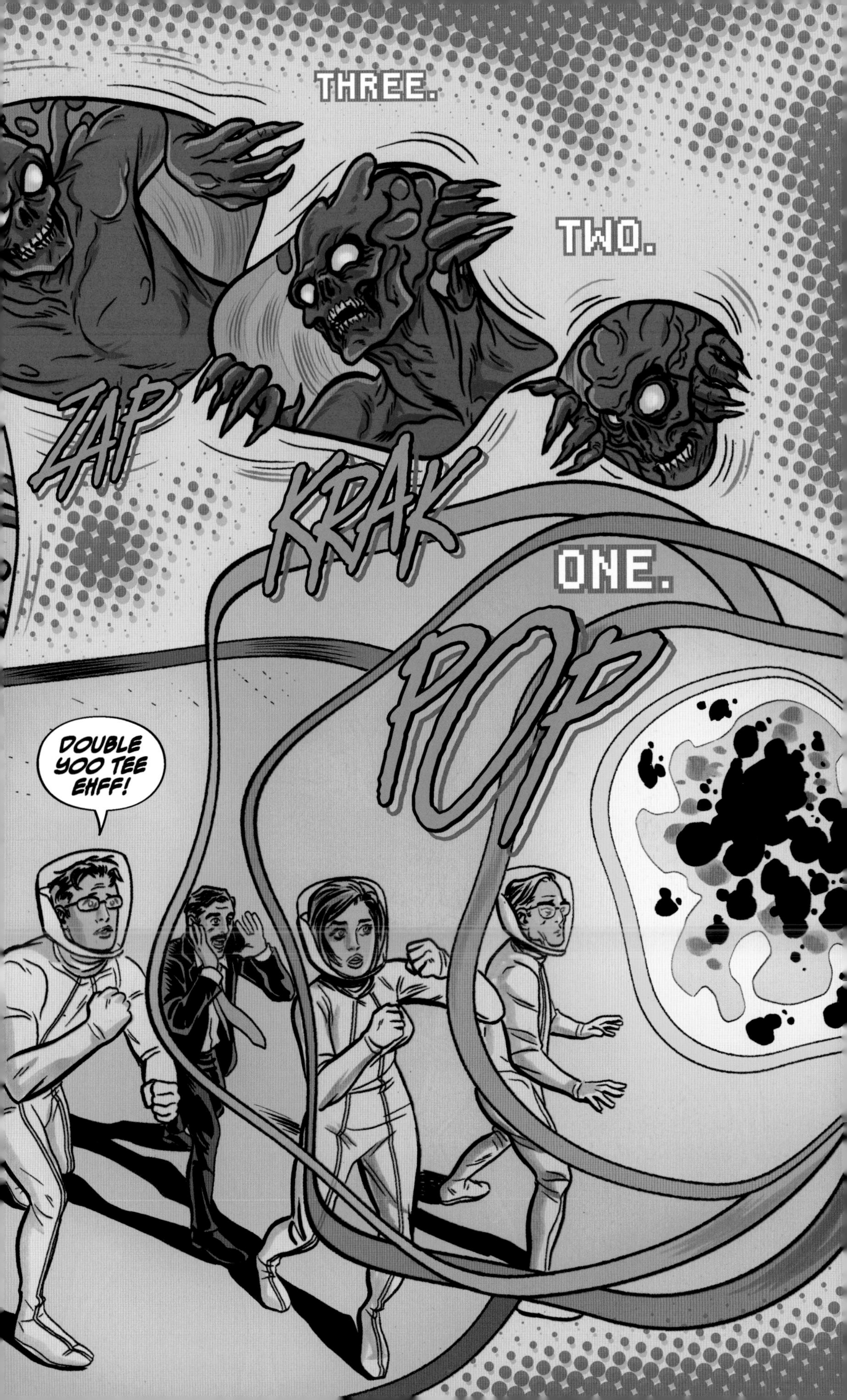
THREE.
TWO.
ZAP
KRAK
ONE.
POP
DOUBLE YOO TEE EHFF!

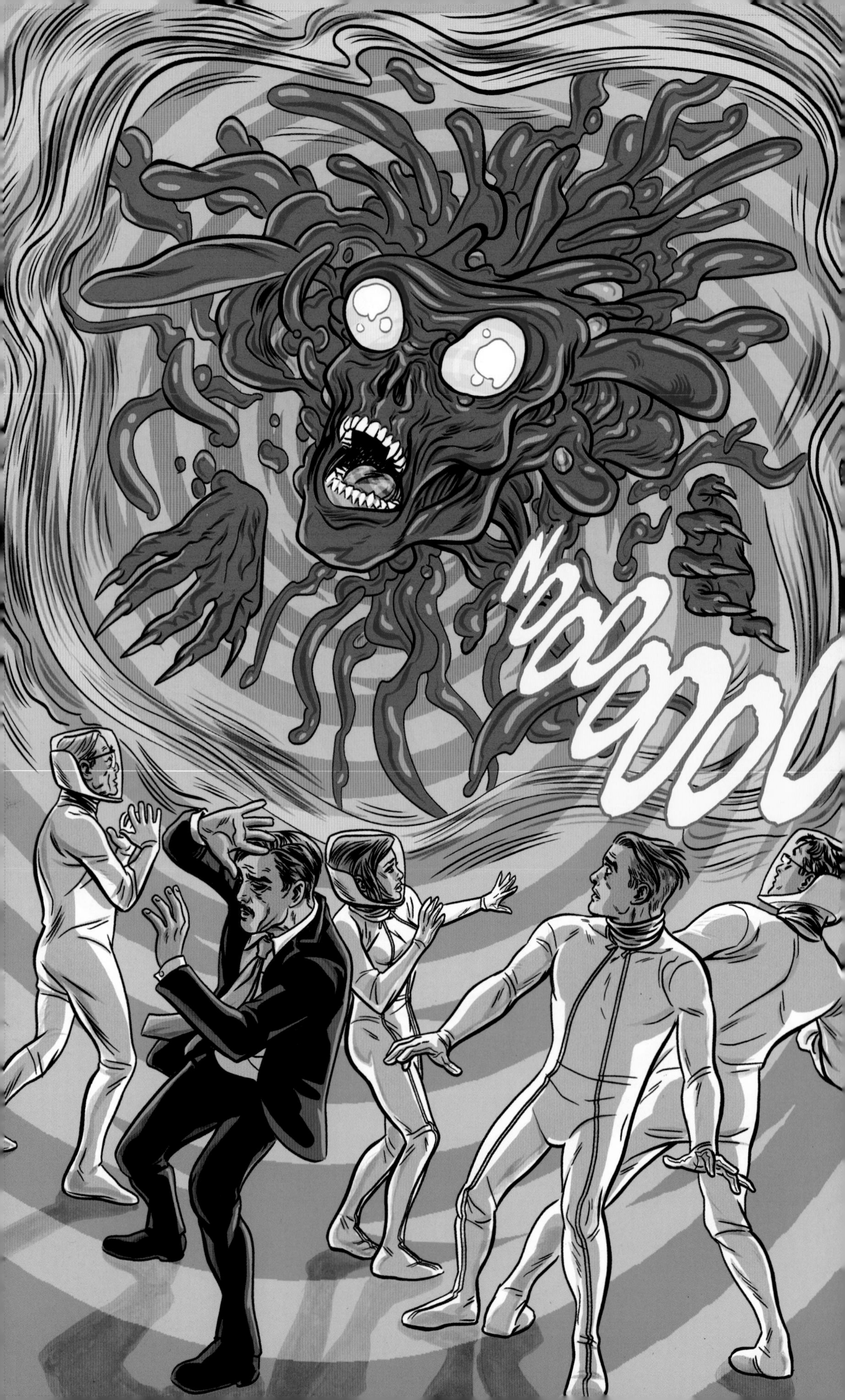
NOOOOOO

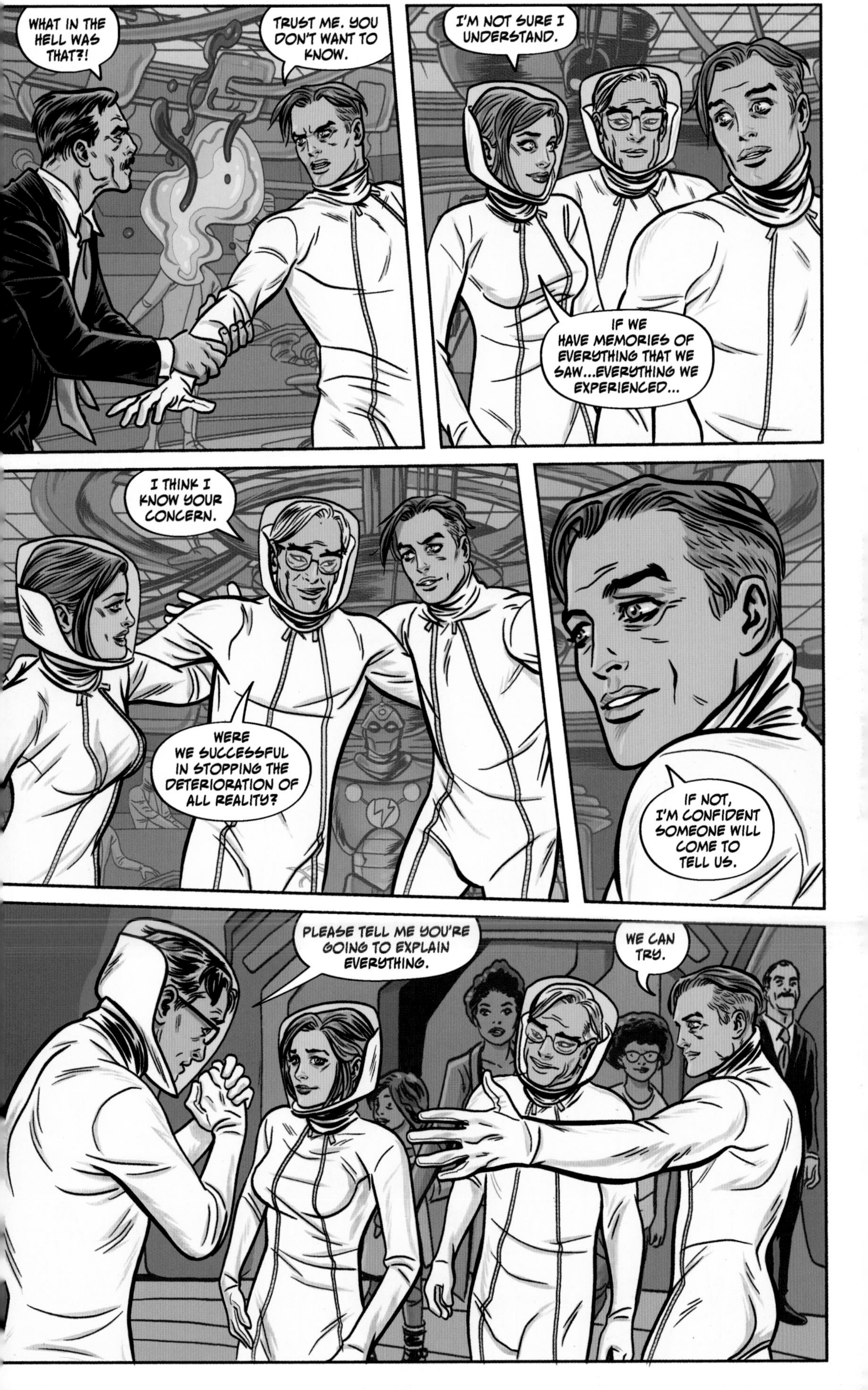

WHAT IN THE HELL WAS THAT?!
TRUST ME. YOU DON'T WANT TO KNOW.
I'M NOT SURE I UNDERSTAND.
IF WE HAVE MEMORIES OF EVERYTHING THAT WE SAW...EVERYTHING WE EXPERIENCED...
I THINK I KNOW YOUR CONCERN.
WERE WE SUCCESSFUL IN STOPPING THE DETERIORATION OF ALL REALITY?
IF NOT, I'M CONFIDENT SOMEONE WILL COME TO TELL US.
PLEASE TELL ME YOU'RE GOING TO EXPLAIN EVERYTHING.
WE CAN TRY.

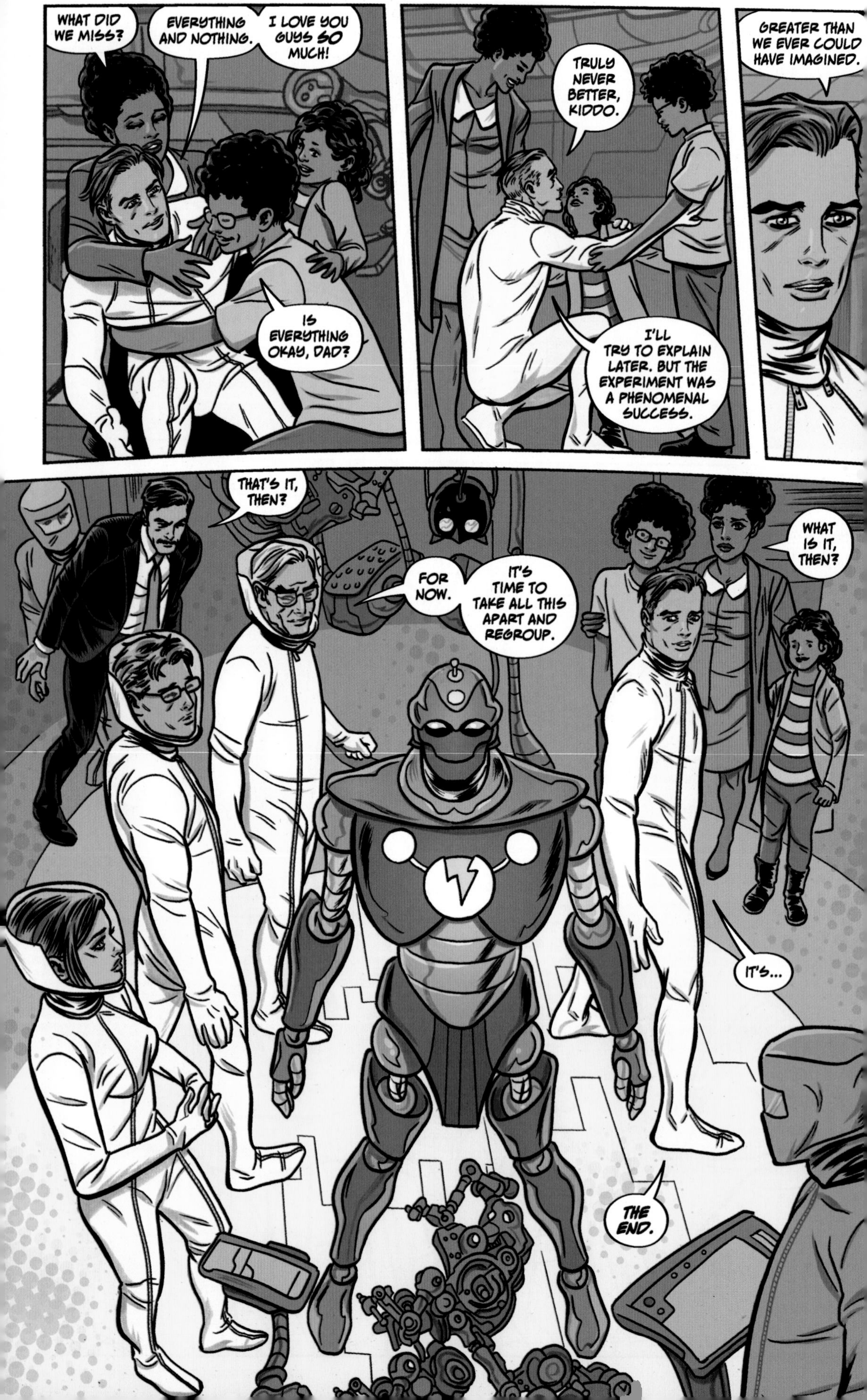
WHAT DID WE MISS?
EVERYTHING AND NOTHING.
I LOVE YOU GUYS SO MUCH!
IS EVERYTHING OKAY, DAD?
TRULY NEVER BETTER, KIDDO.
I'LL TRY TO EXPLAIN LATER. BUT THE EXPERIMENT WAS A PHENOMENAL SUCCESS.
GREATER THAN WE EVER COULD HAVE IMAGINED.
THAT'S IT, THEN?
FOR NOW.
IT'S TIME TO TAKE ALL THIS APART AND REGROUP.
WHAT IS IT, THEN?
IT'S...
THE END.

VARIANT COVER FOR X-RAY ROBOT #1 BY
CHRIS SAMNEE WITH MATTHEW WILSON

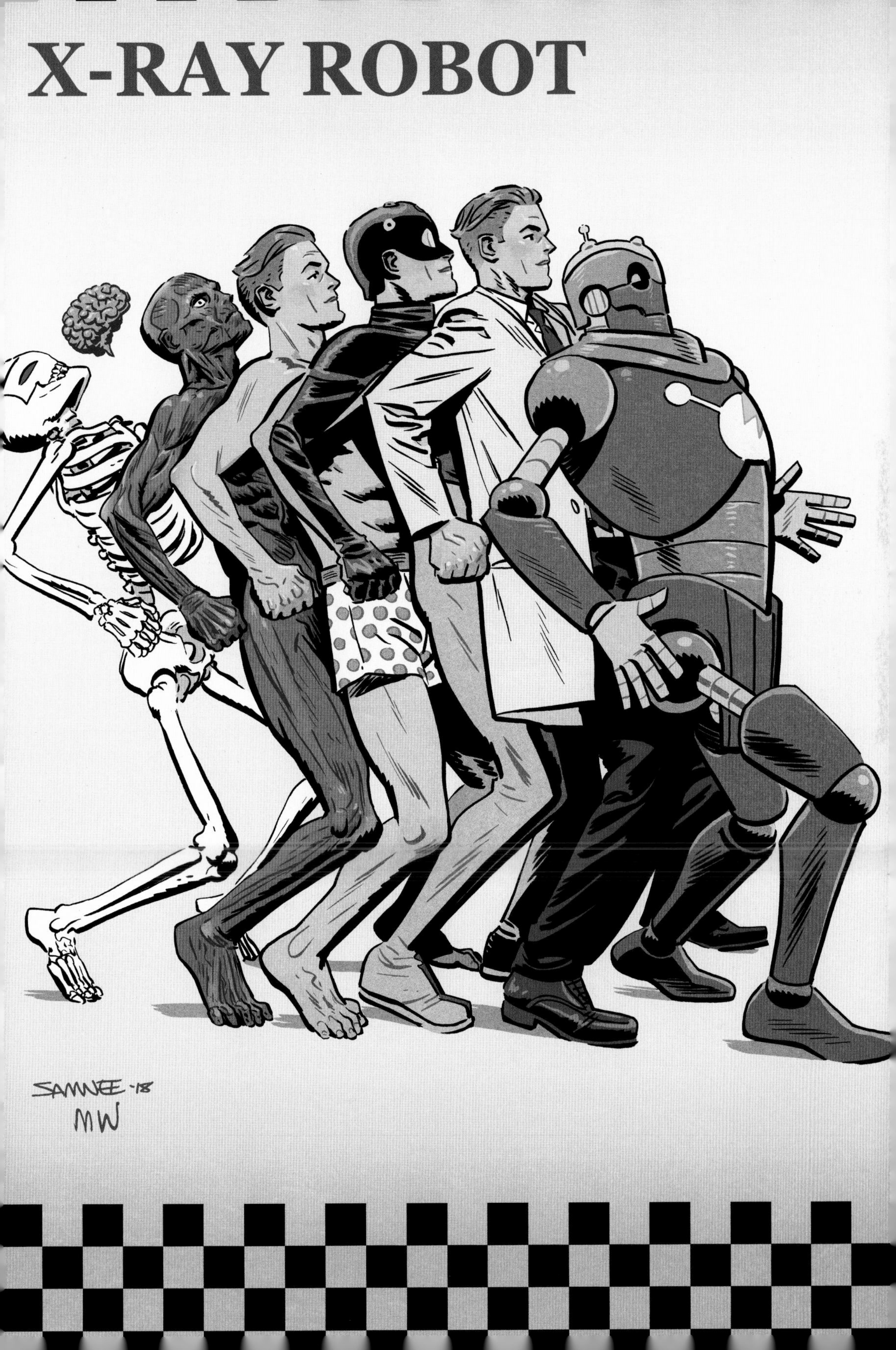
X-RAY ROBOT
SAMNEE -18
MW

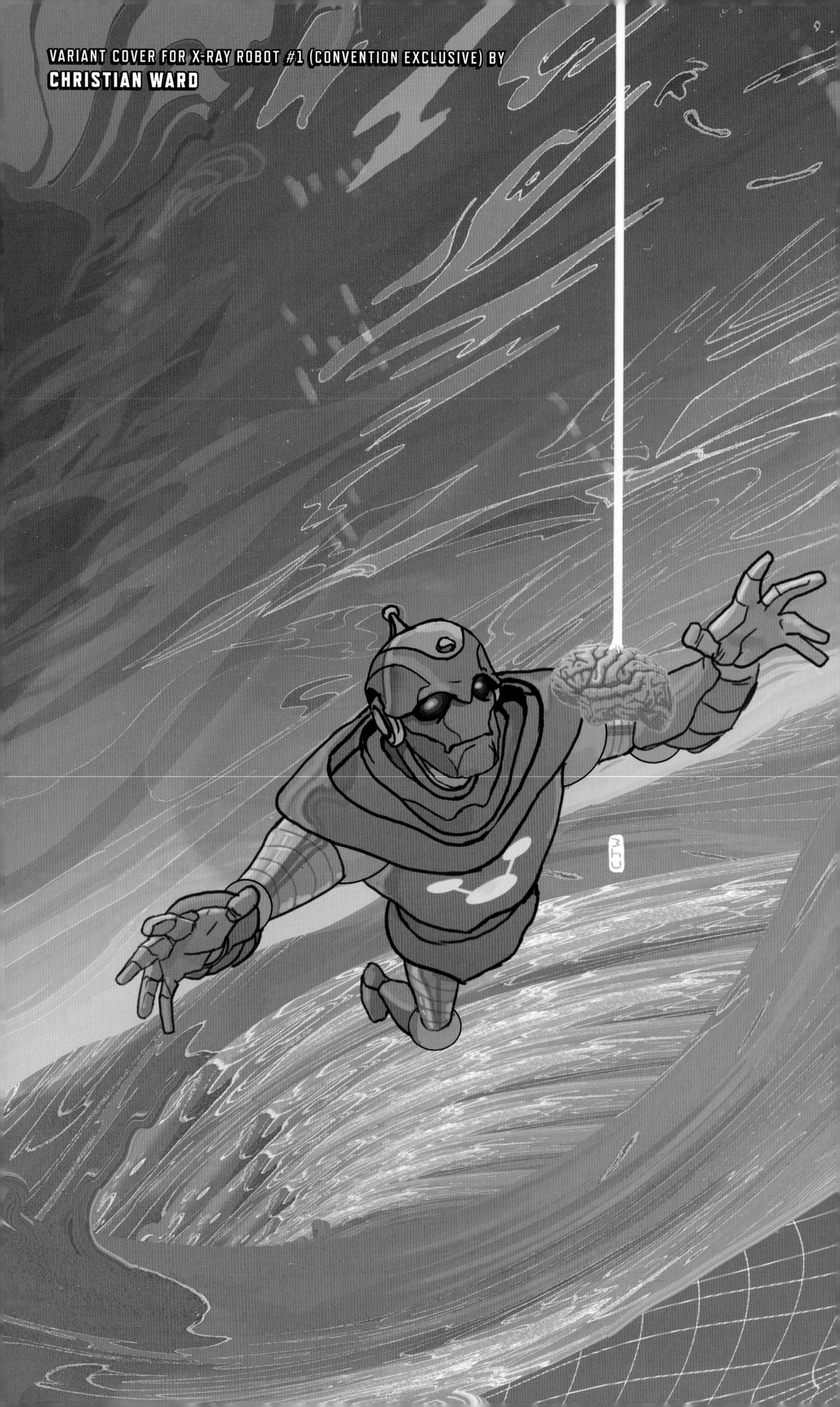

VARIANT COVER FOR X-RAY ROBOT #1 (CONVENTION EXCLUSIVE) BY
CHRISTIAN WARD

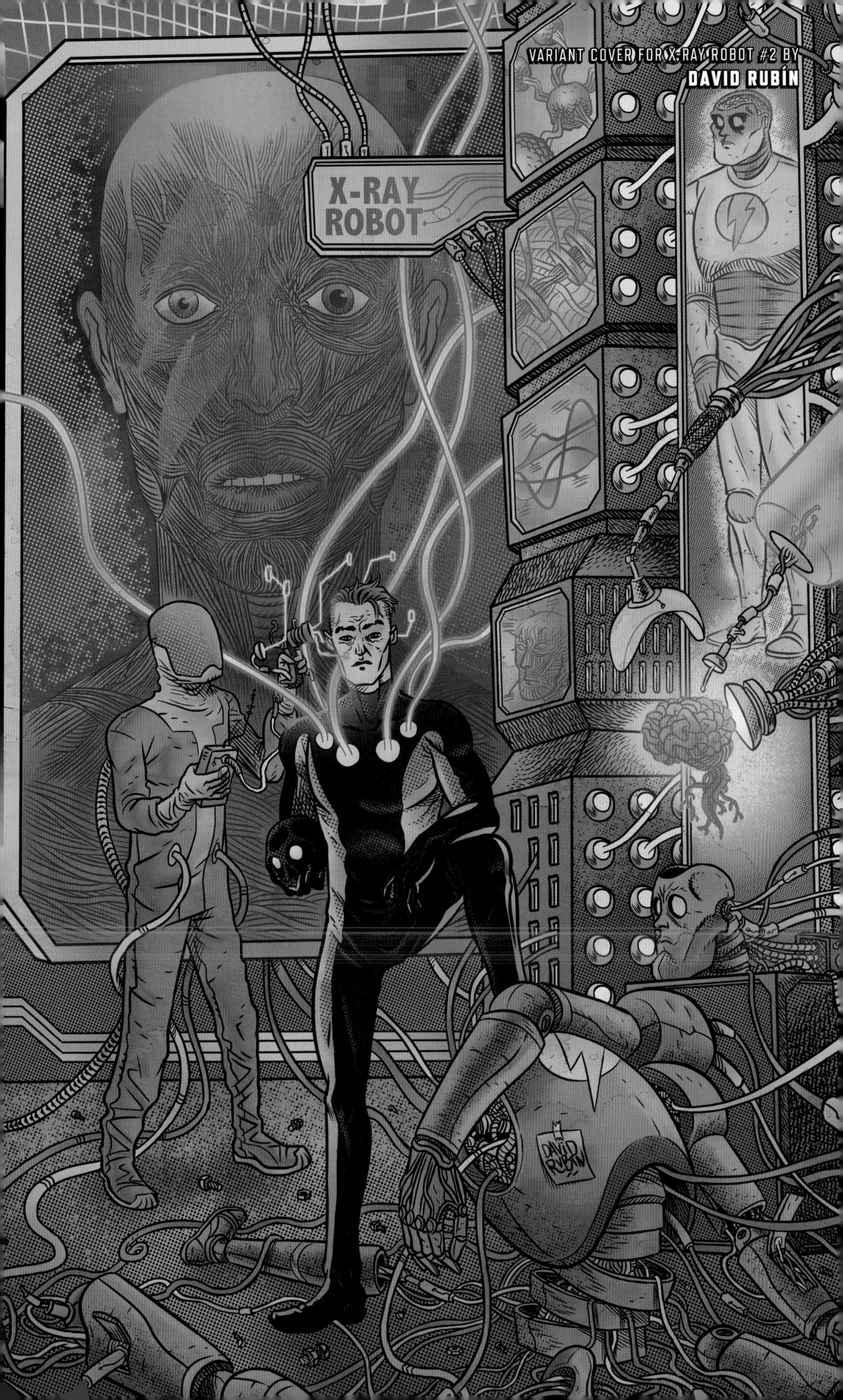
X-RAY
ROBOT
DAVID RUBÍN

VARIANT COVER FOR X-RAY ROBOT #2 BY
DAVID RUBÍN

FOC VARIANT COVER FOR X-RAY ROBOT #2 BY
PAUL POPE WITH LAURA ALLRED

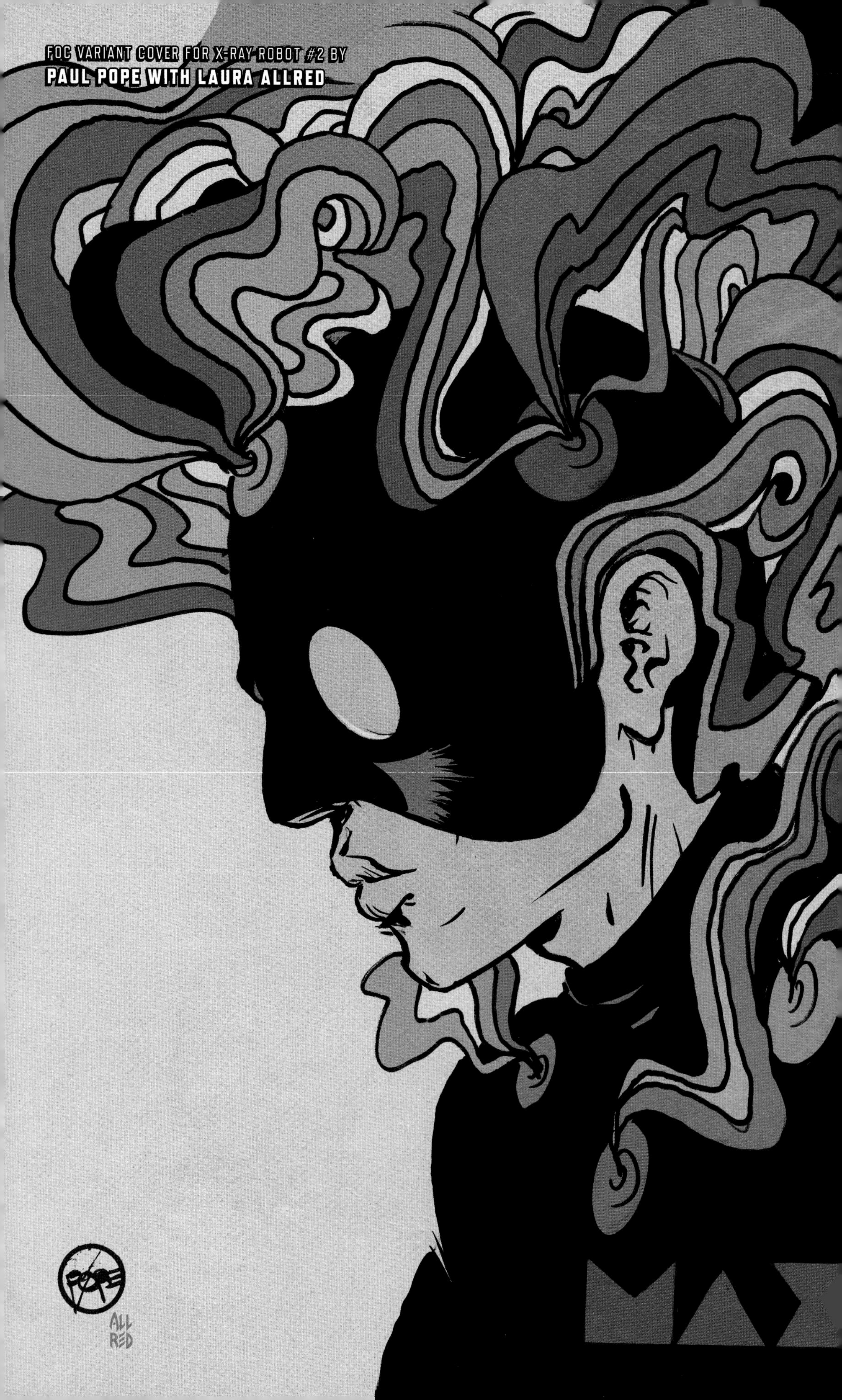
POPE
ALL
RED

VARIANT COVER FOR X-RAY ROBOT #3 BY
GREG SMALLWOOD

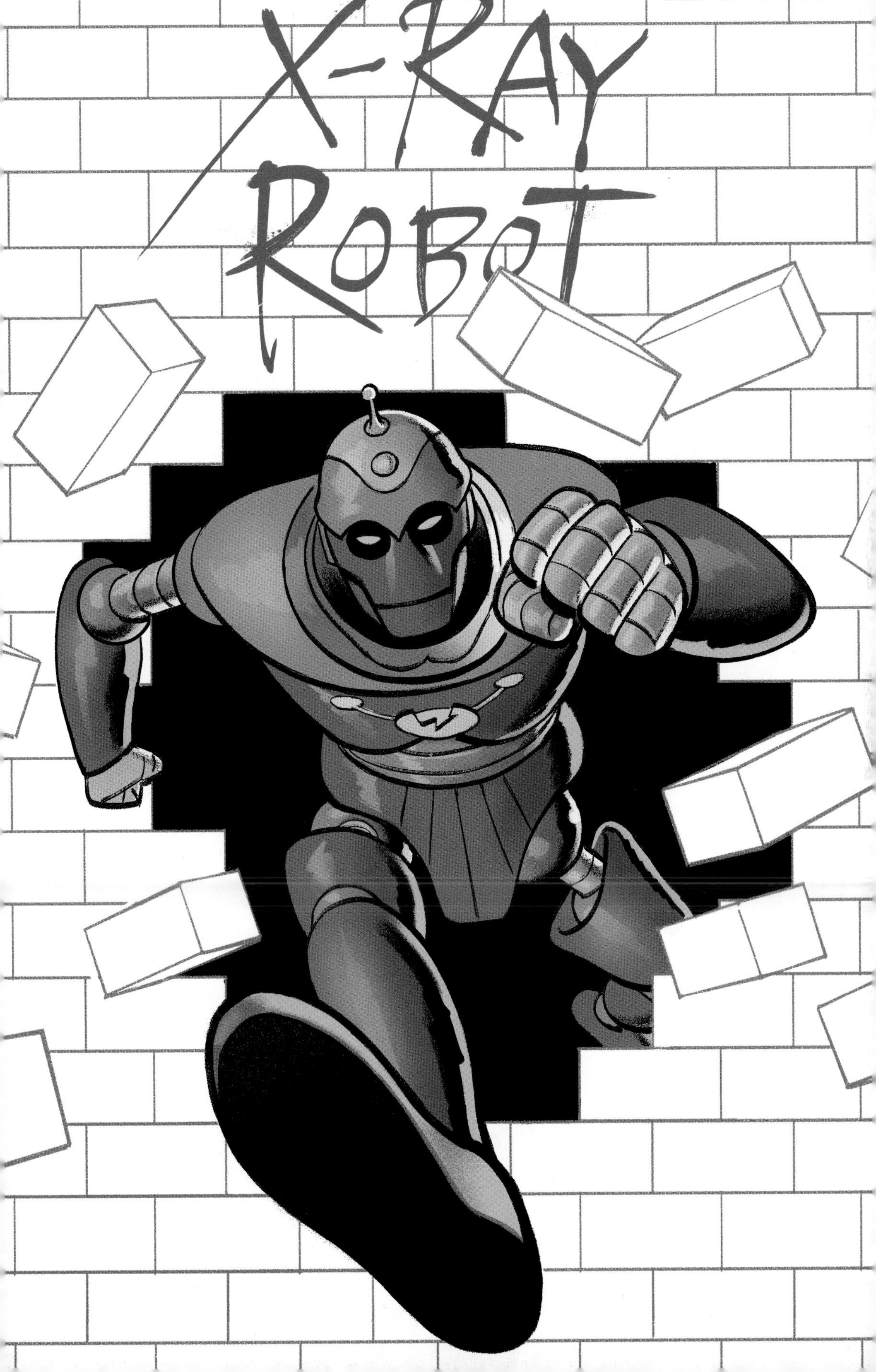
X-RAY
ROBOT

VARIANT COVER FOR X-RAY ROBOT #4 BY
TRADD MOORE
HOMAGE INSPIRED BY ALEX GREY

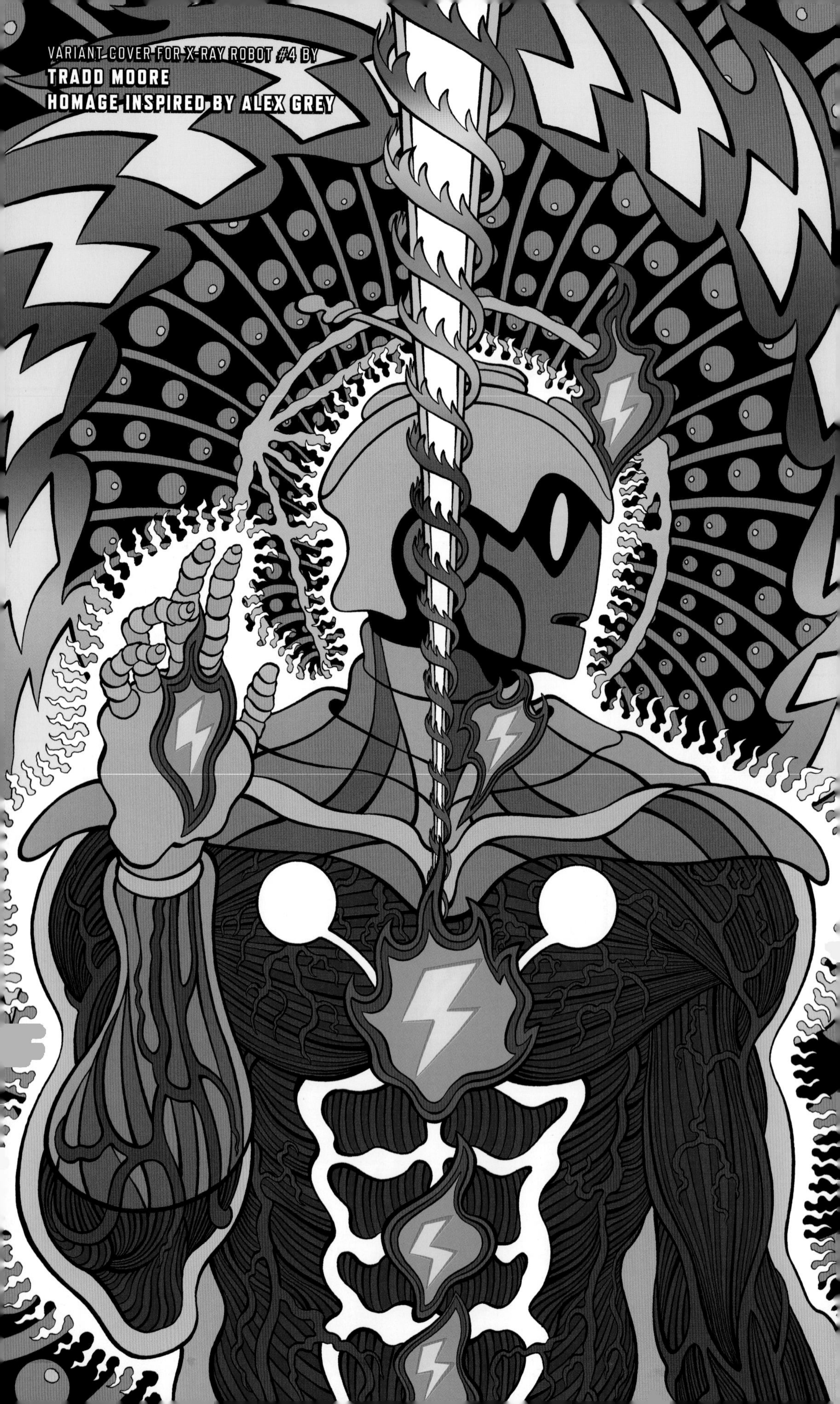

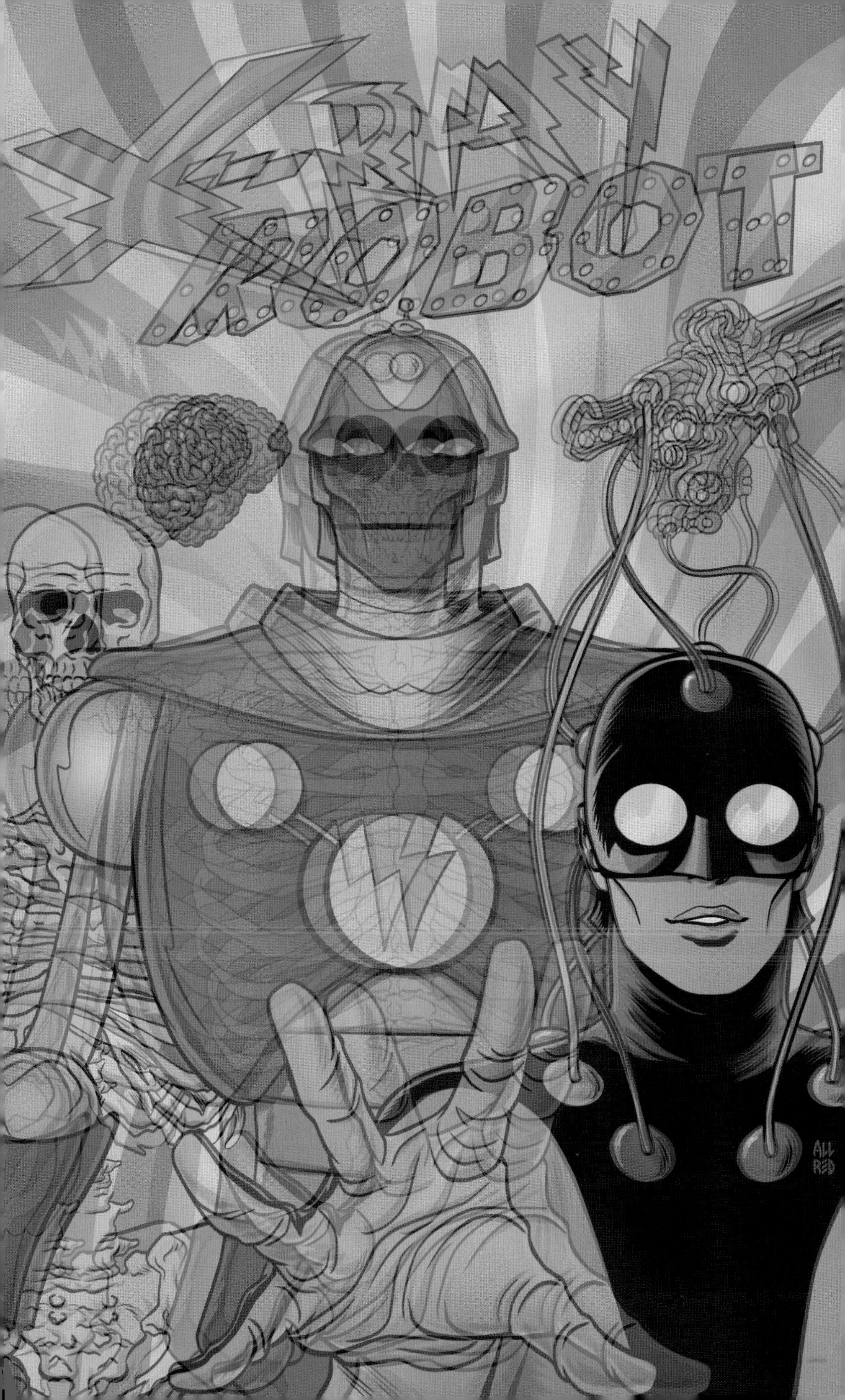
X-RAY ROBOT
ALL RED

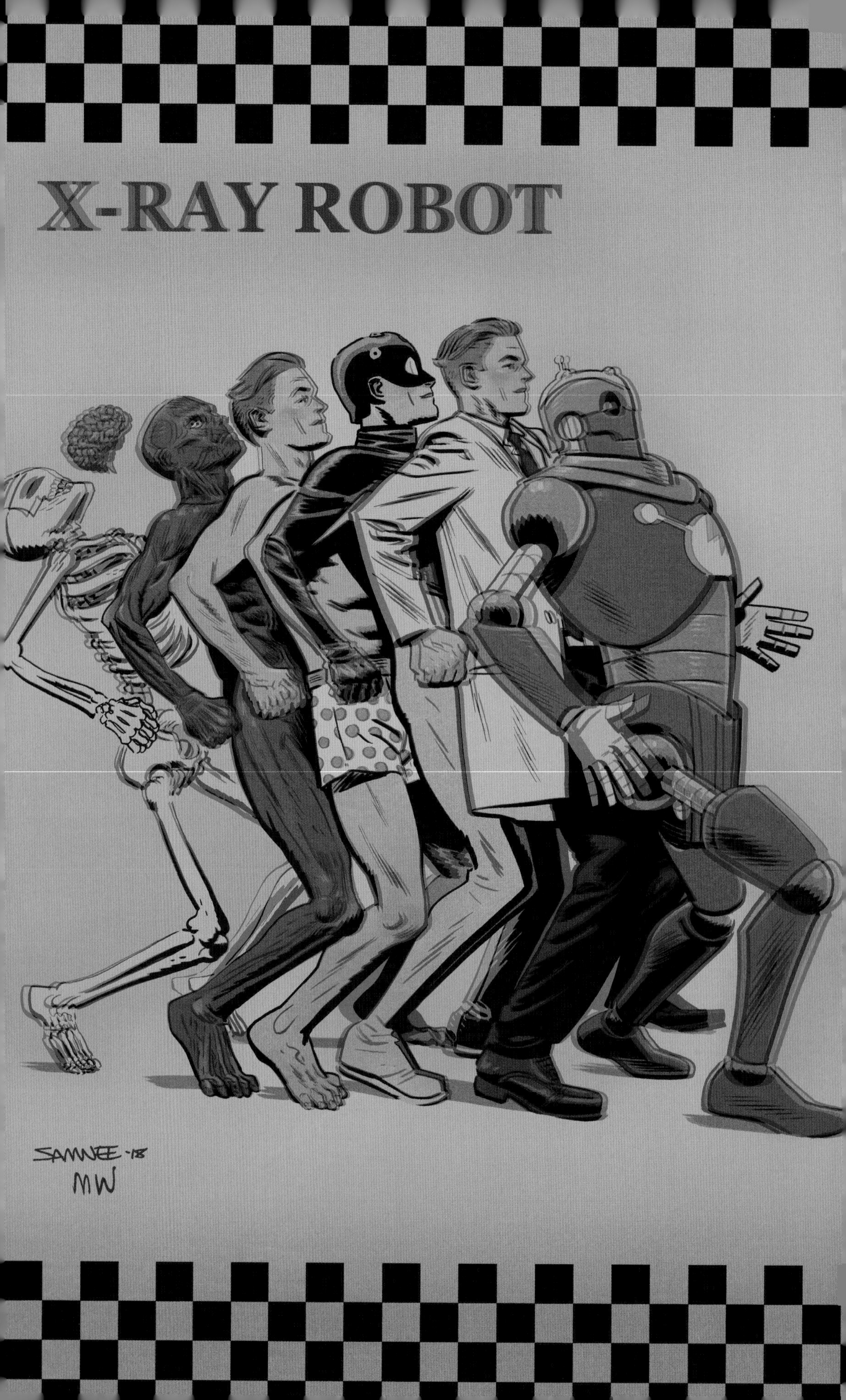
X-RAY ROBOT
SAMNEE -18
MW

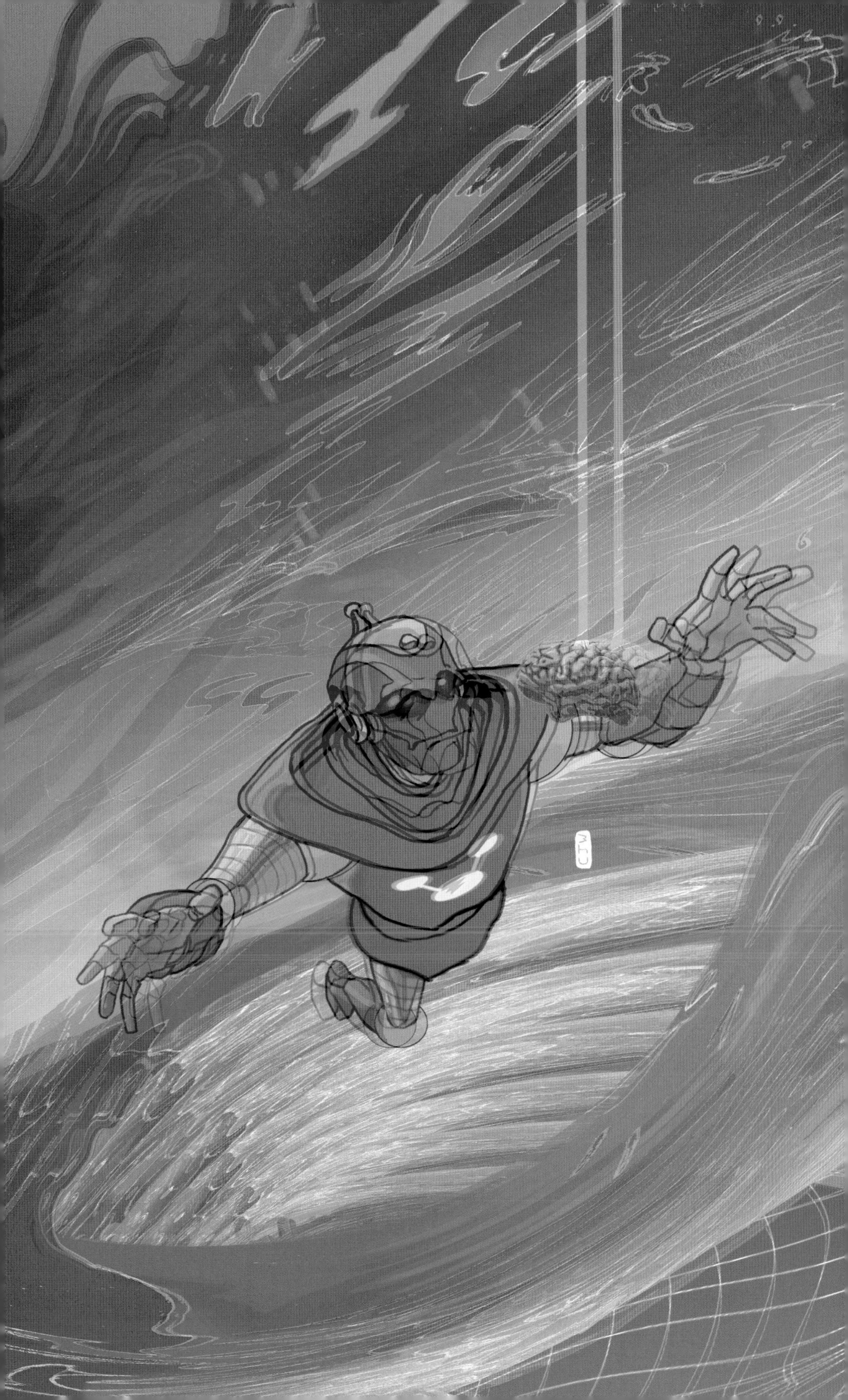

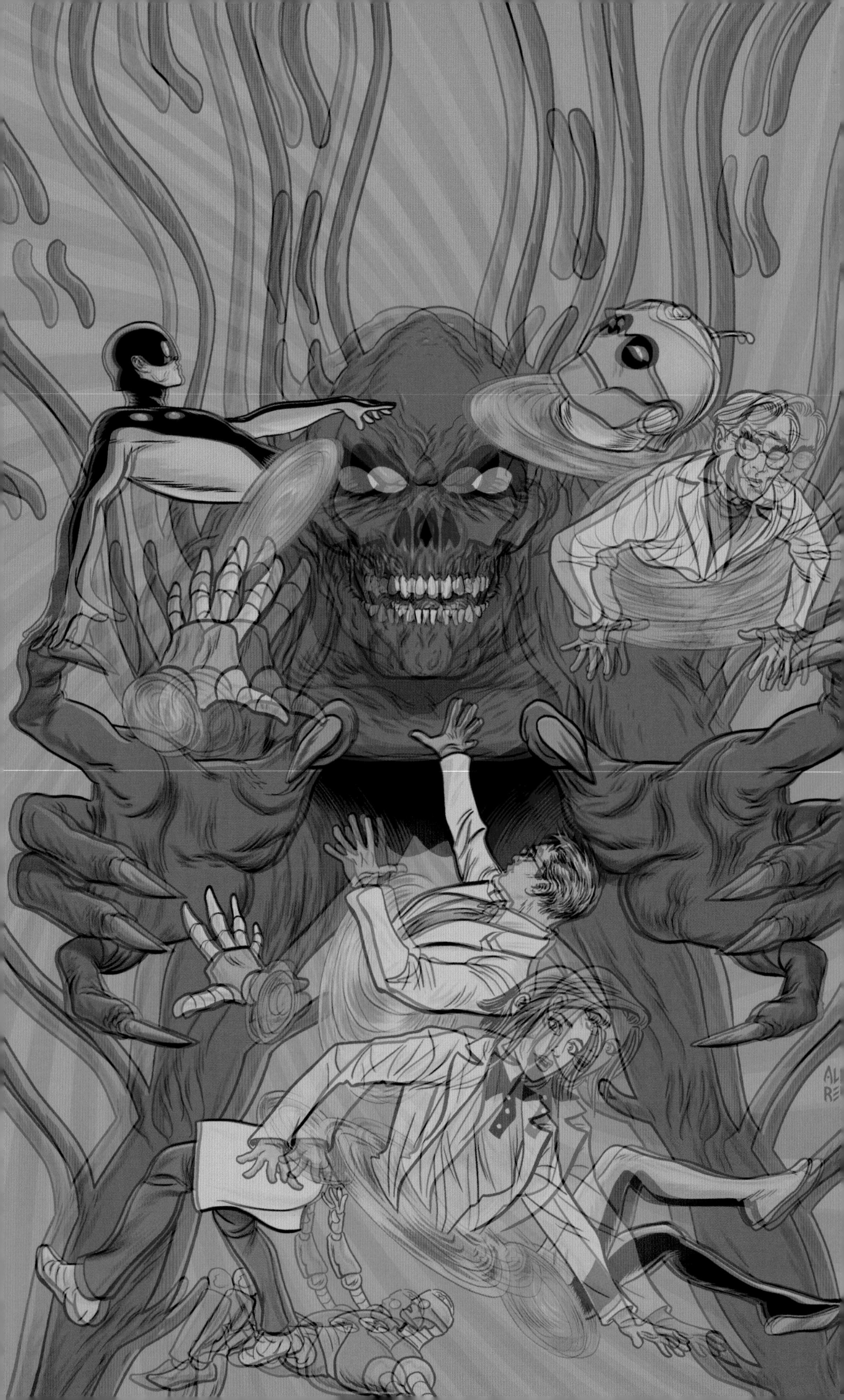

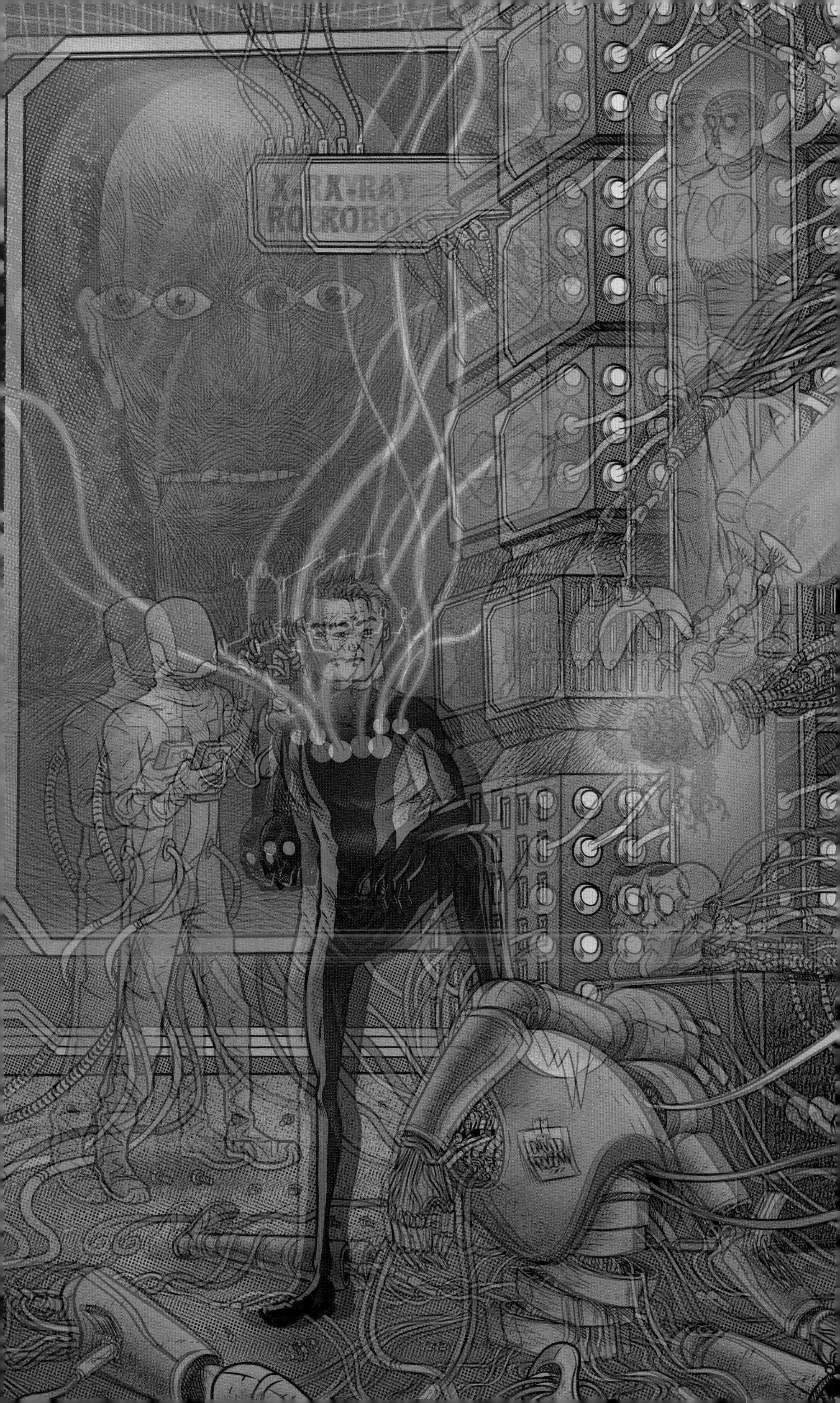
X-RAY
ROBO

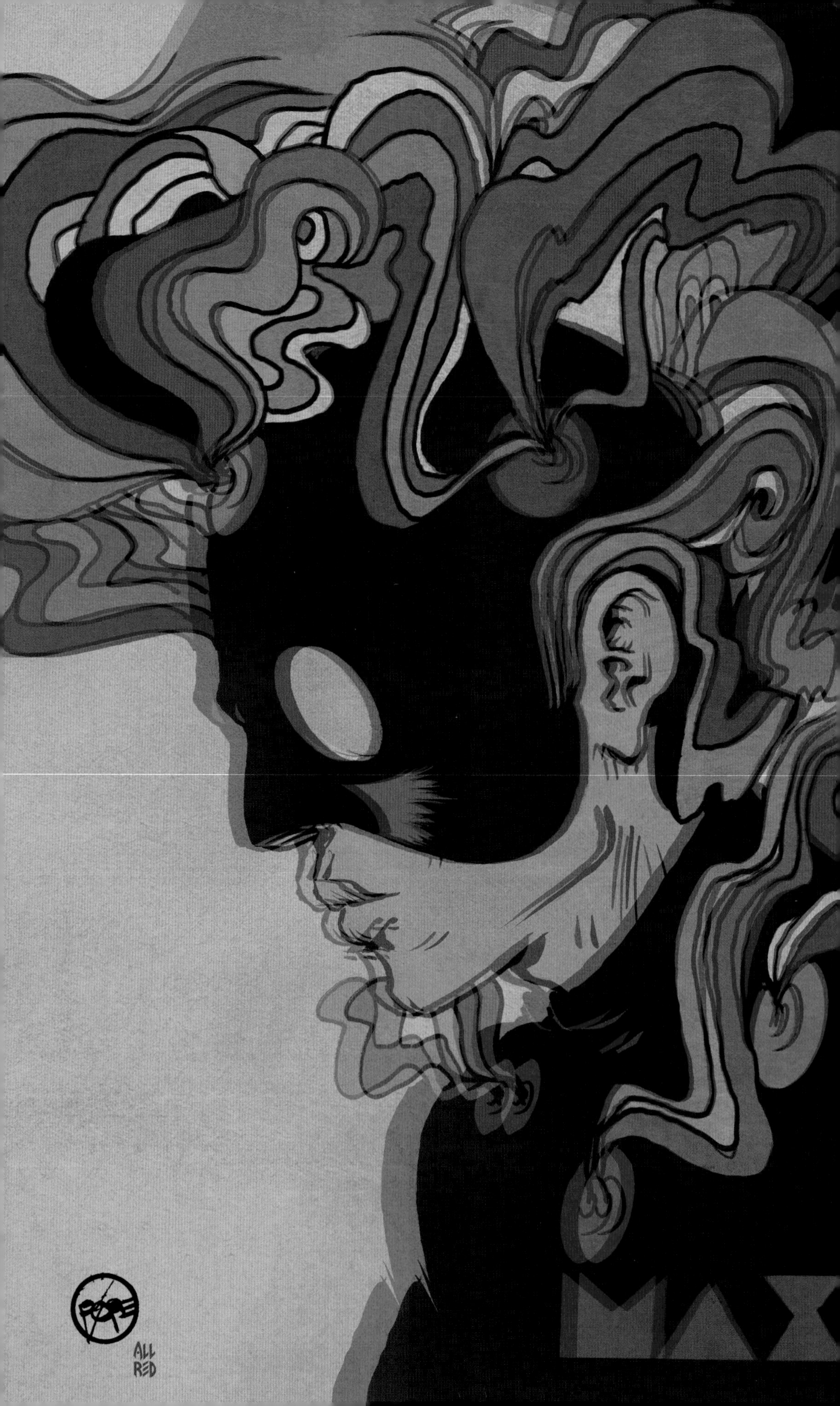
ALL
RED

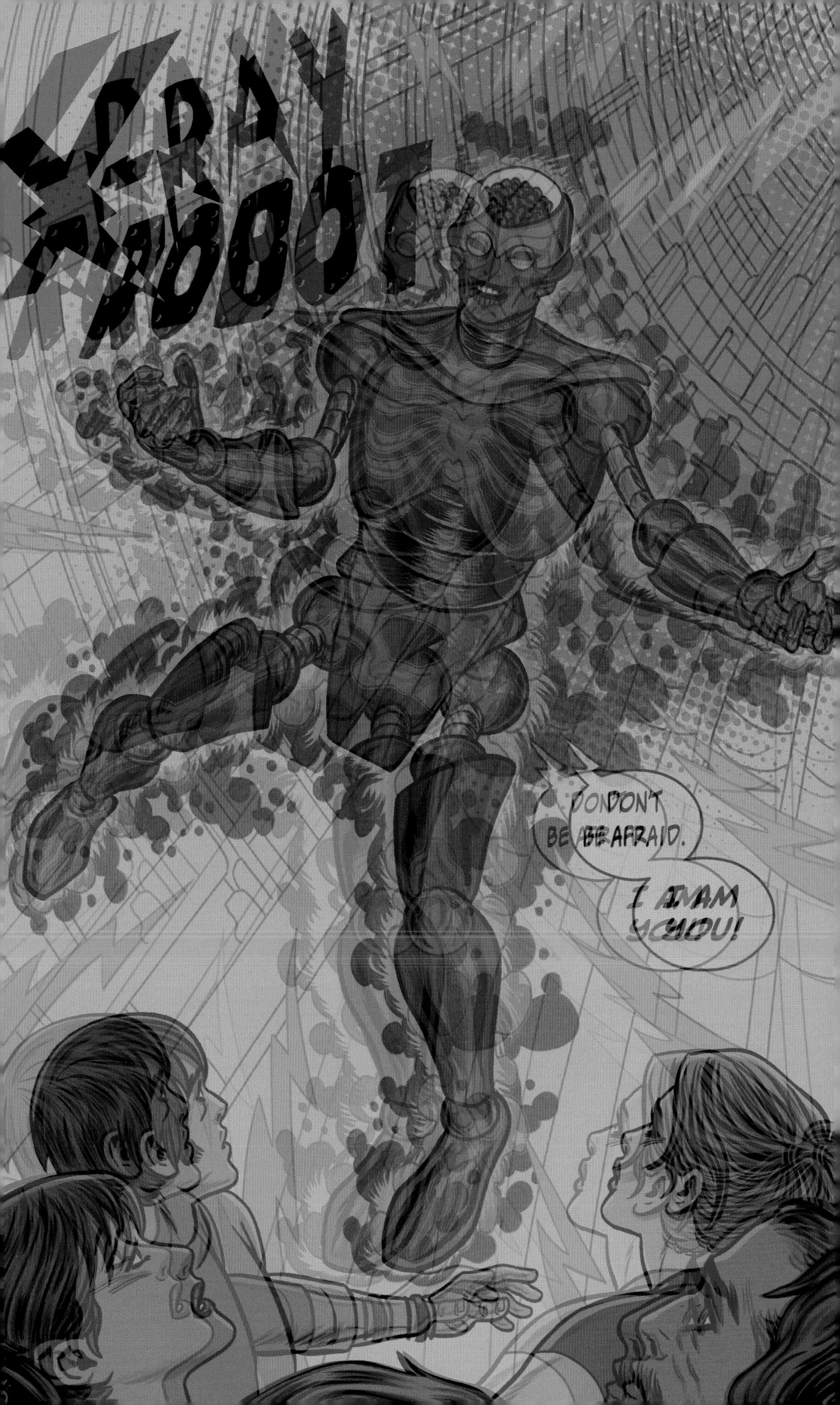
DON'T BE AFRAID.
I AM YOU!

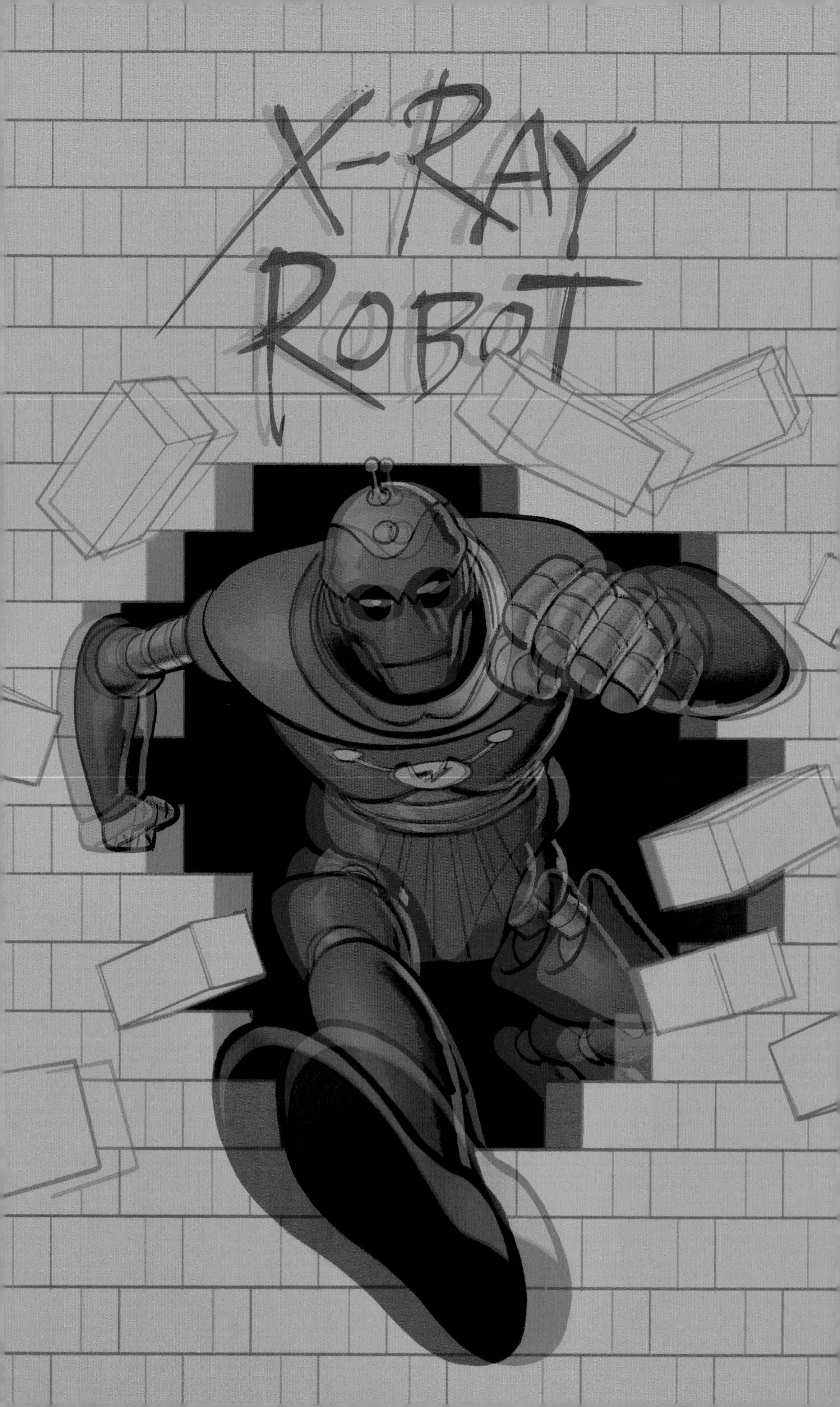
X-RAY
ROBOT

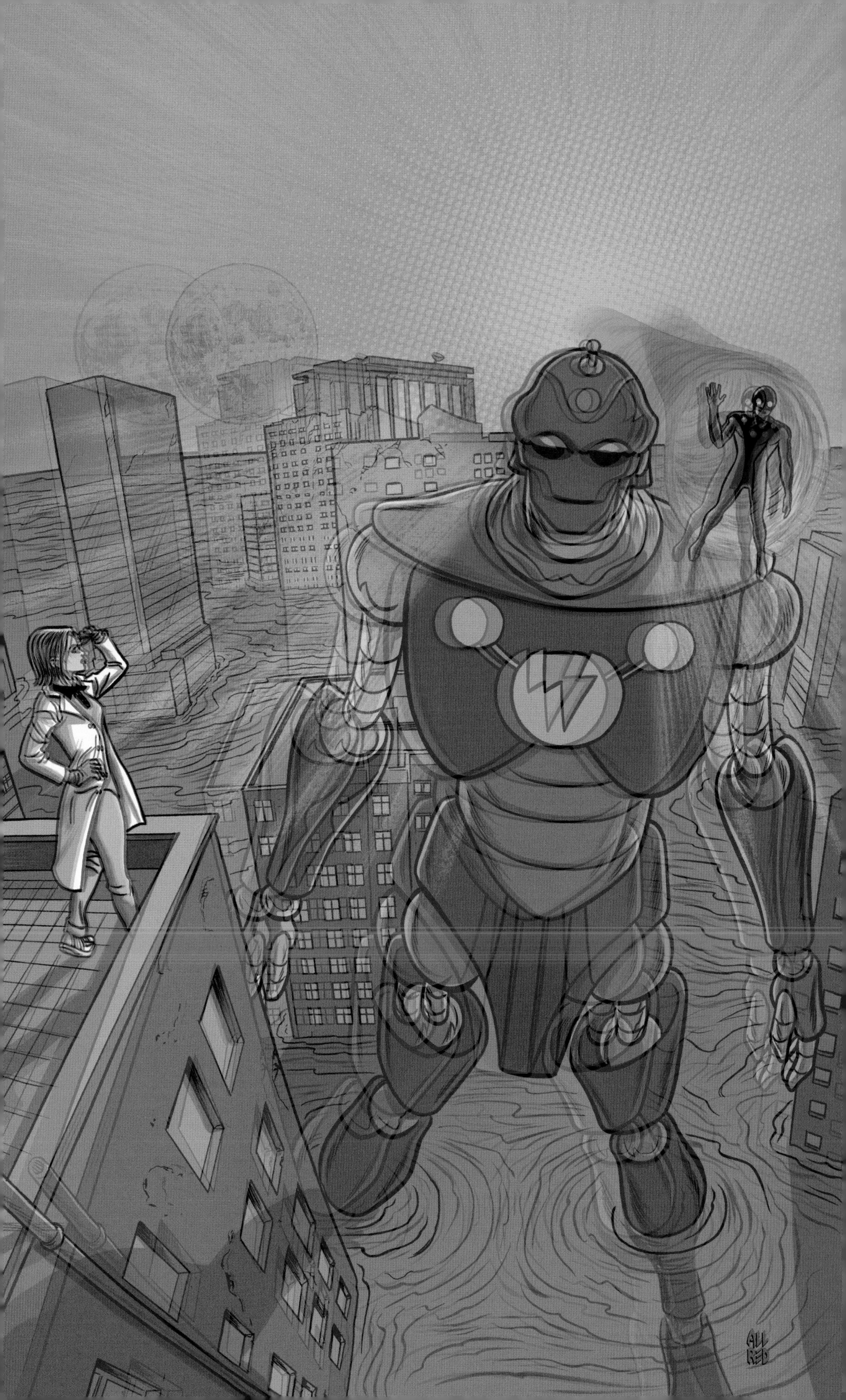

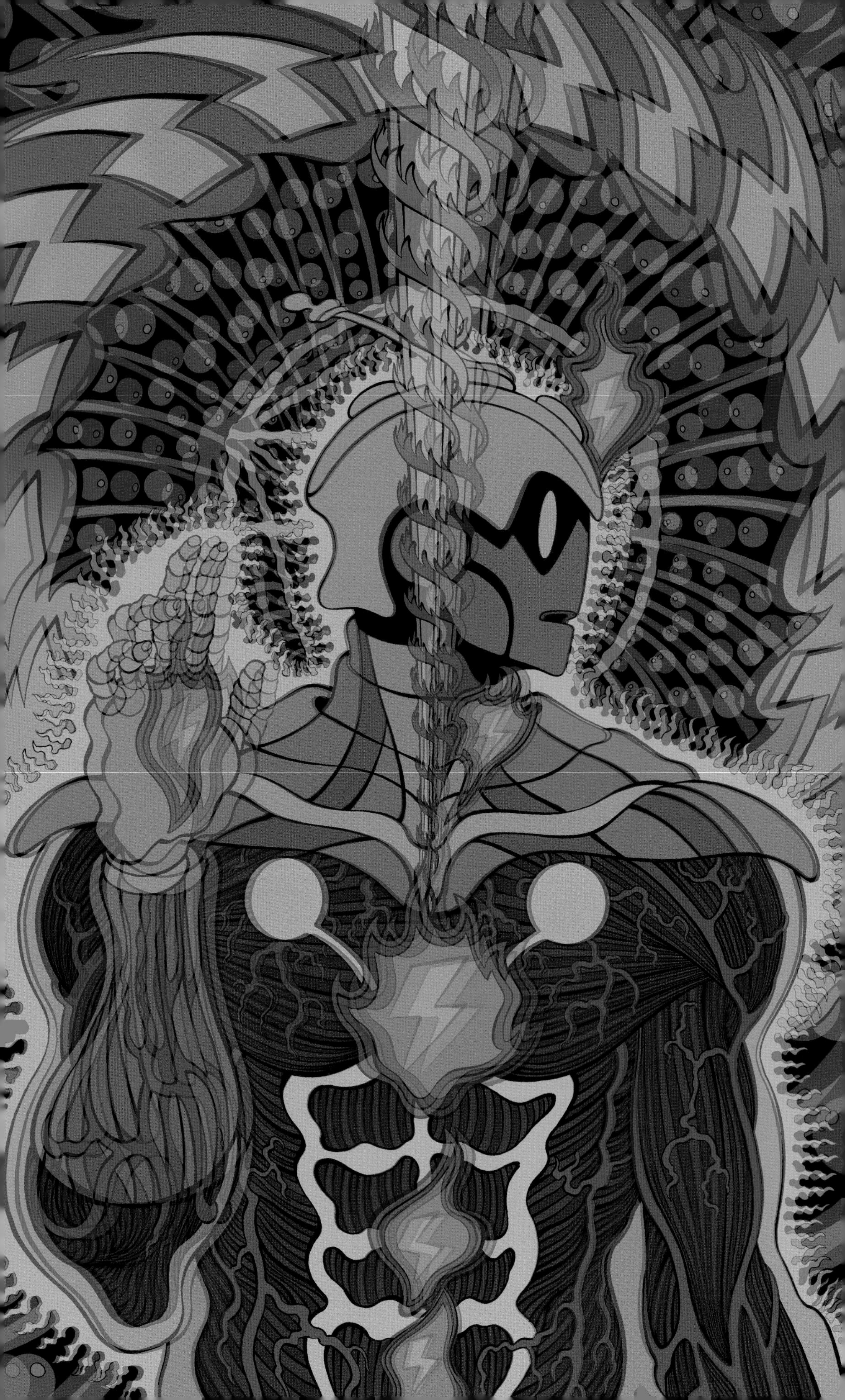

HELLO! **CHRISTIAN HERE, 3D GURU AND VISITOR TO SNAP CITY.**

You may be wondering right about now why there's all these pages of paired images. Well, with a little trick I'm about to teach you, you should be able to view these in 3D, in full color, without the use of any special glasses.

The larger pairs are set up for "crossview," while the smaller pairs are set up for "parallel" viewing. To see the crossview pairs in 3D, first, turn your book sideways so you're looking at them normally. Then, stare right between the two images. Gently start to cross your eyes. Your vision will blur for a second, but then your eyes will "converge" the two images and "fuse" them together into one clear 3D picture. Your eyes should remain locked on this image, allowing you to soak in the whole view in 3D!

To see the parallel images in 3D, you will need to "diverge" your eyes. Start by staring at one of the smaller image pairs, with your face fairly close to the page. You almost need to stare past where you're looking, as if your eyes are looking at something far away—with any luck, the pictures will go blurry and then float toward each other, locking and fusing into one clear 3D image.

This all might take some practice if you've never done it before, but the results are worth it. If you're having trouble, feel free to look up other descriptions of these methods online; maybe the way someone else describes this might "click" with you better. Remember, too: some people are naturally better at seeing crossview than parallel, and vice versa. Lastly: if you get one of these methods to work, but the 3D looks really weird, almost like the depth is completely wrong: you may be using the crossview method to view a parallel pair, or vice versa. ◄━

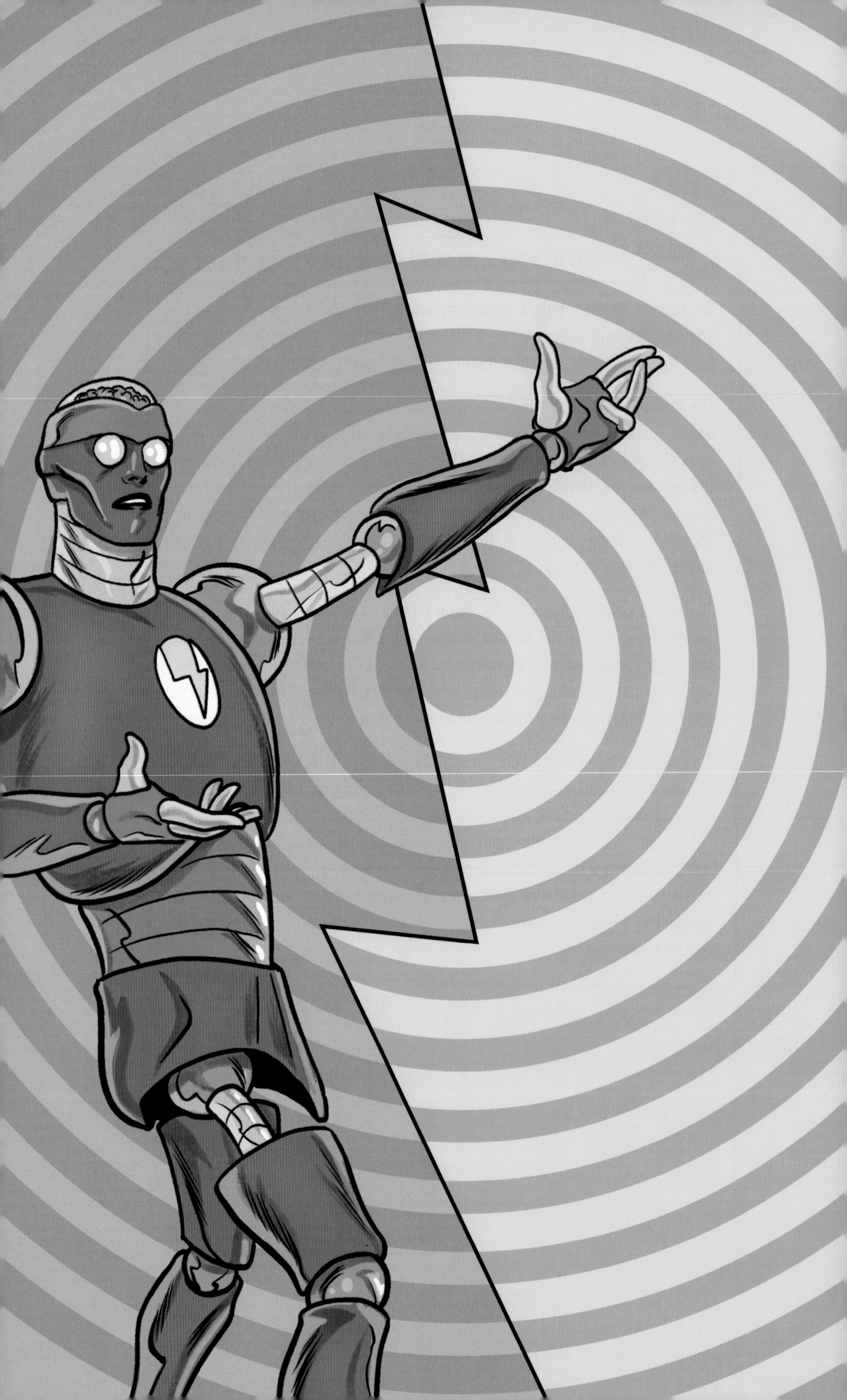

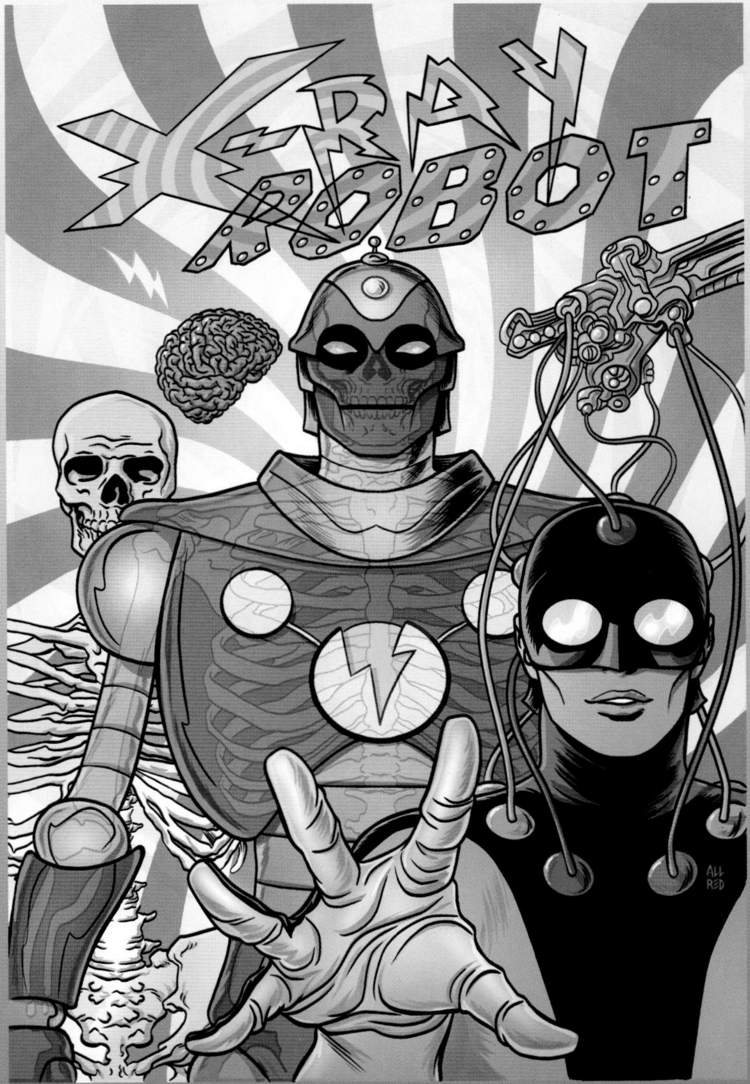
X-RAY ROBOT
ALLRED

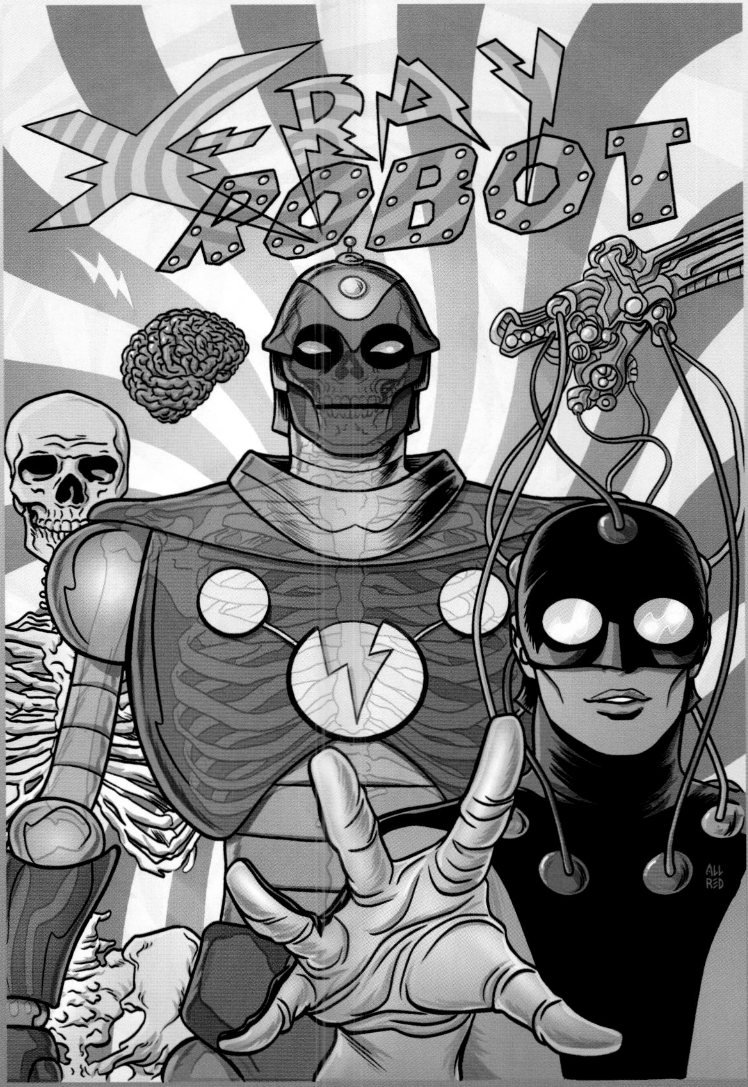
X-RAY ROBOT
ALLRED

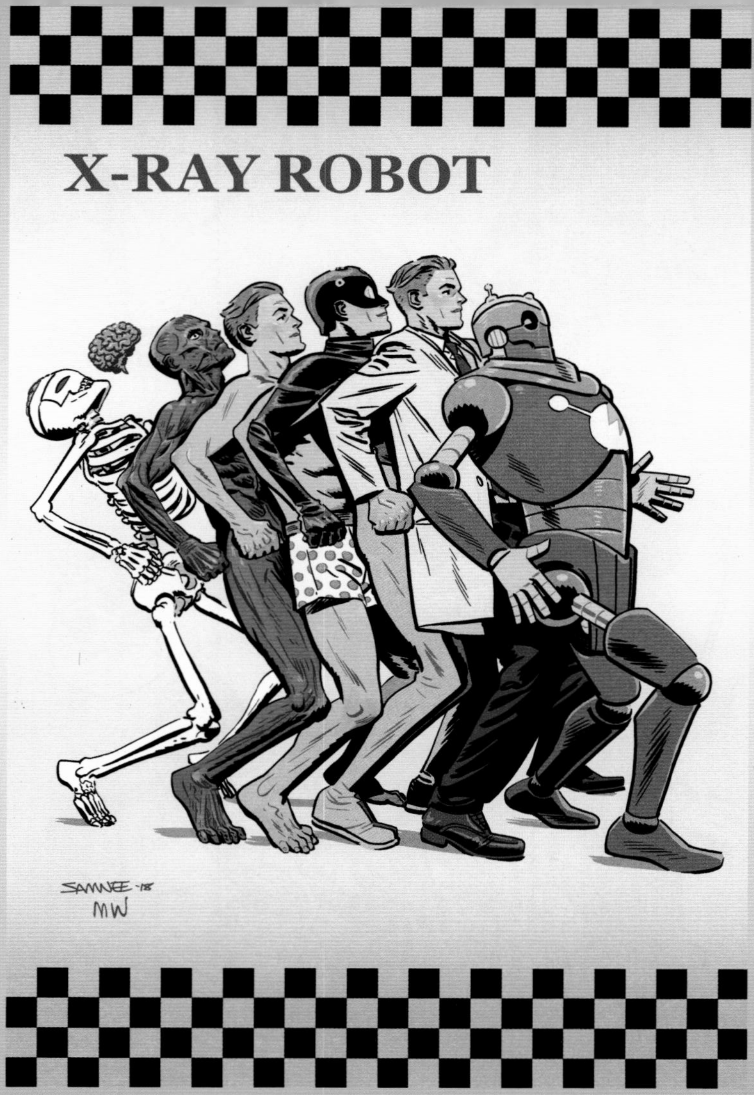
X-RAY ROBOT
SAMNEE -18
MW

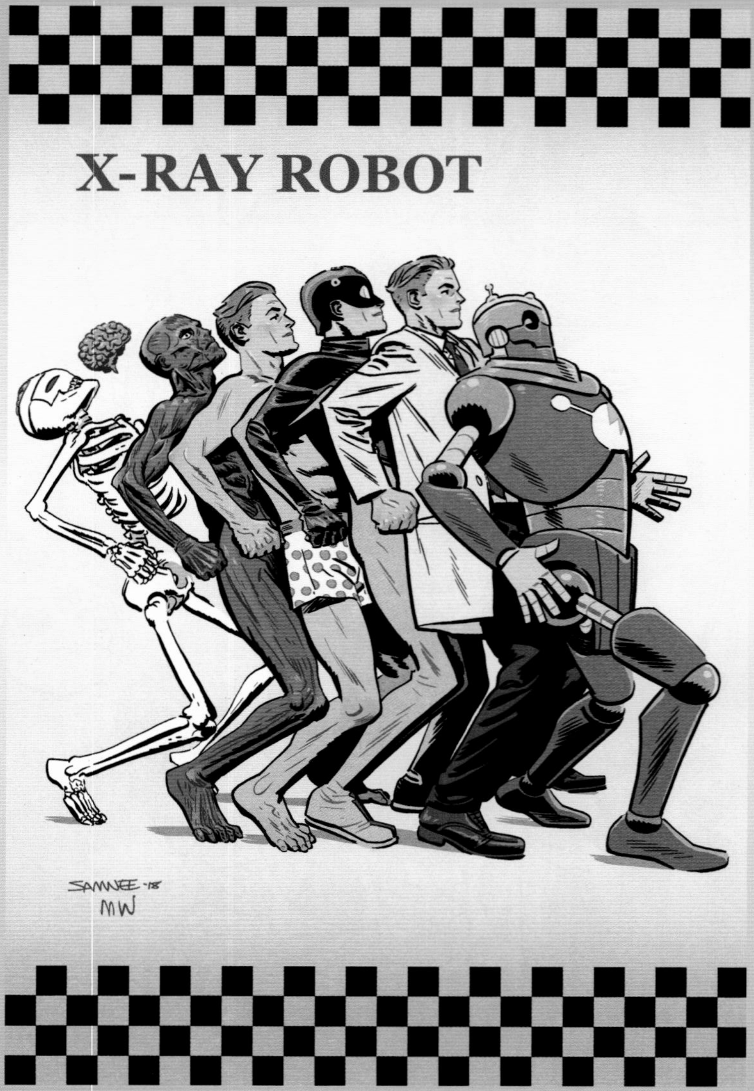
X-RAY ROBOT
SAMNEE -18
MW

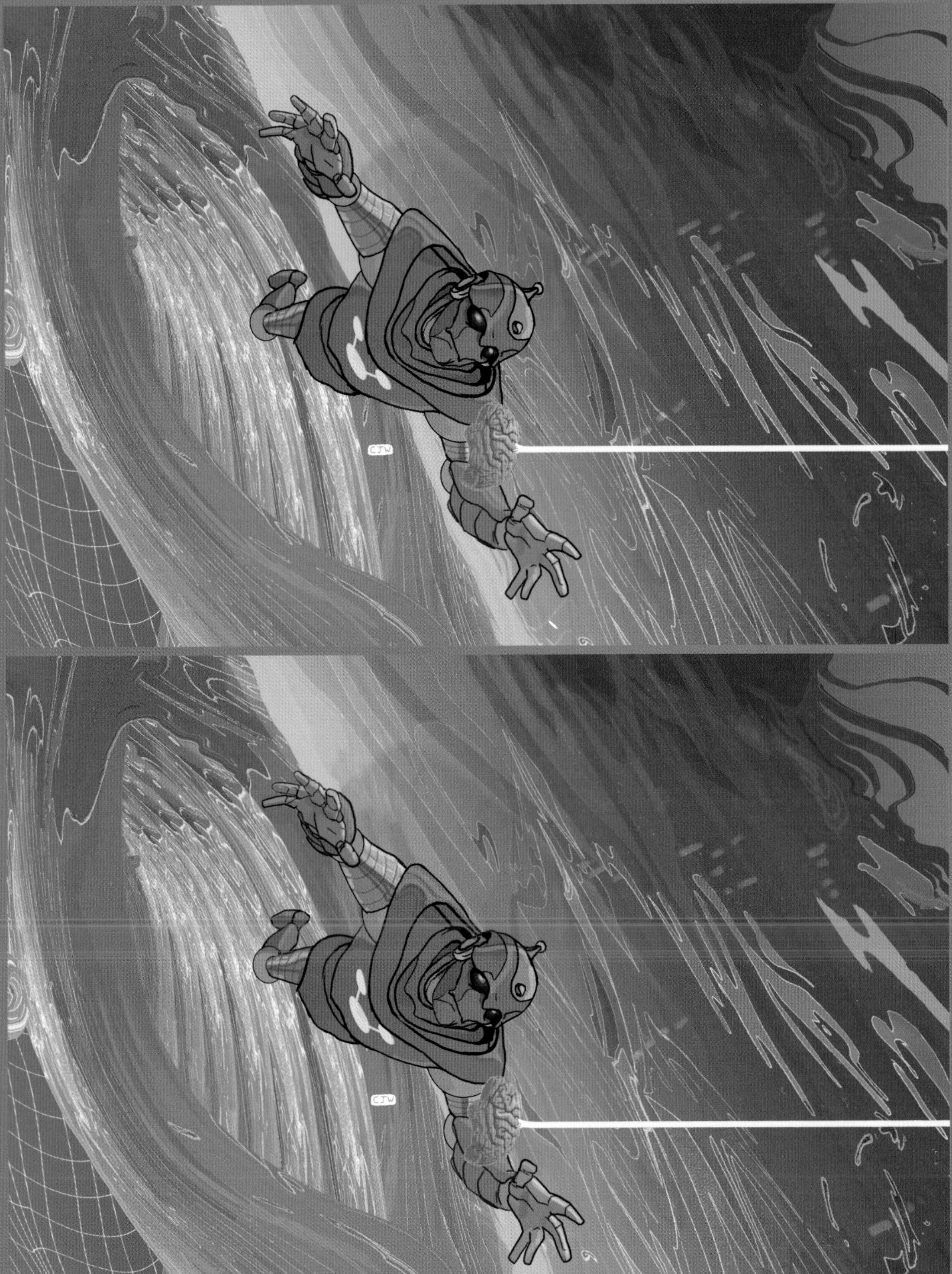
CJW
CJW

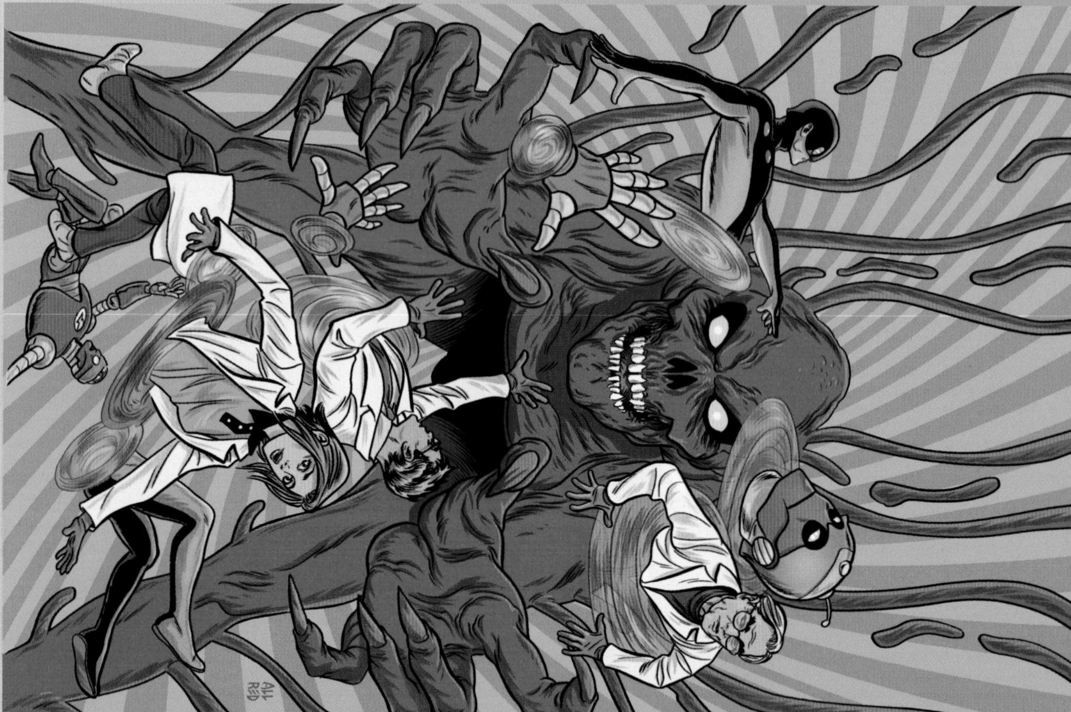
ALL
RED

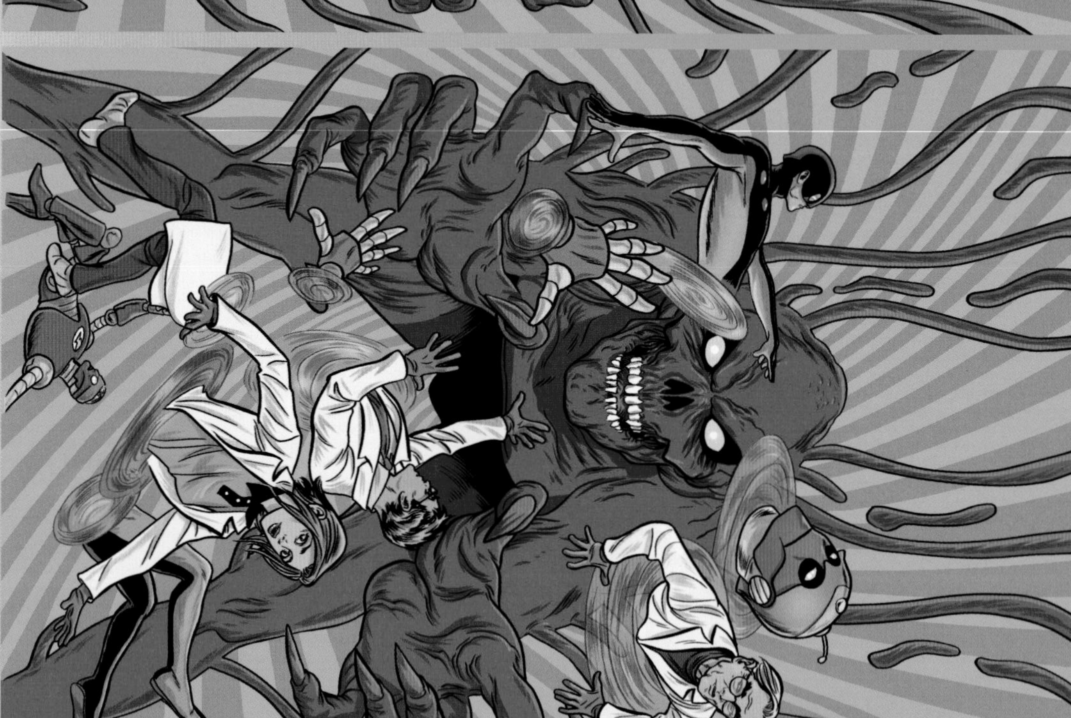
ALL
RED

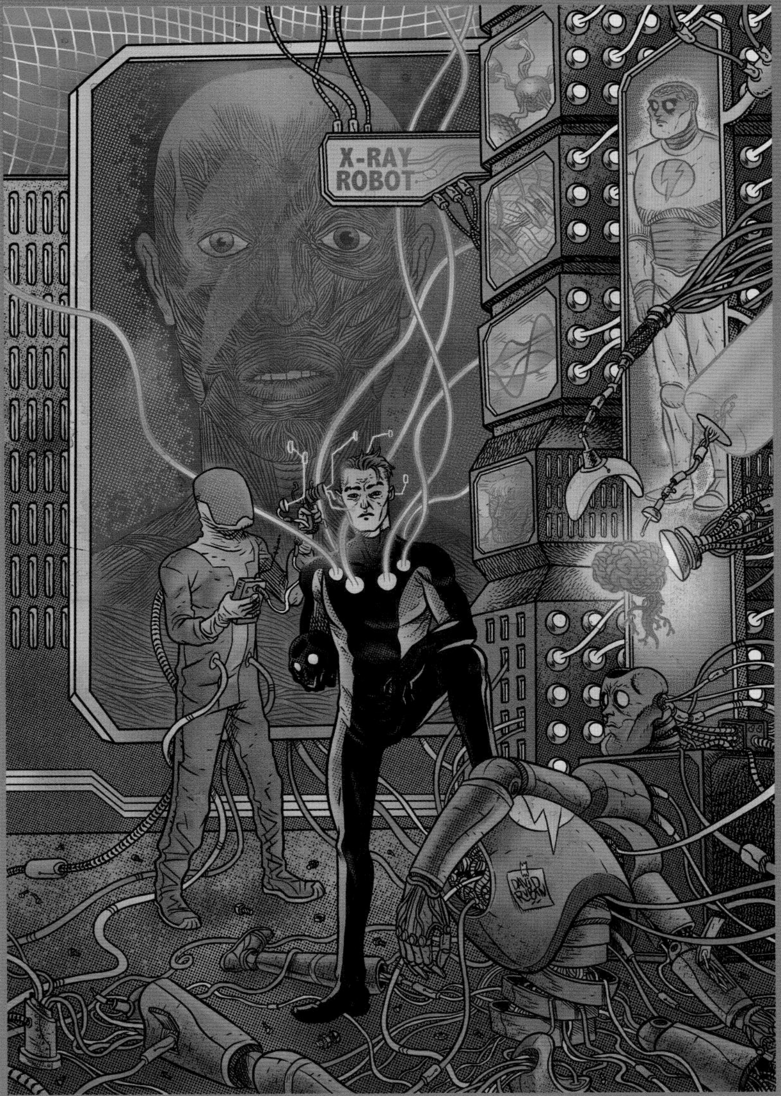
X-RAY ROBOT
DAVID RUBIN

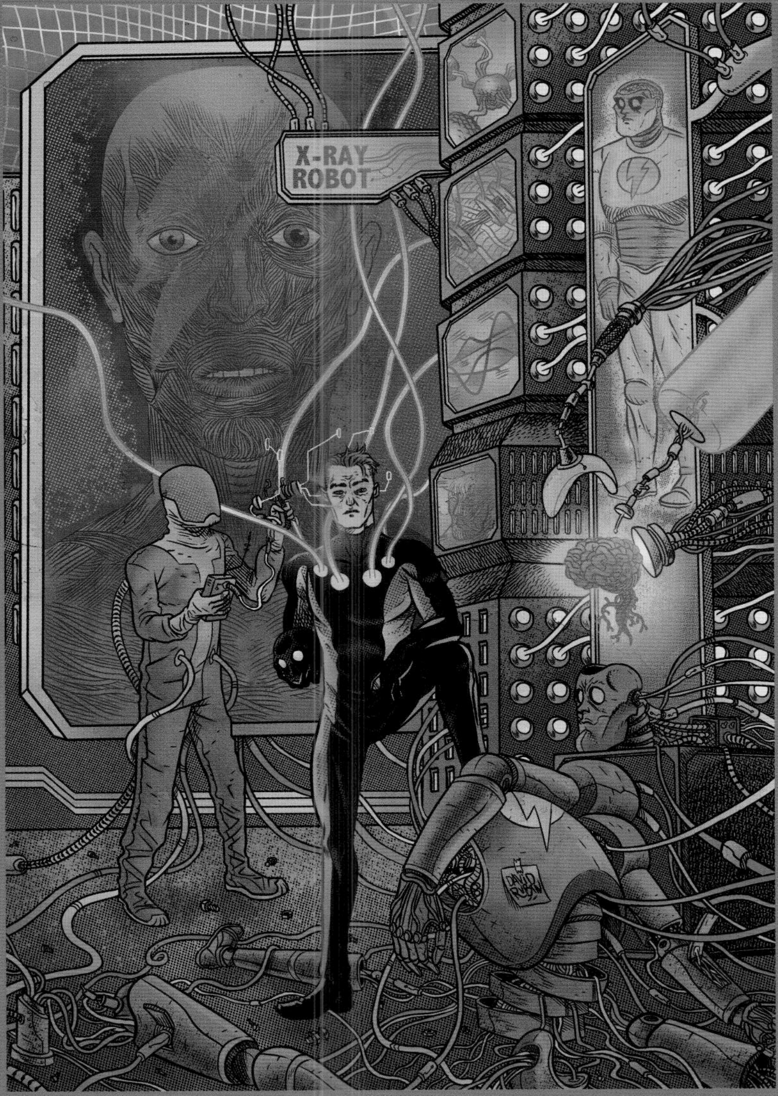
X-RAY ROBOT
DAVID RUBIN

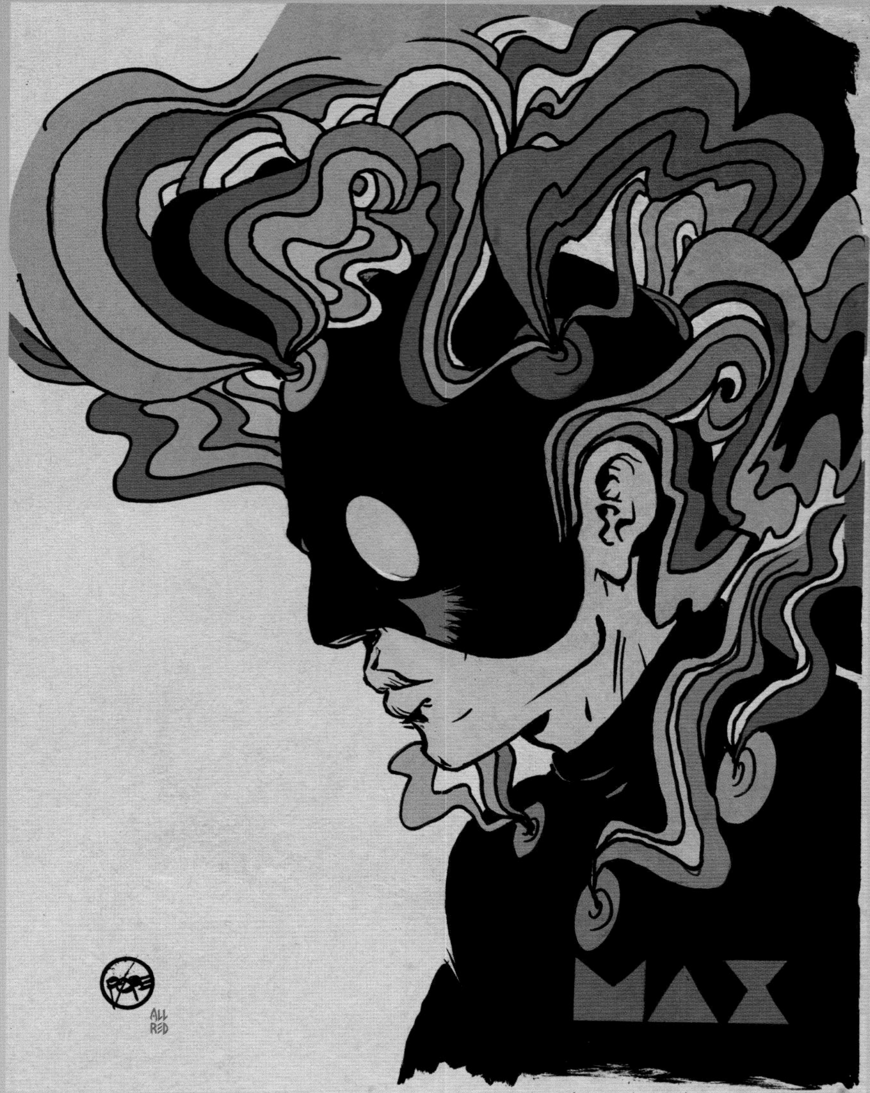
MAX
ALL RED

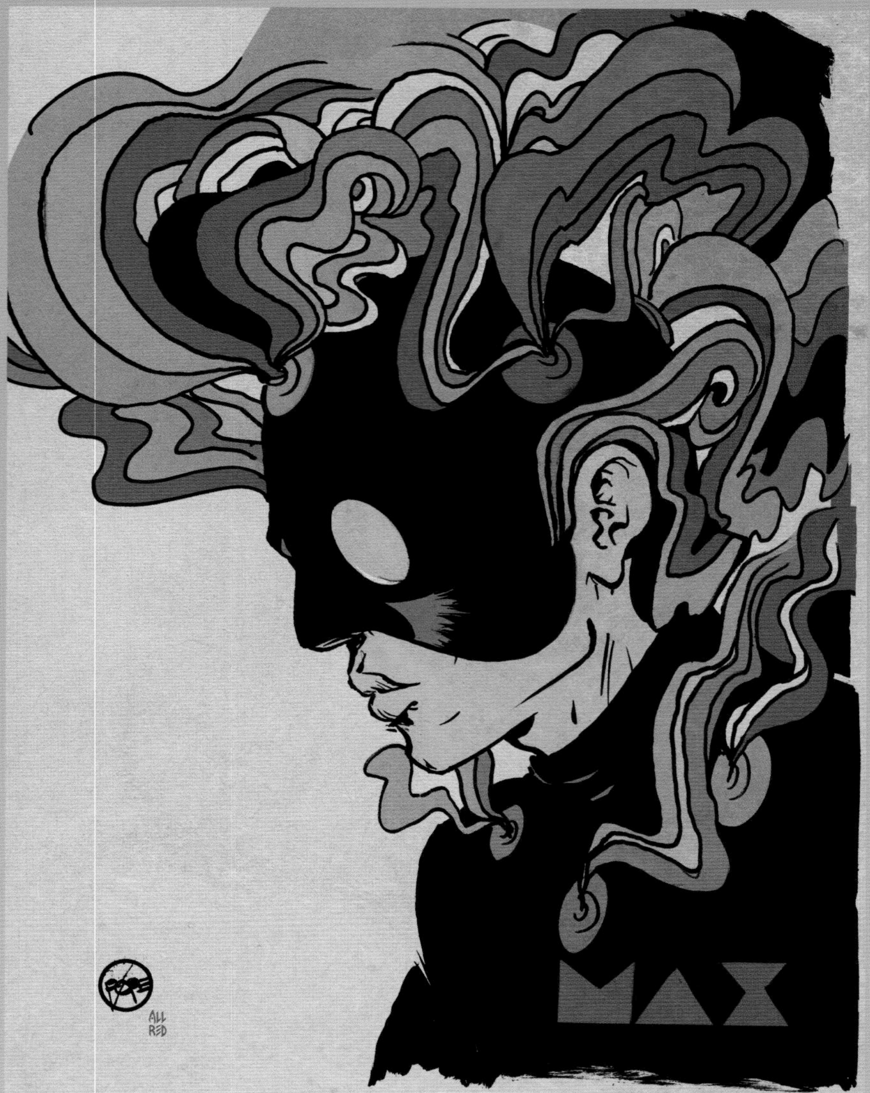
MAX
ALL RED

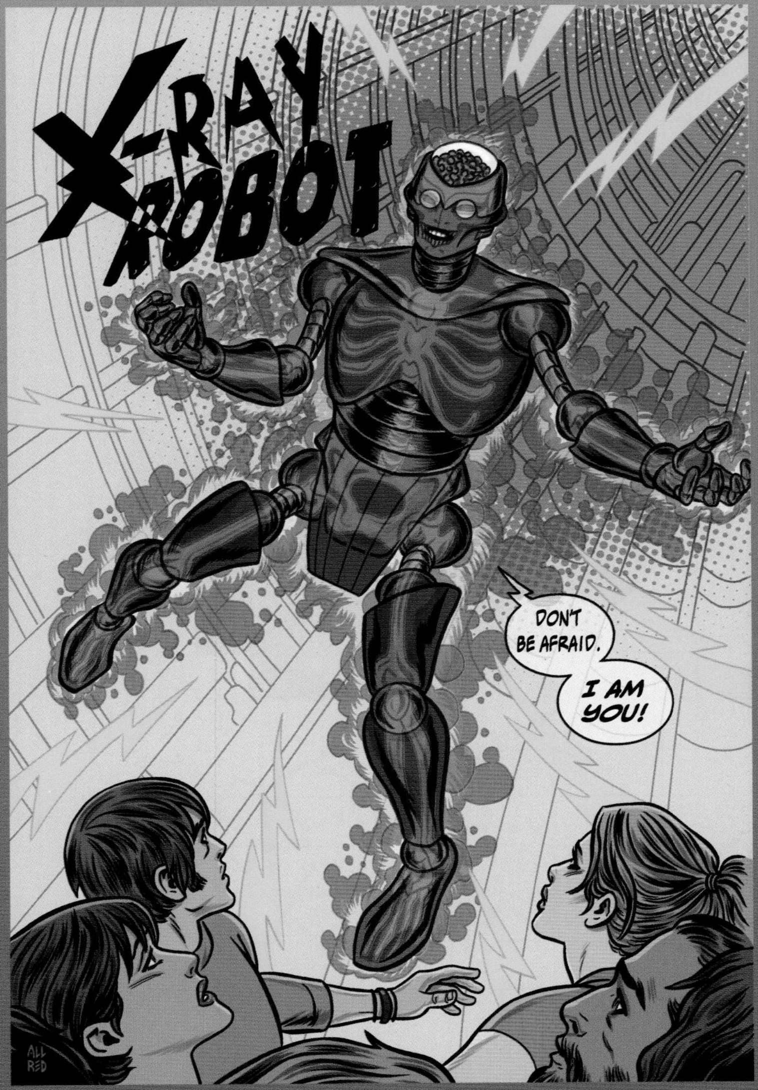
X-RAY ROBOT
DON'T BE AFRAID.
I AM YOU!
ALLRED

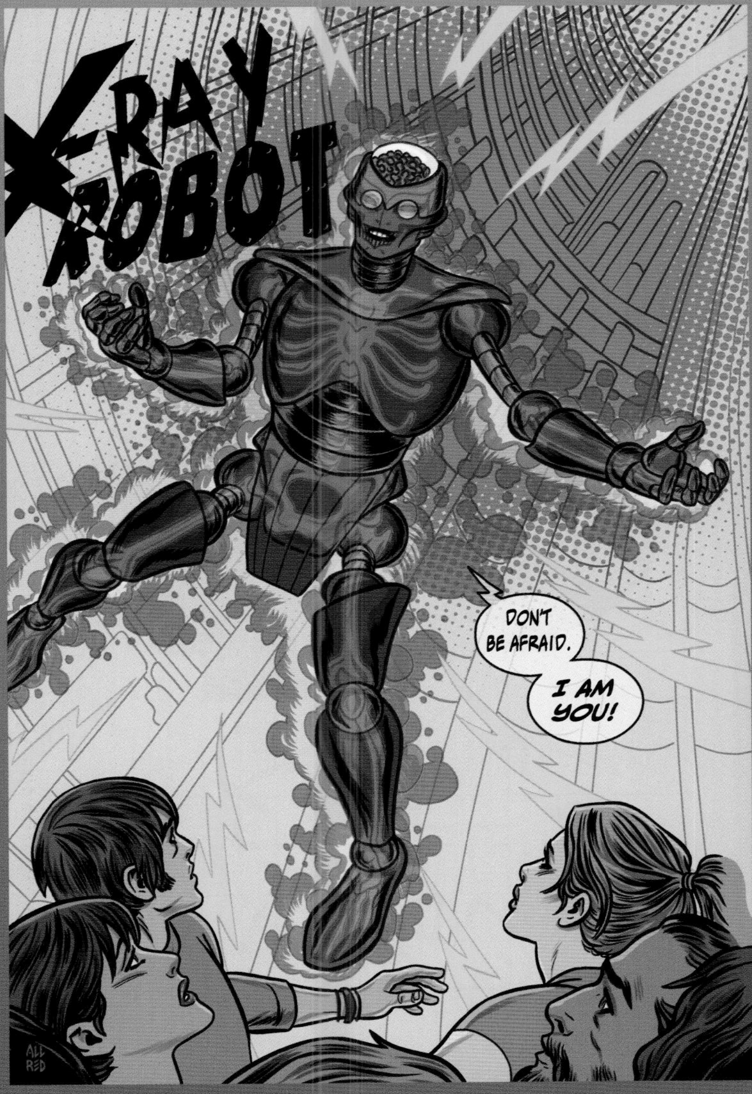
X-RAY ROBOT
DON'T BE AFRAID.
I AM YOU!
ALLRED

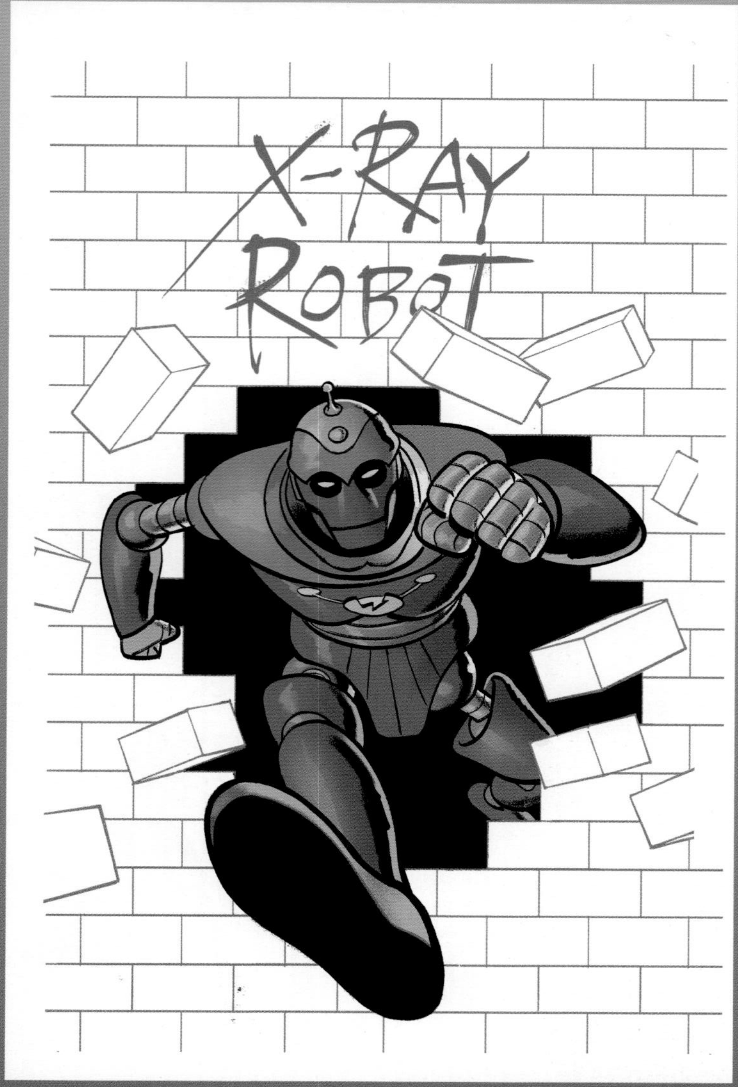
X-RAY ROBOT
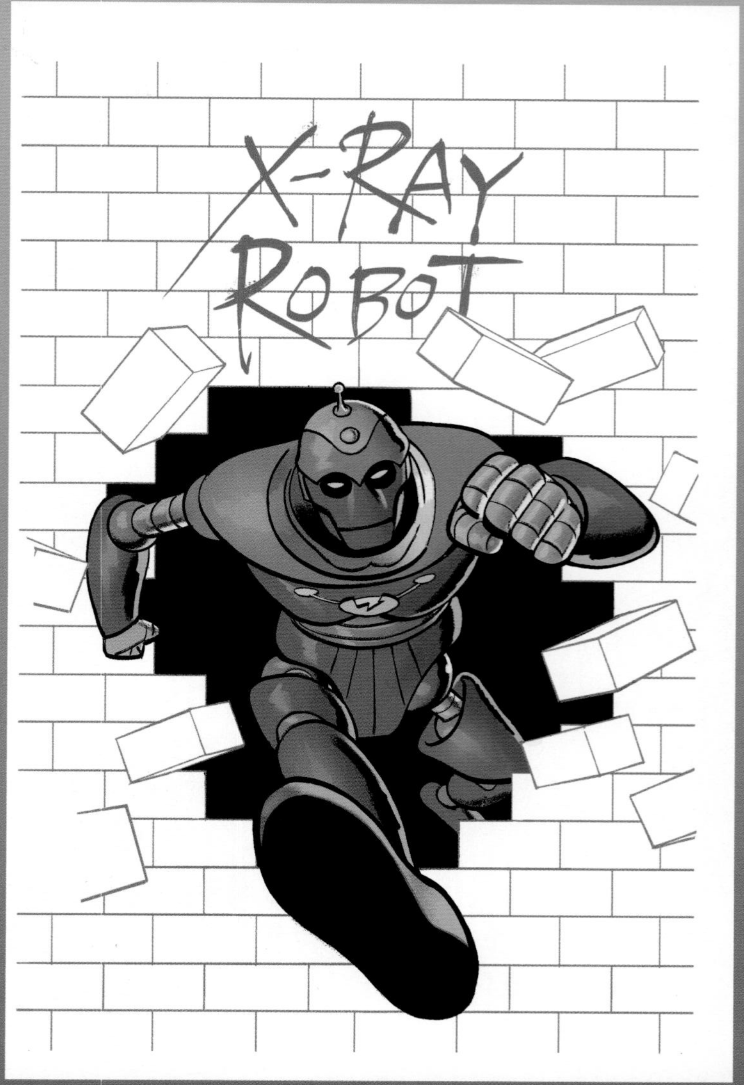
X-RAY ROBOT

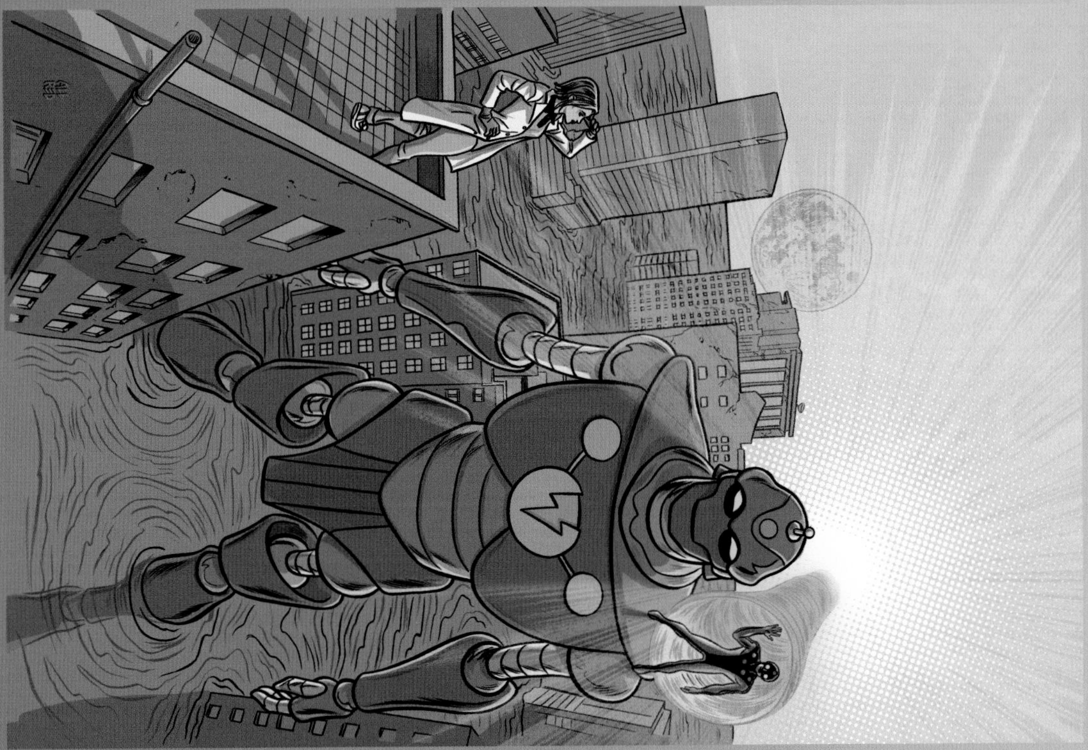

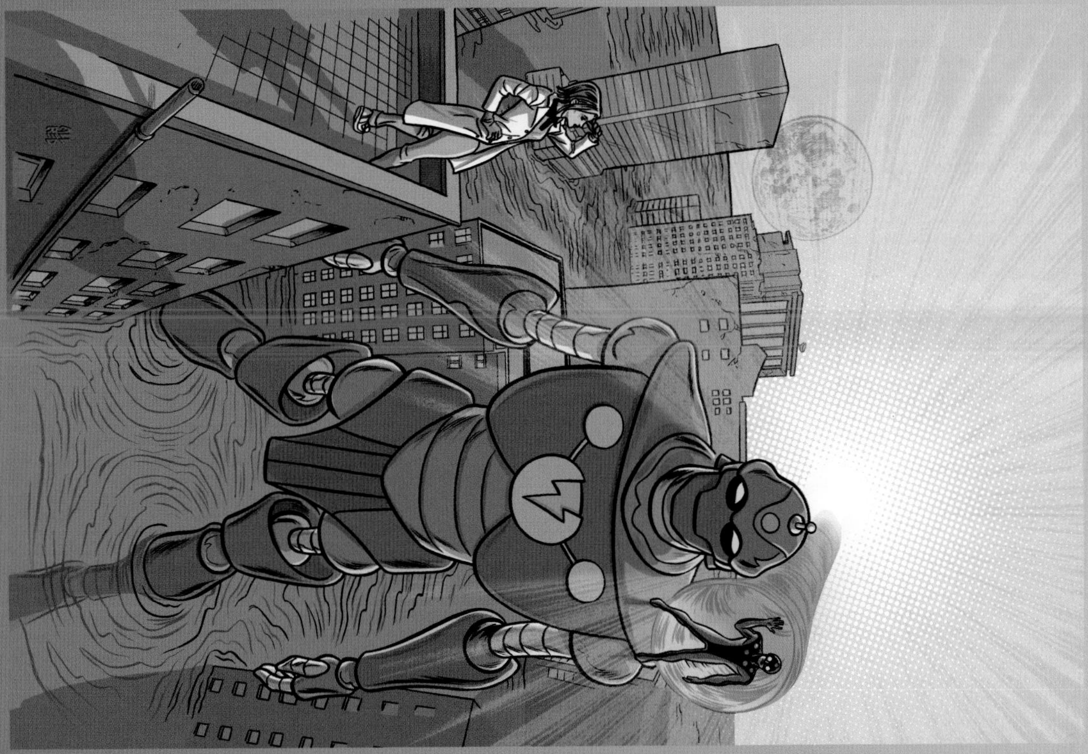

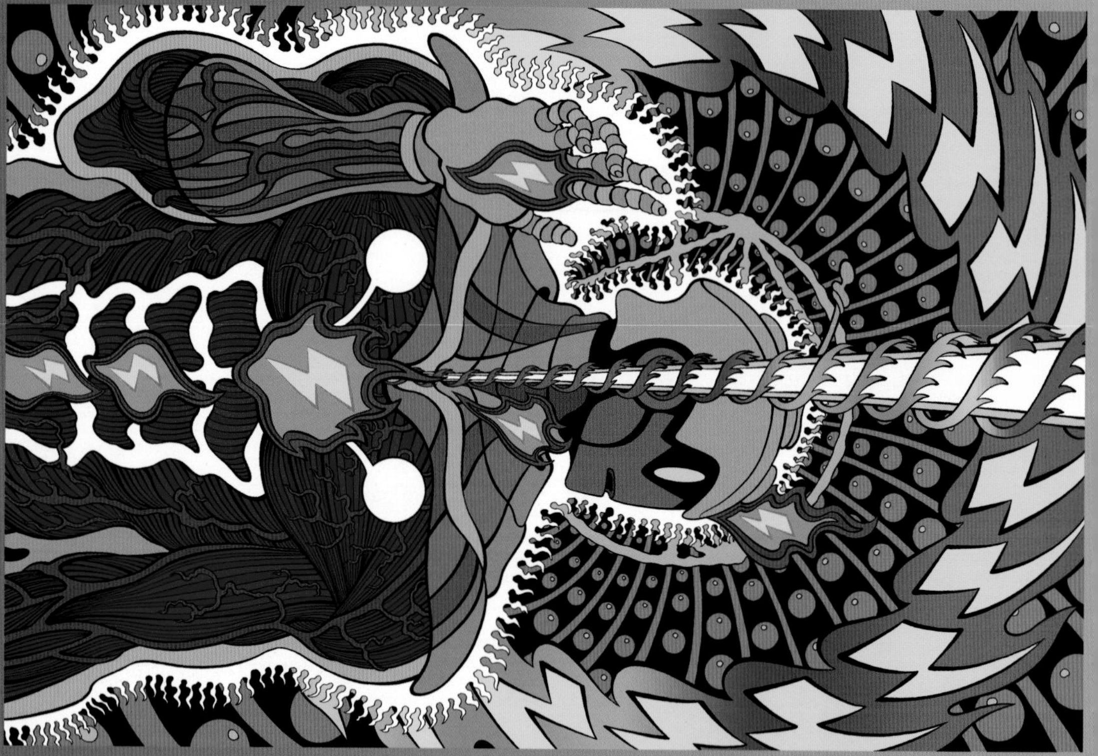

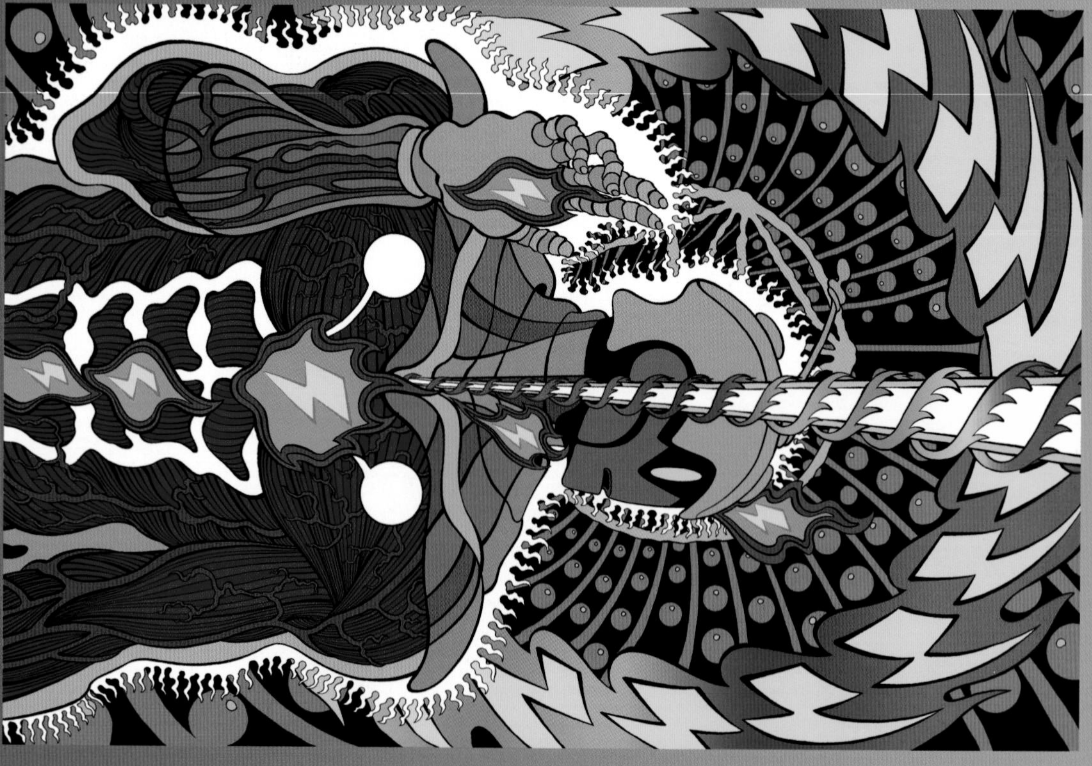

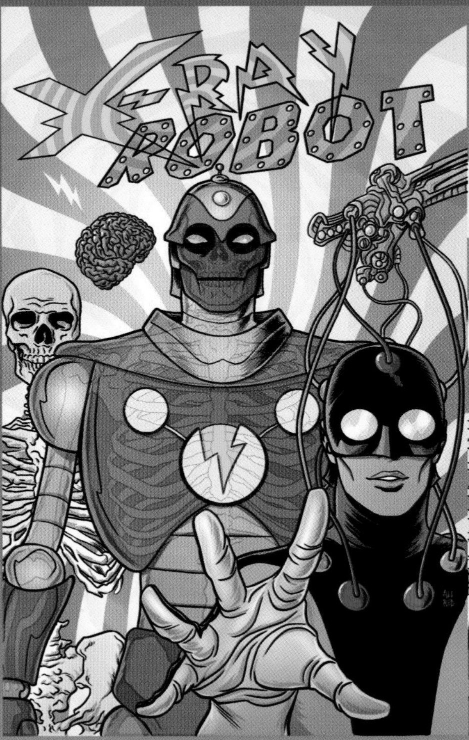
X-RAY ROBOT

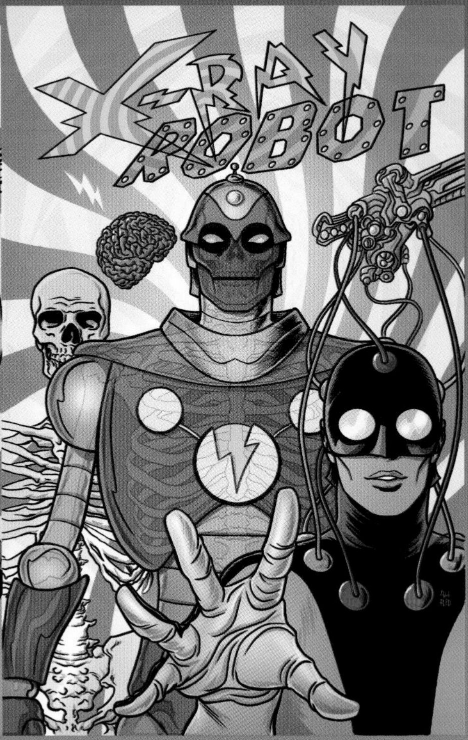
X-RAY ROBOT

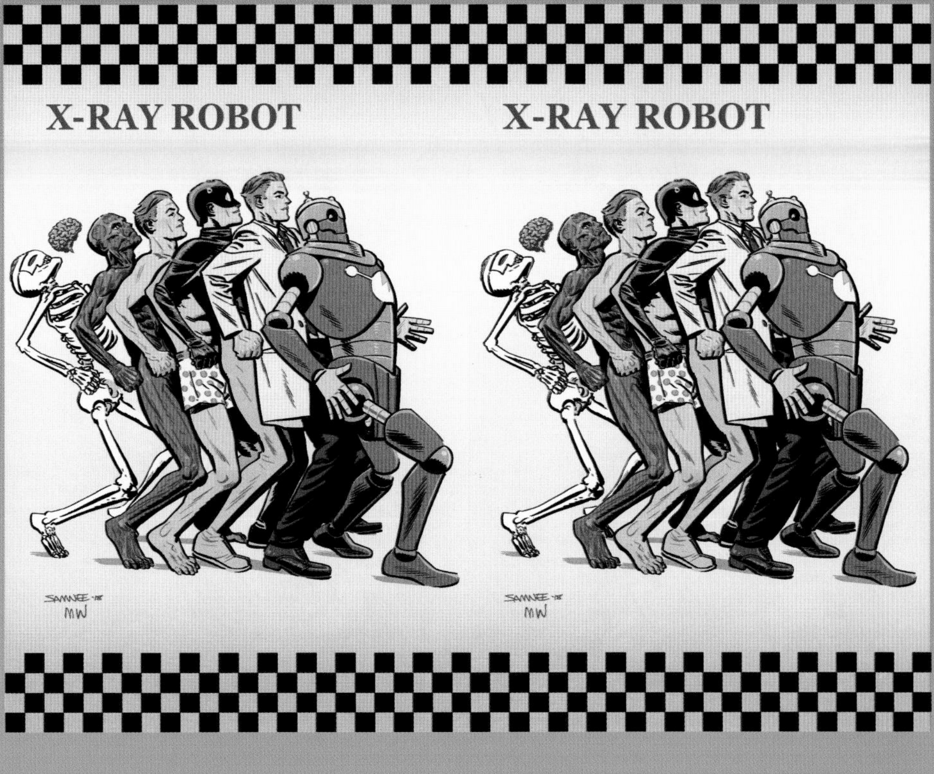
X-RAY ROBOT
X-RAY ROBOT

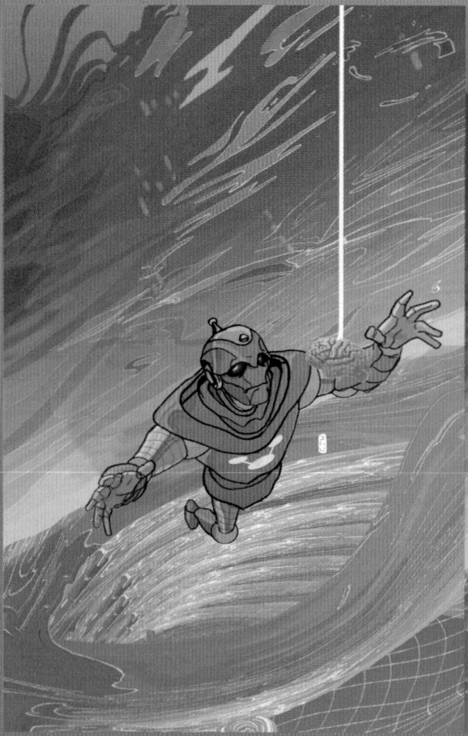

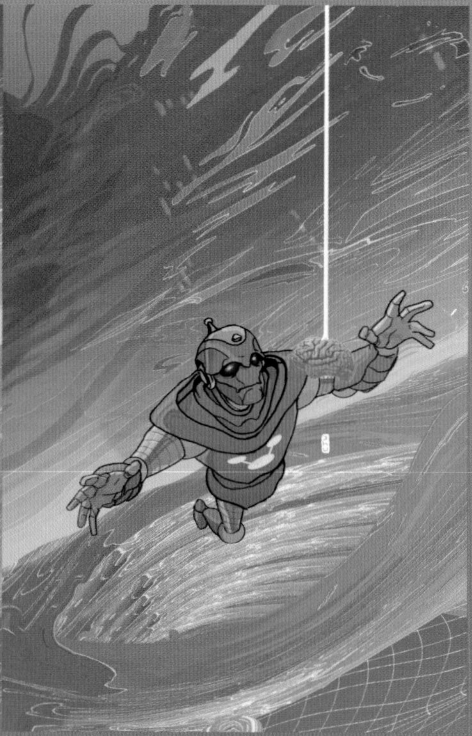

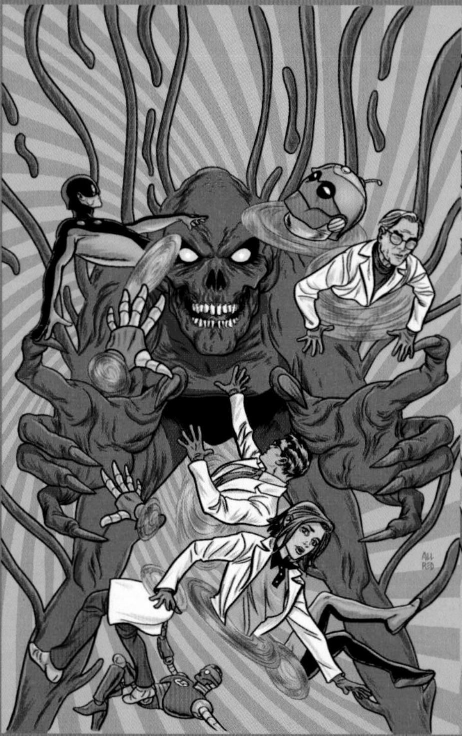

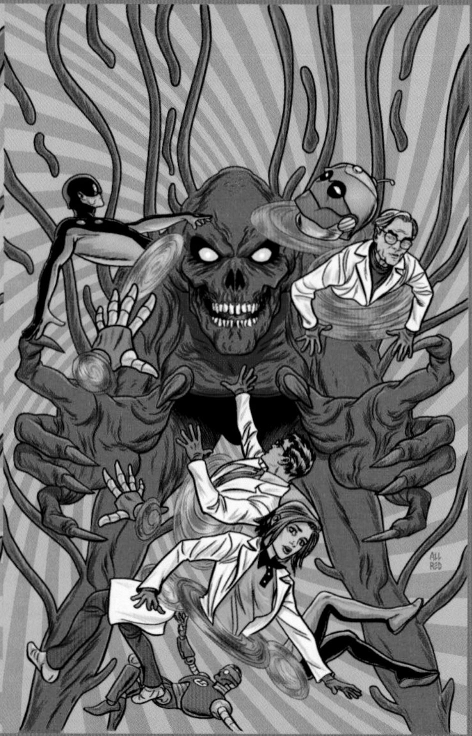

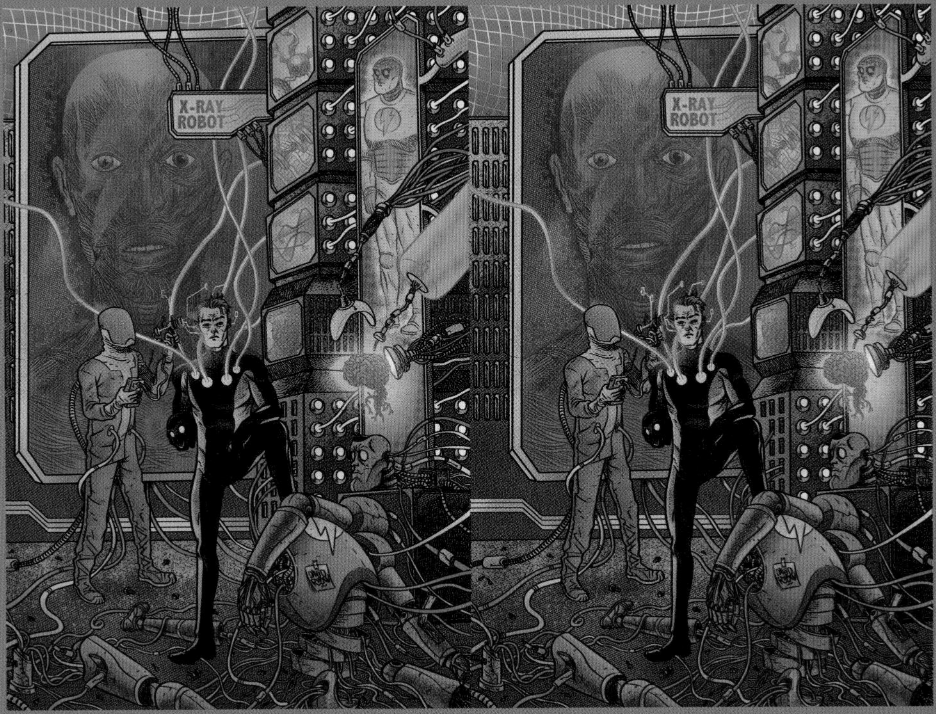
X-RAY ROBOT
X-RAY ROBOT

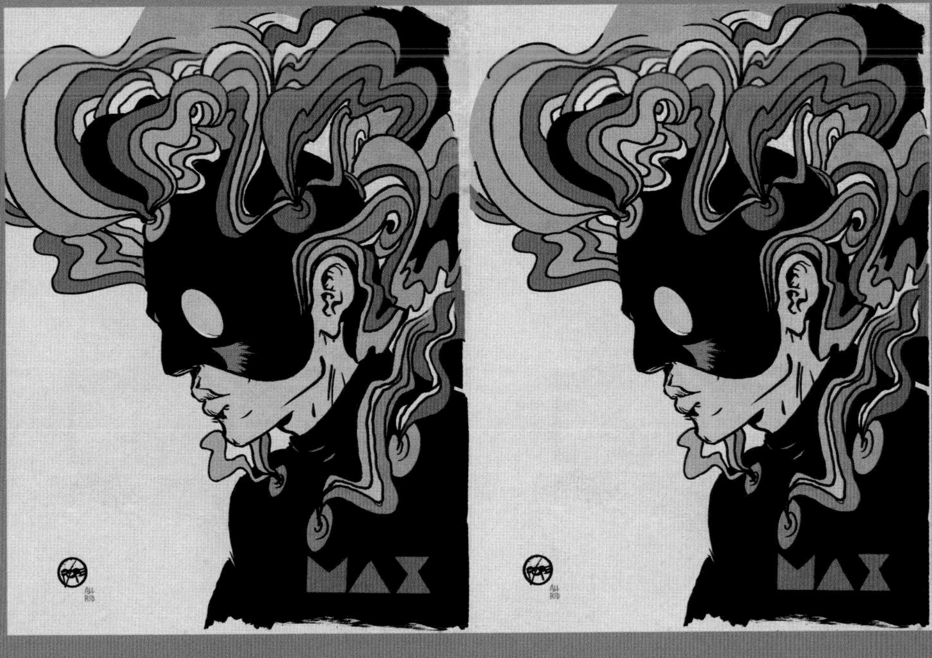

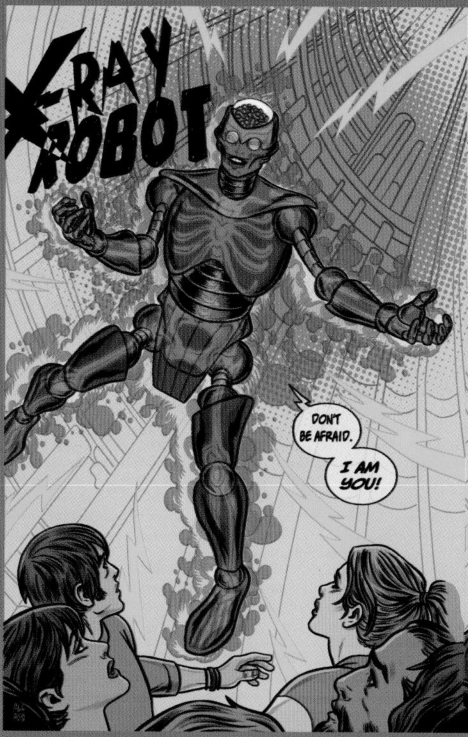
X-RAY ROBOT
DON'T BE AFRAID.
I AM YOU!

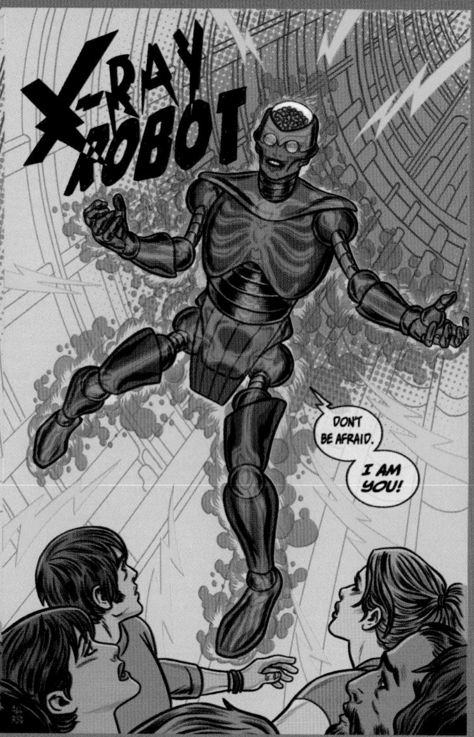
X-RAY ROBOT
DON'T BE AFRAID.
I AM YOU!

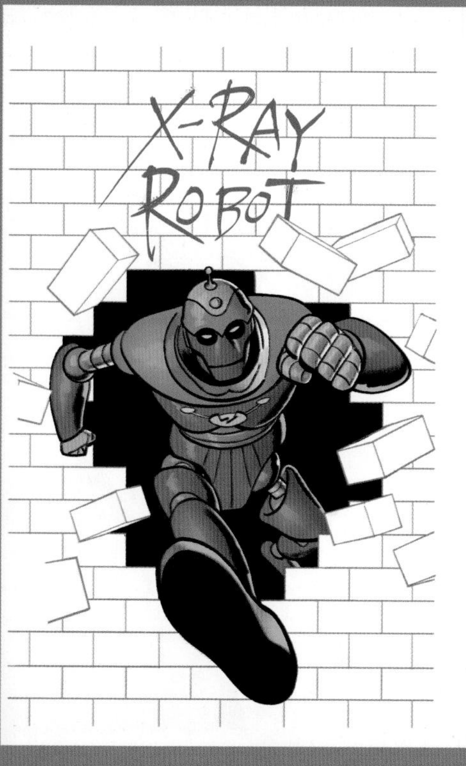
X-RAY ROBOT

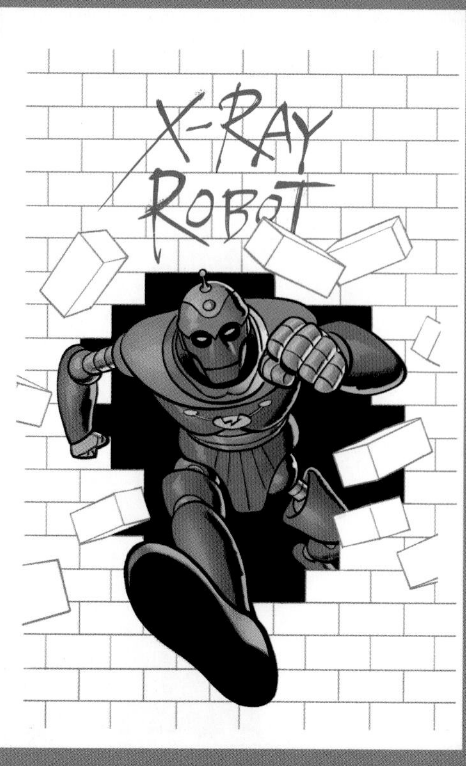
X-RAY ROBOT

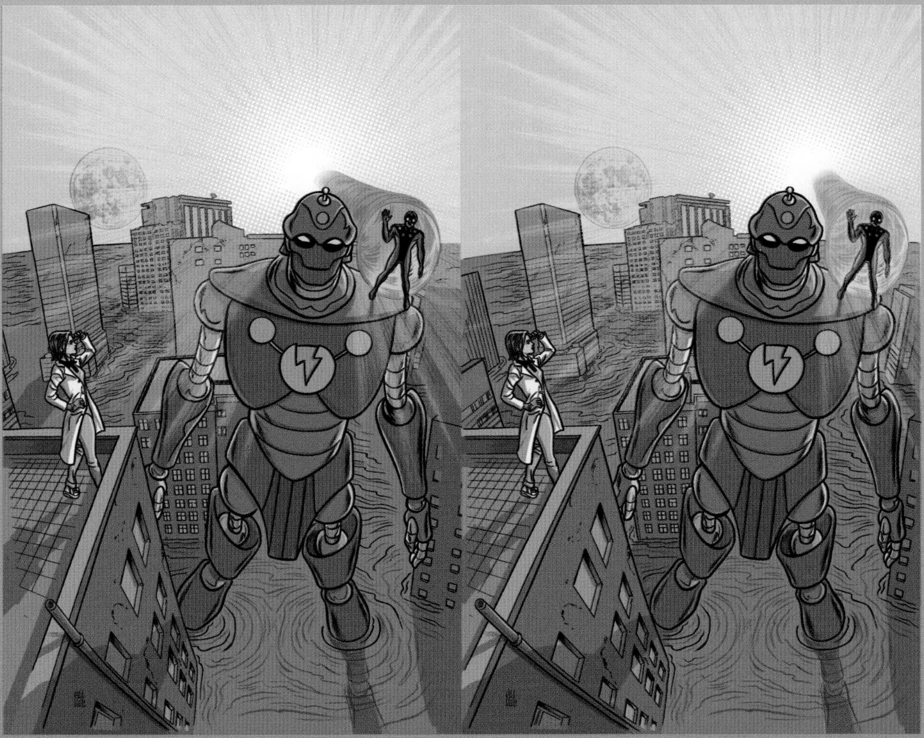

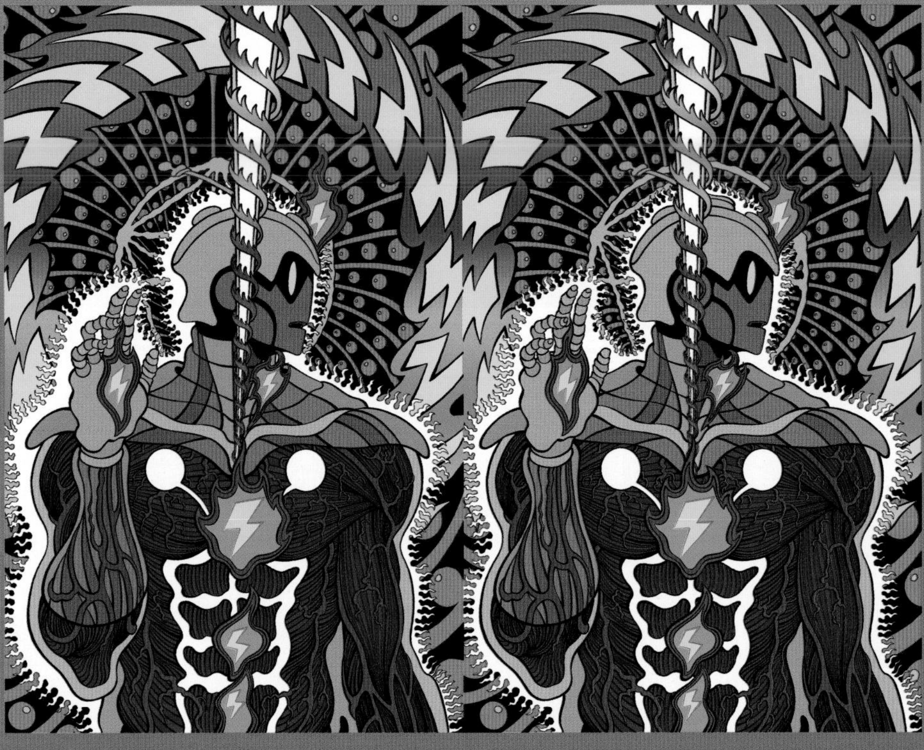

BLACK HAMMER
Jeff Lemire and Dean Ormston
BLACK HAMMER LIBRARY EDITION: VOLUME ONE
ISBN 978-1-50671-073-0 | $49.99
BLACK HAMMER LIBRARY EDITION: VOLUME TWO
ISBN 978-1-50671-185-0 | $49.99
VOLUME 1: SECRET ORIGINS
ISBN 978-1-61655-786-7 | $14.99
VOLUME 2: THE EVENT
ISBN 978-1-50670-198-1 | $19.99
VOLUME 3: AGE OF DOOM, PART I
ISBN 978-1-50670-389-3 | $19.99
VOLUME 4: AGE OF DOOM, PART II
ISBN 978-1-50670-816-4 | $19.99

QUANTUM AGE: FROM THE WORLD OF BLACK HAMMER
Jeff Lemire and Wilfredo Torres
ISBN 978-1-50670-841-6 | $19.99

SHERLOCK FRANKENSTEIN & THE LEGION OF EVIL: FROM THE WORLD OF BLACK HAMMER
Jeff Lemire and David Rubín
ISBN 978-1-50670-526-2 | $17.99

EMPOWERED VOLUME 1
Adam Warren
ISBN 978-1-59307-672-6 | $17.99

THE PAYBACKS COLLECTION
Donny Cates, Eliot Rahal and Geof Shaw
ISBN 978-1-50670-482-1 | $24.99

THE BLACK BEETLE
Francesco Francavilla
KARA BOCEK
ISBN 978-1-50670-537-8 | $12.99

THE COMPLETE ANGEL CATBIRD
Margaret Atwood and Johnnie Christmas
ISBN 978-1-50670-456-2 | $24.99

HELLBOY OMNIBUS
Mike Mignola and others
VOLUME 1: SEED OF DESTRUCTION
ISBN 978-1-50670-666-5 | $24.99
VOLUME 2: STRANGE PLACES
ISBN 978-1-50670-667-2 | $24.99
VOLUME 3: THE WILD HUNT
ISBN 978-1-50670-668-9 | $24.99
HELLBOY IN HELL
ISBN 978-1-50670-749-5 | $24.99

ORIGINAL VISIONS—THRILLING TALES!

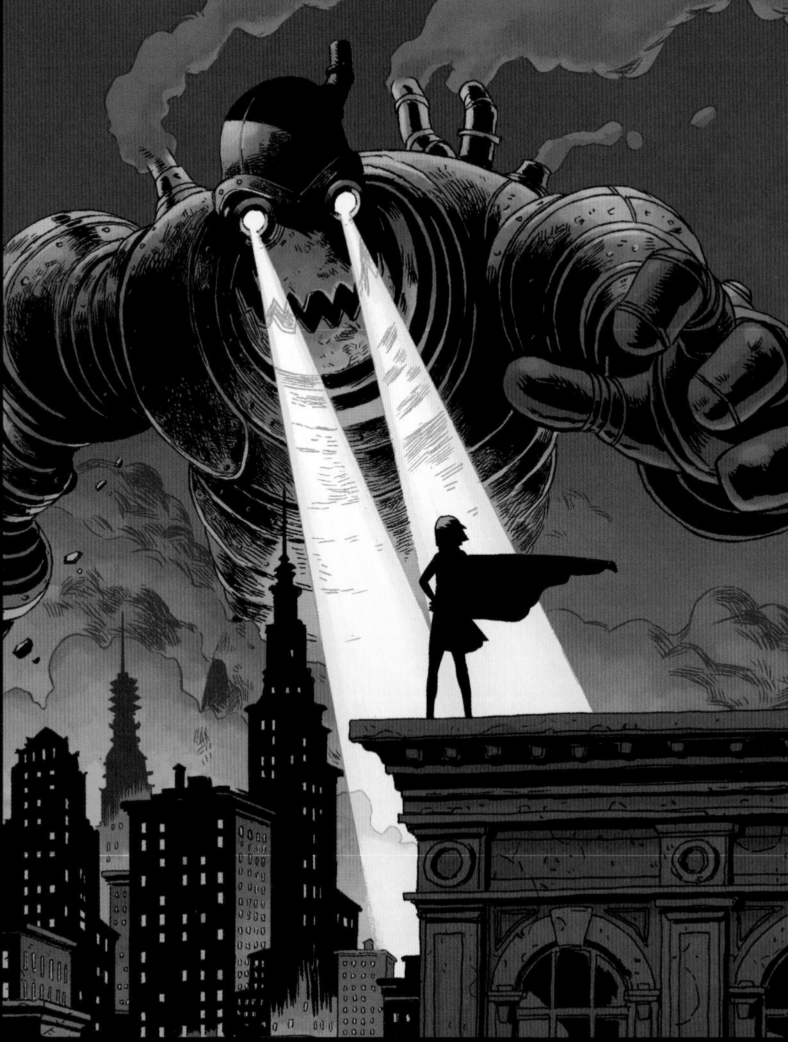

"These superheroes ain't no boy scouts in spandex. They're a high-octane blend of the damaged, quixotic heroes of pulp and detective fiction and the do-gooders in capes from the Golden and Silver Ages."
—Duane Swierczynski

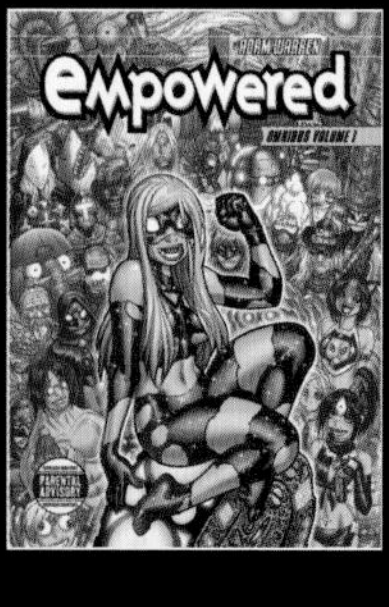
empowered
OMNIBUS VOLUME 1

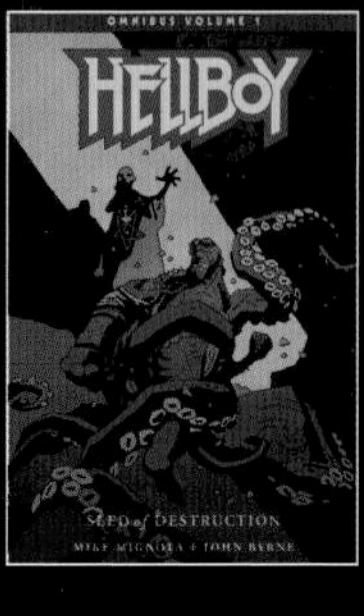
OMNIBUS VOLUME 1
HELLBOY
SEED of DESTRUCTION

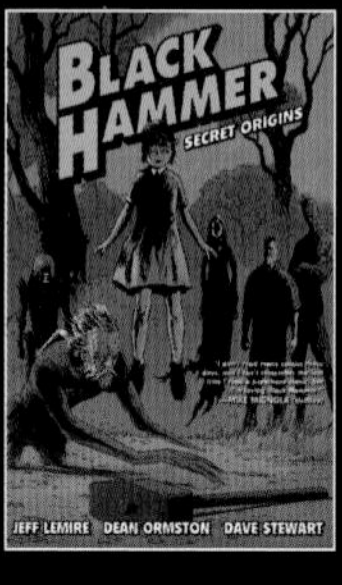
BLACK HAMMER
SECRET ORIGINS
JEFF LEMIRE DEAN ORMSTON DAVE STEWART

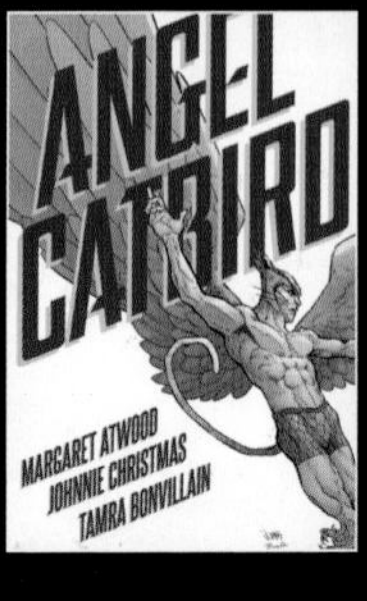
ANGEL CATBIRD
MARGARET ATWOOD
JOHNNIE CHRISTMAS
TAMRA BONVILLAIN

AVAILABLE AT YOUR LOCAL COMICS SHOP OR BOOKSTORE
To find a comics shop in your area, visit comicshoplocator.com. For more information or to order direct, visit DarkHorse.com

PECULATIVE FICTION FROM

darkhorse originals

nique creators with unique visions."—MIKE RICHARDSON, PUBLISHER

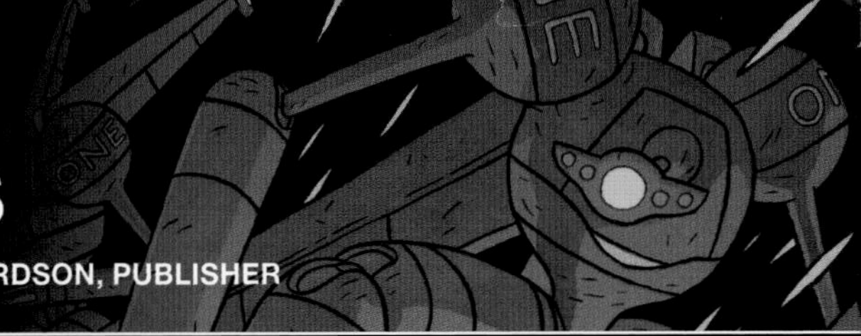

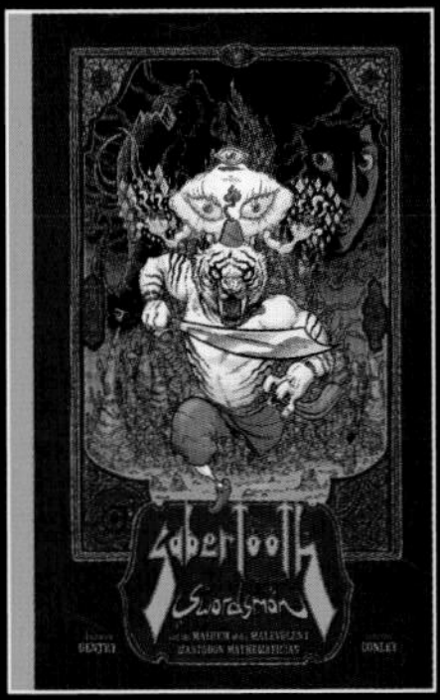
Sabertooth
Swordsman
GENTRY
CONLEY

SABERTOOTH SWORDSMAN

Damon Gentry and Aaron Conley

Granted the form of the Sabertooth Swordsman by the Cloud God of Sasquatch Mountain, a simple farmer embarks on a treacherous journey to the Mastodon's fortress!

ISBN 978-1-61655-176-6 | $17.99

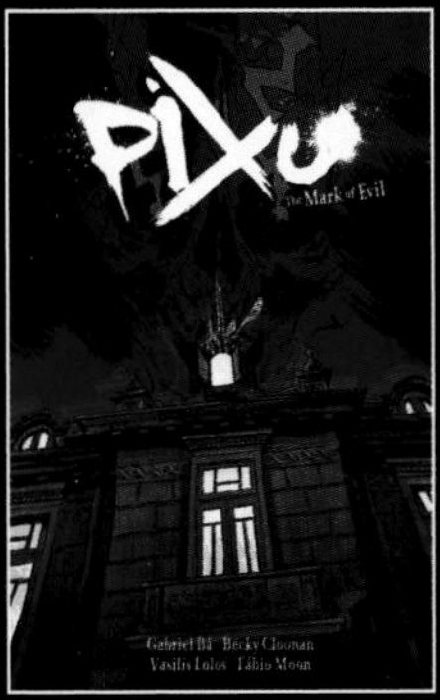
PIXU
the Mark of Evil
Gabriel Bá Becky Cloonan
Vasilis Lolos Fábio Moon

PIXU: THE MARK OF EVIL

Gabriel Bá, Becky Cloonan, Vasilis Lolos, and Fábio Moon

This gripping tale of urban horror follows the lives of five lonely strangers who discover a dark mark scrawled on the walls of their building. As the walls come alive, everyone is slowly driven mad, stripped of free will, leaving only confusion, chaos, and eventual death.

ISBN 978-1-61655-813-0 | $14.99

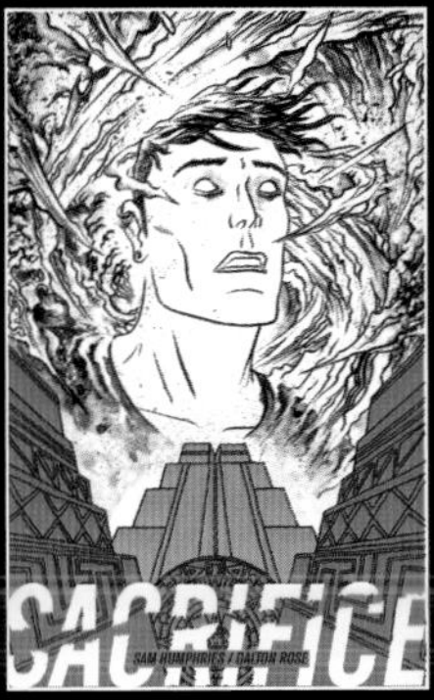
SACRIFICE
SAM HUMPHRIES / DALTON ROSE

SACRIFICE

Sam Humphries, Dalton Rose, Bryan Lee O'Malley, and others

What happens when a troubled youth is plucked from modern society and sent on a psychedelic journey into the heart of the Aztec civilization—one of the greatest and most bloodthirsty times in human history?

ISBN 978-1-59582-985-6 | $19.99

DE:TALES

Fábio Moon and Gabriel Bá

Brimming with all the details of human life, Moon and Bá's charming stories move from the urban reality of their home in São Paulo to the magical realism of their Latin American background. Named by *Booklist* as one of the 10 Best Graphic Novels of 2010.

ISBN 978-1-59582-557-5 | $19.99

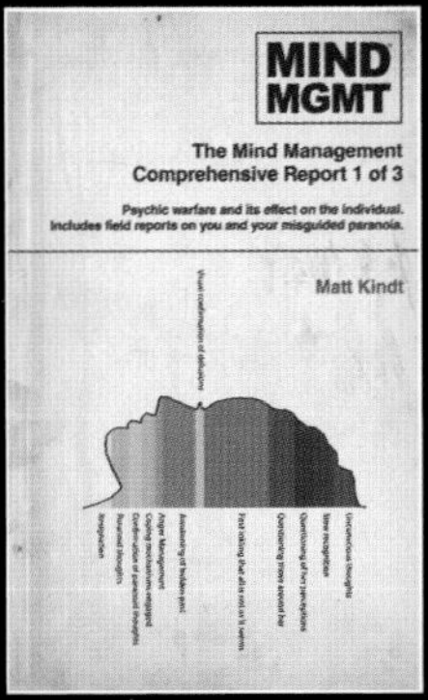
MIND
MGMT
The Mind Management
Comprehensive Report 1 of 3
Psychic warfare and its effect on the individual.
Includes field reports on you and your misguided paranoia.
Matt Kindt

MIND MGMT OMNIBUS

Matt Kindt

This globe-spanning tale of espionage explores the adventures of a journalist investigating the mystery of a commercial flight where everyone aboard loses their memories. Each omnibus volume collects two volumes of the Eisner Award–winning series!

VOLUME 1: THE MANAGER AND THE FUTURIST
ISBN 978-1-50670-460-9 | $24.99

VOLUME 2: THE HOME MAKER AND THE MAGICIAN
ISBN 978-1-50670-461-6 | $24.99

VOLUME 3: THE ERASER AND THE IMMORTALS
ISBN 978-1-50670-462-3 | $24.99

DARK HORSE BOOKS

AVAILABLE AT YOUR LOCAL COMICS SHOP OR BOOKSTORE

To find a comics shop near you, visit comicshoplocator.com • For more information or to order direct, visit DarkHorse.com

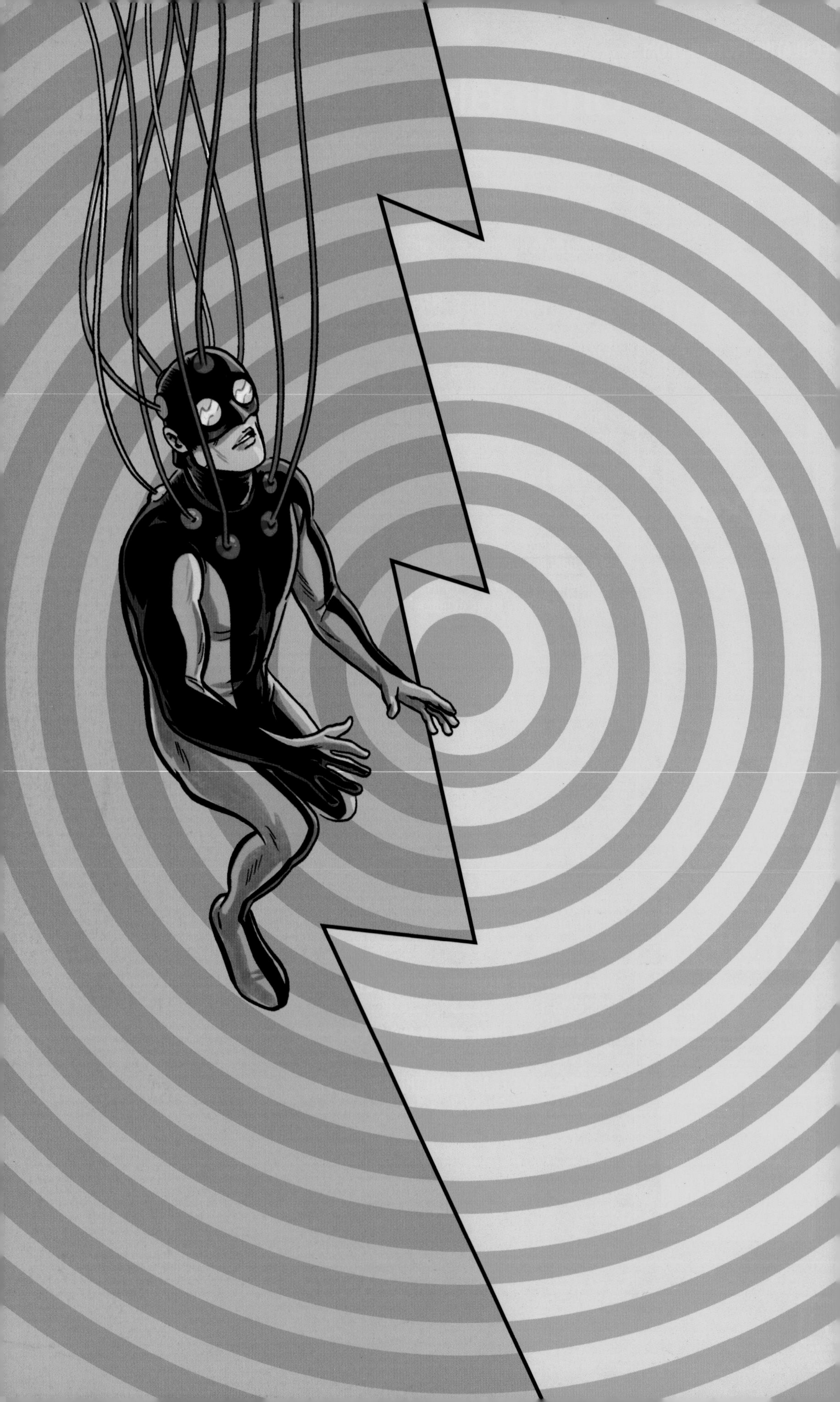